BERNARD SCHWE

RADICALS
ON THE ROAD

The Politics of English Travel Writing in the 1930s

UNIVERSITY PRESS OF VIRGINIA   CHARLOTTESVILLE & LONDON

The University Press of Virginia
© 2001 by the Rector and Visitors of the University of Virginia
Printed in the United States of America on acid-free paper

First published 2001

9 8 7 6 5 4 3 2 1

Library of Congress Cataloging-in-Publication Data
Schweizer, Bernard, 1962–
     Radicals on the road : the politics of English travel writing in the 1930s /
Bernard Schweizer.
          p. cm.
     Includes bibliographical references and index.
     ISBN 0-8139-2069-8 (alk. paper) — ISBN 0-8139-2070-1 (pbk. : alk. paper)
     1. Travelers' writings, English—History and criticism.   2. English prose
literature—20th century—History and criticism.   3. Politics and literature—
Great Britain—History—20th century.   4. Waugh, Evelyn, 1903–1966—
Political and social views.   5. Orwell, George, 1903–1950—Political and social
views.   6. Greene, Graham, 1904– —Political and social views.   7. West,
Rebecca, Dame, 1892– —Political and social views.   8. Radicalism—Great
Britain—History—20th century.   9. British—Travel—Historiography.
I. Title.

PR808.T72 S39 2001
820.9'355—dc21

                                                                    2001033238

To Liang

CONTENTS

PREFACE

MY FASCINATION with travel preceded my interest in travel writing by several years. In 1987 and 1988 I spent fourteen months abroad, backpacking through large tracts of Asia, followed by a stay Down Under and a slow hitchhiking trip up the Alaska Highway. One place in particular left an indelible mark on my memory. Like many Western travelers, in fact in accordance with a long-standing tradition, I felt that Tibet taught me an important lesson.[1] In my case, it was politics rather than Tibet's usual association, with spirituality, that determined the nature of my "epiphany": I arrived in Lhasa at the very moment in 1987 when the smoldering political unrest in this "autonomous region" erupted into open violence. The riots of October 1987 were sparked by the beating and imprisonment of a group of monks who had been caught waving the Tibetan flag and shouting slogans for Tibetan independence. When news broke about their arrest, a mob of Tibetans stormed the police station where the monks were held, freed them, and burned down the building. In response, Chinese troops began to shoot into the crowd from rooftops surrounding the area, killing and injuring scores of Tibetans.[2]

At this point, my relationship to China became quite hostile. While traveling in other provinces of China, I had seen too much of communism's potential for breeding conformity, lethargy, and irresponsibility to be well disposed toward the authoritarian manifestations of Beijing's policy on minorities. As a result, I began to dislike Chinese people and their culture with an intensity that surprised me. In the meantime, I found Tibet to be a land of austere, pure beauty whose inhabitants deserved my unconditional respect and trust.

It took me a while to admit that my political zeal had colored almost all of my perceptions about China in general and Tibet in particular. I came to realize, too, that I may have been wrong-headed in some of my opinions. Although I never changed my stance on Tibet, I began to differentiate between China's governmental policy and the spirit of its people. By one of life's more pleasant ironies, I married a Chinese citizen four years after my troubled journey in her country. And it was in my domestic life, subsequently, that I began a gradual, slow return voyage to her home country. During my actual trip in China, I had been too ideologically biased, my mind already made up, to have an appropriate sociocultural perspective on the country and its people.

Prolonged traveling entails all manner of initiations and often sets the stage for new departures in our lives. One significant outcome of my trip was a growing interest in travel literature. This, in turn, energized my professional life, and I even began my academic career by teaching a seminar on travel literature at Duke University. The two travel writers who, among other authors on my first syllabus, made the most lasting impression on me were Graham Greene and George Orwell. In an intriguing variant of the common pattern, their journeys struck me as ideograms of political conviction, rather than as mere celebrations of adventure or as inventories of foreign anomalies. When I tried to find more examples of this type of travel book, I realized that political travel writing had never flourished better than in the 1930s, that is, precisely when Orwell and Greene (as well as a host of other British intellectuals) had embarked on their radical journeys. This convinced me that something extraordinary had happened in Britain during the 1930s—with regard to both travel and politics—and I wanted to get to the bottom of it. *Radicals on the Road* represents the outcome of my inquiries into the relationship between ideological trajectories and real journeys, between places and their political mapping, and between radical rhetoric and the dictates of experience.

ACKNOWLEDGMENTS

I OWE A GREAT debt of gratitude to Marianna Torgovnick, who essentially taught me the craft of writing and provided expert support and guidance during the early stage of this book. A special thanks also to Fredric Jameson, Michael Moses, Thomas Pfau, and Ian Baucom for their helpful criticisms of my project.

At the University of Zurich, my work was energized by the astonishing intellectual presence of Peter Hughes, whom I would like to thank very much for his stimulating input during the reconceptualization stage of this study. I also want to thank Allen Reddick, who gave me the opportunity to address the Research Colloquium at the University of Zurich with my work-in-progress. Further, Raphael Newman has earned my gratitude and respect for his inestimable help in editing a draft manuscript of this work. During the final stage of manuscript preparation, Dennis Marshall, an excellent copy editor, showed a keen eye for argumentative coherence and offered stimulating feedback. Finally, I am indebted to Sandra Orsulic whose English translation of Serb texts enabled me to add the finishing touches to my treatment of Rebecca West.

This book has been with me in Durham, North Carolina, in Zurich, Switzerland, in Tulsa, Oklahoma, and in New York. During these peregrinations, I was always accompanied by my loving wife, Liang, and our daughter, Lyra, both of whom I want to thank most cordially for being such terrific traveling companions.

• • •

My thanks also go to two journals for permission to reprint material that previously appeared in their pages: "Graham Greene and the Politics of Travel," *Prose Studies* 21, no. 1 (April 1998): 95–124, and "Ethiopia and Dystopia in Evelyn Waugh's African Books," *Journal of African Travel Writing* 7 (October 1999): 17–34.

RADICALS ON THE ROAD

INTRODUCTION

GOING ON A JOURNEY often involves fantasies of rebellion and renewal. Paul Hollander declares that "travel and revolution have something in common. Both are routine-shattering, seen as open-ended and leading to some, not fully definable, transformation of personal lives" (33). Georges Van den Abbeele argues similarly that "to call an existing order (whether epistemological, aesthetic, or political) into question by placing oneself 'outside' that order, by taking a 'critical distance' from it, is implicitly to invoke the metaphor of thought as travel" (xiii). According to such views, traveling means not only leaving one's emotional tangles, old habits, and stale relationships behind, but also engaging with new orders of knowledge and, perhaps most importantly, embracing new social and political possibilities. It is needless to say that such a progressive model of travel has been thoroughly challenged by the work of those postcolonial cultural critics who emphasize the authoritarian and normalizing nature of much travel writing. Under their scrutiny, travel is seen as an extension of colonialism,[1] and travel writing as an ideological construction of alterity in the service of political and economic hegemony. *Radicals on the Road* complicates the issue of travel writing's inherent and actual political potentialities. In the first place, it aims to situate the politics of travel historically by exploring the manifold ways in which 1930s travelers engaged problems of race, social class, gender, culture, history, and place. Then, by working through a set of interrelated contemporary issues, especially the connection between travel, ideology, anxiety, and dualistic thinking, this study resets the parameters for a critically productive, contextualized approach to travel writing.

The rationale for focusing on the 1930s is twofold: political and sociohistoric. Politically, the 1930s are relevant because most of the travelers of that period were also political radicals. In fact, the ideological connotations of the term *fellow traveler* came into usage during the 1930s. Although the term has acquired a broader meaning over the course of time (it originally designated someone who sympathized with the communist program for social revolution without actually being a party member),[2] in the 1930s *fellow traveler* had not merely a figurative meaning but a literal one as well. Indeed, the term aptly captures the link between traveling as a physical activity and as a state of mind or radical political orientation. The authors chosen for this study were fellow travelers in both senses of the term: they were restless voyagers and they took up ideological causes that represent the whole ideological spectrum of the time: Evelyn Waugh was a declared conservative and fascist sympathizer; George Orwell was a dedicated socialist; Graham Greene wavered between his bourgeois instincts and his liberal, left-wing sympathies; and Rebecca West maintained strong feminist and liberationist convictions.

Historically, the 1930s evolved what could be properly termed a "travelling culture," to use James Clifford's suggestive term. Indeed, a whole generation of English intellectuals between the ages of thirty and forty traveled compulsively during the decade before World War II. Those who, like C. Day-Lewis, stayed at home, were almost an anomaly. Besides being constantly on the move, these 1930s intellectuals generated a body of travel books that constitutes a cultural narrative in its own right, reflecting the dominant historical parameters of the time as well as its most influential psychocultural theories. Thus, for students of political traveling, the 1930s provide an ideal terrain for investigations into the ideological and psychological workings of journey narratives.

• • •

Travel writing was, of course, not invented in the 1930s. As early as the fourteenth century, Marco Polo's account of his journeys to the East became a popular source for tall tales as well as a reference manual for traders along the Silk Road to China. During the Elizabethan age, several collections of explorers' logbooks—Hakluyt's *The Principal Navigations, Traffics and Discoveries of the English Nation* (1589–1600) is an example—presented the activity of traveling "not in isolation but as part of a corporate enterprise to master space through a systematic accumulation of facts about unknown or imperfectly known lands" (Gingras, 1305). Mark Cocker argues similarly that the advancement of knowledge and the expansion of empire have been closely allied in the modern era: "The scramble by Europe's scientists to attach their labels and enforce their names on elements of the natural world was at times as hotly contested as the geopolitical scramble for territory" (31). As a result of this conspicuous alliance between travel, politics, and natural history, there emerged in the seventeenth and eighteenth centuries what Mary Louise Pratt has called the "planetary consciousness" (5), as conceptual system that helped Europeans to realize their cognitive and political domination over the "rest" of the world.

During the eighteenth century, the concern with natural history was temporarily eclipsed by the explorers' sociological interest. Indeed, travel books by Cook and Bougainville became a vehicle for the first anthropological studies and a means of voicing novel ideas about the social and cultural constitution of mankind. During the romantic period, travel was adopted as a mold for registering personal transformation and *Bildung,* a phenomenon most insistently manifested in the concept of the Grand Tour. In the Victorian age, travel writing increasingly served to consolidate imperial authority, as in the case of James Anthony Froude's account of the West Indies, or as a means to advocate the extirpation of African "darkness," as in the case of Sir Morton Stanley and others. In the first quarter of the twentieth century, finally, travelers such as Eric Bailey perfected the role of the eccentric and wily amateur spy who gathered intelligence in remote areas like Tibet and thereby single-handedly influenced the Great Game of power politics.[3]

Travelers in the 1930s added their own share to the "historical taintedness" (Clifford, 39) with which the modern history of travel and travel writing has come to be associated. But they also pioneered a new tradition by employing travel writing self-consciously as a platform for voicing radical political ideas. Simultaneously, they abandoned the documentary, pseudoscientific, journalistic method that had dominated the writing of travel books in the past and instead opted for the more imaginative, introspective, essayistic, and argumentative kind of travel book that clearly aspired to be recognized as a form of literature.

From a commercial perspective, these innovations were highly successful. Compared with the first two decades of the twentieth century, the number of newly published English travel books reached an unprecedented height during the 1930s.[4] Valentine Cunningham states in his extensive study of 1930s literature that "there was a huge audience for travel books. The thirst for news from elsewhere scarcely let up" (349). By capturing the public imagination, travel writers tapped into a lucrative market, and Samuel Hynes's observation that "the journey itself [was] the most insistent of 'thirties metaphors'" (229) is well supported by such facts. Further confirmation for the importance of traveling in the 1930s can be found in essays such as "Travelling in the Thirties," by Richard Johnstone, or "The Views of Travellers: Travel Writing in the 1930s," by Philip Dodd. Also, Paul Fussell's landmark study *Abroad: British Literary Travel between the Wars* (1980) draws mostly on 1930s travel books.[5] These scholarly treatments of 1930s travel writing, however, have largely neglected aspects of political radicalism and the question of ideology's function in shaping the discourse of travel during that time. It is precisely these topics that *Radicals on the Road* sets out to explore and clarify.

Let me state bluntly, then, that travel and politics are not antagonistic, as Paul Fussell suggests, but rather inseparable companions, especially during periods of instability and crisis like the 1930s. This truth is nowhere more clearly expressed than in the travel books by Greene, Waugh, Orwell, and West, all of whom felt compelled to travel because of their ideological convictions. As Robert Kaplan aptly put it, "frontiers test ideologies like nothing else" ("What Makes History," 18), and 1930s travelers felt the need to test their ideologies more urgently than travelers of other periods. Clifford Geertz goes one step further, claiming that travel and displacement not only test ideologies but verily generate them: "It is a loss of orientation that most directly gives rise to ideological activity" (219). Geertz specifies this statement by adding: "It is in country unfamiliar emotionally or topographically that one needs poems and road maps. So too with ideology" (218). What Geertz stipulates in *The Interpretation of Cultures* (1973) is directly echoed by a remark in Evelyn Waugh's African travel book *Remote People* (1931): "It is very surprising to discover the importance which politics assume the moment one begins to travel" (137). No statement could capture the atmosphere of 1930s travel more accurately.

• • •

The dominant historical factors that caused the 1930s to be such a turbulent historical period—namely, the polarization of political ideology, the economic depression, and the growing threat of war—were responsible for the emergence of three basic phenomena in England's public consciousness: radicalism, dualism, and anxiety. Although these aspects can be said to determine the general mood of the 1930s, the period's body of travel writing is the locus classicus for the expression and the study of these phenomena. Among the three factors named above, political radicalism is the element most directly determined by the writers' conscious designs and initiatives. More often than not, 1930s travelers used the vehicle of travel writing to advance specific political arguments, whether they were in favor of the British Empire, in defense of Roman Catholic hegemony, against fascist aggression, or for a socialist transformation of society.

Part 1 locates these explicit political arguments in the period's travel writing and thereby charts the major ideological parameters of the 1930s. I demonstrate how travel books by Evelyn Waugh, George Orwell, Graham Greene, and Rebecca West reflect contemporary historical developments and how, in turn, these travelers' impressions were shaped by their respective ideological positions. In other words, the focus of the first four chapters is on what David Harvey has named the activity of "place construction": "Representations of places have material consequences in so far as fantasies, desires, fears and longings are expressed in actual behavior. Evaluative schemata of places, for example, become grist to all sorts of policy-makers' mills. . . . The political-economic possibilities of place (re)construction are, in short, highly coloured by the evaluative manner of place representation" (22).

But it would be simplistic to assume a straightforward relationship between ideology and discursive place making. In fact, travel also has an inherently destabilizing, disorienting quality, a phenomena identified by Patricia Yaeger as "the strange effects of space" (25). As Yaeger tells us, these effects result from the experience that "space is a fragmentary field of action, a jurisdiction scattered and deranged, which appears to be negotiable or continuous but is actually peppered with

chasms of economic and cultural disjunctions" (4). The ambivalence
between place as the scene of (supposed) cognitive mastery and simultaneously as the locus of a traveler's most unsettling experiences
is a central topic in this study. While part 1 focuses on the political-
historical aspects of place making, part 2 deals with the fact that
"space has an additional political-psychological dimension" (Yaeger,
4) that can lead to "strange effects" and a loss of control.

Chapter 5 shows how 1930s travelers tried to shore up their ideological beliefs by appeal to binary distinctions. The most important
of these binaries was, of course, the distinction between the political
Left and Right. Other binaries were those between imperialism and decolonization or between theory and action. Orwell addresses the latter
dilemma in *The Road to Wigan Pier:* "On the one hand you have the
warm-hearted unthinking Socialist, the typical working-class Socialist,
who only wants to abolish poverty.... On the other hand, you have the
intellectual, book-trained Socialist, who understands that it is necessary to throw our present civilisation down the sink" (181–82). This
dualism reflects the pervasive paradox of intuitive activism and intellectual apathy at odds with one another. Traveling can be seen as a
symptom to resolve this dilemma, because it allowed 1930s intellectuals to enter into a more concrete, more physical relationship with
historical and political realities than if they remained immured in their
intellectual towers. Thus, in the humanist tradition, travel brought together the heart and the head—it spoke as much to the rational ability
as it engaged the determination to act.

The focus of chapter 5 is on yet another dominant polarity of the
1930s; namely, that between optimism and pessimism. The conflict
between these two attitudes found its expression in the period's travel
literature in frequent and often paradoxical references to utopia and
dystopia. Very often, the search for a "good place" or political utopia
caused many travelers to pack their bags in the first place. They were
inspired by the optimistic certainty that other places would offer an
antidote for England's depressed and conflicted situation. Paul Fussell
calls this the "I-Hate-it-Here" condition, which dominated the attitude of English travelers between the wars. But besides the flight mo-
tive, the politically conditioned attraction to specific places also played
an important role. The utopian impulse was particularly strong among
leftist travelers to Russia at the beginning of the thirties. As Paul Hollander has documented in *Political Pilgrims* (1981), their travel ac-

counts are suffused by a virtually unbounded trust in the felicitous nature of Soviet communism. Once the attractiveness of Russia as a social and economic heaven began to pale, the Spanish civil war briefly revived the hopes of leftist travelers that an adequate political system could be established on European soil. Very often, however, the hope of finding a good place quickly dissipated once these travelers were faced with the realities of crisis and conflict. Then they realized that utopia had a way of turning into its opposite—namely, dystopia.[6] And the result, as can be expected, were strong feelings of estrangement and anxiety.

The prevalence of anxiety, the topic of chapter 6, can be interpreted as a sign of strain, especially the strain of trying to maintain socio-economic and racial binaries that seem to be spurious in actual experience. For one thing, what travelers found abroad was often perceived as a disorienting or uncanny reflection of their own home. Such cultural anxieties were further compounded by the feeling of permanent crisis that pervaded the decade. Indeed, many intellectuals and artists gave expression to their conviction "that the form of society in which they had grown up could not possibly last" (Symons, 21). This atmosphere of anxiety was not merely a result of Britain's internal problems. A strong international focus developed, as people followed political developments across the Channel and in distant countries as much as they concerned themselves with domestic affairs: "At no time in English history had so much information on foreign affairs been available in popular form, nor so many conflicting views on policy and prospects. The result was less enlightenment than a permanent feeling of crisis, an expectancy of worse things to come, which grew blacker and blacker until its monstrous climax in September 1938" (Graves and Hodge, 330). Throughout the decade, but especially at its beginning and ending, there was a widespread feeling that the United Kingdom (and the Western world in general) was standing at a pivotal historical threshold. While the Roaring Twenties had contributed to obliterating the cultural pessimism engendered by World War I, the Wall Street crash marked a return of the repressed.

The ensuing global slump challenged hopes for increasing prosperity and technological progress such as were nurtured during the twenties. The latent feeling of anxiety was enhanced by the growing military threat of fascism. In *Journey to a War* (1939), Christopher Isherwood expresses the military threat of fascism in terms of a sickness that is spreading throughout the body politic. While watching a formation of Japanese bombers from a rooftop in Hankow, China, he comments: "The searchlights criss-crossed, plotting points, like dividers; and suddenly there they were, six of them, flying close together and high up. It was as if a microscope had brought dramatically into focus the bacilli of a fatal disease. They passed, bright, tiny, and deadly, infecting the night. The searchlights followed them right across the sky; guns smashed out; tracer-bullets bounced up towards them, falling hopelessly short" (71). The very same words could serve, later on, to describe the London Blitz. Indeed, World War II marked the acute stage of a global sickness that had been incubating during the entire decade that preceded it, causing people to feel restless and apprehensive.

One response to the period's anxiety about domestic and global developments was a resurgence of cultural pessimism. This is evident in the antihumanistic tendency of Evelyn Waugh's works (both fictional and nonfictional) and in the skeptical tenor of books such as Stephen Spender's *The Destructive Element,* where the reader is told that "the nationalist European state does not provide a sense of historic purposiveness" (223). But pessimism was too passive an attitude to suit the dynamic, rebellious impulses of young intellectuals who had been educated in the nation's elite public-school system during the 1920s. It is no surprise, therefore, that many members of the so-called "Auden generation" turned to various forms of spiritual and ideological beliefs in search of affirmative values. Writers such as Waugh and Greene converted to Catholicism. Others, such as Auden and Orwell, "went over" to socialism.[7] These beliefs were sought as an antidote to the anxieties and perplexities of the period, just as travel was pursued as a means to clear the fogs of political confusion and to bring about ideological clarifications. But as this study shows, British travelers of the 1930s often got more (or perhaps I should say less) than they bargained for, returning home with a heightened sense of political anxiety and with less confidence in the values of their own social system than they had set out with.

• • •

Given the crucial importance that political factors assume in the public life of the 1930s, any discussion of the period's travel writing needs to acknowledge the prevailing historical parameters, both in Britain and in the larger world. Eric Hobsbawm has insisted that the 1930s "can be best understood, not through the contest of states, but as an international ideological civil war. . . . It was an international war, because it raised essentially the same issues in most Western countries. It was a civil war, because the lines between the pro- and anti-fascist forces ran through each society" (144). The situation in Britain, with all its historical specificity, was as much a symptom as an embodiment of the overriding forces of the decade, especially "the Great Slump, fascism and the steadily approaching war" (Hobsbawm, 190).

In accordance with this diagnosis, several historians, critics, and creative writers consider the 1930s in Britain as a decade with certain clearly definable properties. *Britain in the Nineteen Thirties* (1971) by Branson and Heinemann, Charles L. Mowat's influential study *Britain between the Wars, 1918–1940* (1955), and Alan Jenkins's illustrated social history *The Thirties* (1976) have solidified the status of the decade as a distinct epoch in Britain's sociopolitical, economic, and cultural life.

But the 1930s were not only a reasonably coherent historical period: these years have also been treated as a separate era in Britain's literary history. This notion was given prominence in Robin Skelton's anthology *Poetry of the Thirties* (1964) and in critical studies such as Richard Johnstone's book *The Will to Believe: Novelists of the Nineteenthirties* (1982). Furthermore, Valentine Cunningham's encyclopedic *British Writers of the Thirties* (1988) did much to map the literary history of the 1930s. Another, if by now dated, contribution to the study of 1930s literature is Samuel Hynes's *The Auden Generation: Literature and Politics in England in the 1930s* (1976). Julian Symons and Malcolm Muggeridge, both contemporaries of the 1930s, have published separate accounts of the period, each one entitled *The Thirties*. The neglect of female writers in such studies was redressed in Janet Montefiore's recent *Men and Women Writers of the 1930s* (1996), which closes several gaps in the male critics' approaches to the period. Montefiore's book is particularly useful for those interested in questions of sexual politics and canon building, as well as in the cultural and political dimensions of collective memory.

• • •

During the first seven years of the 1930s, the economic slump was the single most decisive historical determinant in England. In the early

1930s, mass unemployment and falling wages caused widespread social distress and political unrest. In 1933, official unemployment rose to a staggering 23 percent, meaning that almost three million insured workers in Britain were out of work. Due to the extremely uneven distribution of unemployment, though, some towns and districts reported a rate of up to 80 percent unemployment, whereas in other places almost everyone had a job. Hardest hit by the depression were the lower and middle classes who worked in basic industries—mining, shipbuilding, and textile production. These industries had gradually lost ground in international competition due to insufficient investment and a general lack of modernization (most of the available capital in Britain had been channeled into colonial properties). The resulting decrease in the competitiveness of the nation's basic industries, together with an accelerated monopolization, caused many marginally profitable plants to shut down (often the economic sustenance of entire towns).

Paradoxically, the fall of prices in raw materials and import goods actually raised living standards for those who were able to work: "The fall in the cost of living meant that the middle class and salaried workers, and the better-paid workers in relatively sheltered occupations, began to have some extra purchasing power. This contributed to the expansion from 1934 onwards of consumption industries" (Branson and Heinemann, 4). Thus, while the deflation raised some people to new levels of prosperity, it pushed millions of others into utter poverty. It was precisely this disparity and its resulting sense of social guilt among members of the upper-middle classes that caused the period's left-wing intelligentsia to make such ostentatious displays of sympathy for the plight of the lower classes.

At first, the Labour government (elected in 1929) did little to improve matters in the basic industries. The economic policy of Prime Minister Ramsay McDonald could not alter the course of the deepening recession. McDonald's credibility among leftists was further undermined when he decided in 1931 to form the National Government, a coalition of Conservatives and Labour. This deprived the entire sector of leftist radicals of a proper political representation, leading to the foundation of the Independent Labour Party (ILP), the radical offshoot of the Labour Party.

The political alienation between the Labour Party and the working

classes may have fostered one of the decade's most insistent phenomena—the political engagement of artists and writers on behalf of
the poor and disenfranchised. But intellectuals not only took up the
cause of the working classes, they also took sides on a variety of ideological issues, ranging from sexual morals to international politics.
Most of the leftist intellectuals were young graduates of Oxford and
Cambridge: "In the universities there was political ferment (dating
back to the early thirties), most of it boiling up on the left and in pacifist societies; socialist, and especially Marxist ideas had permeated
even anti-socialists, it was reported" (Mowat, 525). A number of publications and artists' groups, such as the *Left Review,* the Left Book Club,
and the Unity Theatre, founded between 1933 and 1936, all centered
around the idea of propagating ideological messages through art, especially the popularization of leftist theories. Nevertheless, most leftist
intellectuals of the 1930s had been brought up in bourgeois house-
holds and still adhered to a middle-class ethos. For them, social revolution and collectivization remained largely intellectual gambits, not
issues they could relate to wholeheartedly.

The powerful impact of leftist opinion in the public sphere was
occasionally challenged by aggressive displays of rightist ideology.
When Sir Oswald Mosley founded the British Union of Fascists in 1934,
the political polarity between the Right and the Left became openly
visible. Even though some writers took a cynical perspective on this
struggle, claiming that both fascism and socialism were simply "two
expressions of the same spirit of romantic materialism" (Muggeridge,
45), it is certain that "more and more this conflict came to provide the
underlying pattern of thought, whether in politics, literature, or religion" (Muggeridge, 46). The conflict was further aggravated by Mosley's ruthless methods in dealing with people of differing opinions and
by news of Hitler's systematic purges among social democrats, Jews,
pacifists, artists, and other minority groups. But the United Kingdom
was neither Germany nor Italy. Mosley's fascist movement could never
overcome the handicap of looking like a foreign import (beginning
with their outlandish black outfit) and so never posed a serious threat
to Britain's liberal tradition. Moreover, the National Government, with
its broad parliamentary basis among the Labour and Conservative
parties, presented such a solid block of political consensus that it
was hardly susceptible to right-wing or left-wing political agitation.

Even the Popular Front movement, that conglomerate of various leftist groups, was not powerful enough to pose a serious threat to the political status quo.

After 1936, just when the economic depression was easing up and industrial recovery began to get under way, a number of military and political situations escalated. Several sites of smoldering political tension suddenly became acute crises in the years 1936 and 1937: Hitler occupied the demilitarized Rhineland, Japan waged war against China, Italy invaded Ethiopia, and the Spanish civil war began. In all four theaters, the aggressor was a fascist regime, a circumstance that triggered a vast antifascist response in Britain. Nevertheless, the successive governments of Prime Ministers Baldwin and Chamberlain stuck to a resolute noninterventionist policy regarding these crises. In the case of Spain, this policy may have contributed to the escalation of the conflict, since it pitted Russia against the two fascist regimes of Hitler and Mussolini, each side supporting one partner in the civil war. Moreover, Britain's passive stance brought forth such strange flowers as the Hoare-Laval plan, designed to end the Italo-Ethiopian conflict. This cynical initiative, hatched with combined British and French diplomatic efforts at the League of Nations, would have given more than two-thirds of Ethiopia's territory to Mussolini in exchange for Italy's promise not to swallow up the rest of Ethiopia. This was the beginning of England's ill-advised appeasement policy, designed to prevent fascist regimes from entering into a coalition by granting them their most immediate territorial claims.

When the Spanish civil war broke out in 1936, a flare of hope ran through the leftist camp. Besides opposing fascism, the Spanish civil war provided leftists with an opportunity to combat their sense of isolation from the working classes and to get down to the realities of proletarian life. But all the hopes associated with the struggle in Spain were dashed when Franco's forces triumphed in 1939. Moreover, the British communists who had cheered the achievements of the USSR at the beginning of the decade began to feel uneasy about their political convictions when news broke about Stalin's purges and the Moscow trials of 1936. The disillusionment deepened when the communist faction in the Spanish civil war began its persecution of socialists and anarchists in Barcelona. The decisive shock, however, was the Nazi-Soviet pact of 1939. The military cooperation between two nations supposed to be archenemies pulled the rug out from under all those who had been arguing for the well-intentioned, progressive character of the Soviet regime.

As if the rise of fascism and the dire effects of the Great Depression were not enough to worry about, there was another fundamental change in the making, threatening the very core of British national identity. The 1930s marked the beginning of the transition from the British Empire to the Commonwealth of Nations, a voluntary association of self-ruled states. By the beginning of the 1930s, five white Colonies (New Zealand, Australia, Canada, Ireland, and South Africa) had attained the status of dominions. According to a key passage in the Balfour Declaration of 1926, this meant that they were "autonomous Communities within the British Empire, equal in status, in no way subordinate one to another in any aspect of their domestic or external affairs. . . . Every self-governing member of the Empire is now the master of its destiny." This principle of decolonization, which was enacted into law by the Statute of Westminster in 1931, applied only to a few of the total number of British colonies during the 1930s. But England's intelligentsia expected the process to be irreversible—that soon the number of dominions would grow and the colonies would disappear one by one.

What travelers of the 1930s did not yet realize was the extent to which their journeys were predicated upon the specific advantages they enjoyed as envoys from the imperial metropolis. Vast tracts of Africa, Asia, and South America offered British travelers an infrastructure and social network they could depend on. Once the empire went into decline, the very same travelers who had taken their privileges for granted during the 1930s sounded the alarm. In 1947, Evelyn Waugh wrote famously that "there is no room for tourists in a world of 'displaced persons.' Never again, I suppose, shall we land on foreign soil with letter of credit and passport (itself the first faint shadow of the great cloud that envelops us) and feel the world wide open before us" (*When the Going Was Good,* 9). In the post–World War II context, "displaced person" had a restrictive meaning, referring to prisoners of fascist regimes or to victims of forced labor. They were the vanguard of postcolonial migrants whose movements were, though not a direct result of war, similarly determined by global developments beyond their control.

But in the same measure that decolonization started a massive centripetal flow of people toward the former colonial metropoles, it hindered the centrifugal outflow of metropolitan travelers to the margins of empire. Once World War II came to a close and the dismantling of the British Empire began in earnest, the letter of credit and passport no longer fulfilled their function as guarantors of social privilege and as tickets to roam freely within, and to some extent without, Britain's huge empire. In 1951, a distraught Peter Fleming wrote that "the horizons of the British have been sharply contracted. The whole of China is out of bounds. Persia would hardly attract the casual traveller. The Indian peninsula, though still accessible, is no longer dotted with a dependable network of Government Houses and Residencies and dark bungalows, hill-stations and cantonments, between which residents and visitors formerly drifted almost without effort" (7–8). Fleming's acute sense of disappointment demonstrates not only the mutual involvement of imperialism and travel; it also explains to some degree why those who began to travel in the 1930s needed some time to find their bearings in a world that seemed suddenly thrown into political disarray. Most of them actually ceased to write travel books, thereby making room for a new generation of postwar travel writers whose itineraries were more eclectic and whose books were no longer attuned to particular political beliefs.

PART ONE

1   GEORGE ORWELL

FOR GEORGE ORWELL, both the act and the rhetorical figure of traveling were linked with the idea of social and political transformation. Because of his intense awareness of social differences, it was enough for him to migrate from one social class to the next to feel the kind of estrangement typically experienced by travelers to distant places. Orwell needed to go no further than to London's East End or to the industrial north of England to feel a strong sense of border-crossing or, as Valentine Cunningham put it, of "going over:" "No wonder 'going over' was contemplated by Orwell and his kind as a sort of exile, a self-alienation from most of what was familiar to one's own region and class" (241). But for Orwell, traveling involved not only a social and ideological, rather than a geographical, displacement, it was also tied up with a sense of responsibility, of promoting a silenced perspective, and of making sociopolitical confessions.

As a committed socialist and self-declared member of the "lower upper middle class," Orwell traveled whenever he left the confines of his bourgeois social turf. Thus, for Orwell, travel was never a matter of self-gratification or escape. On the contrary, he used it to get to the bottom of things, even if that bottom turned out to be pretty nasty. In his essay "Why I Write," Orwell argues that "the opinion that art should have nothing to do with politics is itself a political attitude" (422). If one substituted traveling for art, the statement would reflect another of Orwell's deeply held convictions. Indeed, Orwell considered both art and travel as expressions of one's politics. In the course of his career as a traveler and travel writer, it became increasingly clear that travel and social criticism, even revolution, sprang from the same source. To be more specific: travel for Orwell was a means to transcend the boundaries of his "native" bourgeois ideology, and thereby to promote a revolutionary consciousness in the members of his own class.

In order to appreciate the uniqueness of Orwell's readiness to "lower" his social status by traveling, one has to recognize that the opposite is usually achieved when Westerners pack their bags. In his Mexican travelogue, for instance, Aldous Huxley argues that "it is never wise to establish a reputation for what must seem to [rural Mexicans] inordinate and fantastic wealth. . . . Our host was doubtless one of the richest men in the village; but his whole annual income would probably not have bought a single first-class ticket across the Atlantic" (243). Paul Fussell argues that mass tourism is a form of (temporary and reversible) upward mobility in a global context: "The escape is also from the traveler's domestic identity, and among strangers a new sense of selfhood can be tried on, like a costume. The anthropologist Claude Lévi-Strauss notes that a traveler takes a journey not just in space and time, but 'in social hierarchy as well': and he has noticed repeatedly that upon arriving in a new place he has suddenly become rich (travelers to Mexico, China, or India will know the feeling) (13). In this analysis, the degree of personal mobility is correlated with the degree of personal privilege. The greater the privilege, the further the range of one's journey. In light of this tendency, George Orwell goes against the grain, first by limiting his mobility and choosing destinations that are closer to home, and second by willingly leaving behind his middle-class milieu to experience life in underprivileged contexts. Of course, he does not do so gratuitously; in fact, nothing less than a change of his own identity is what he pursues.

This revolutionary tendency manifests itself in Orwell's travel writing in a sustained effort to construct a political persona for himself that is of one piece with the ethos of liberation and egalitarianism that he promotes. In order to do so, Orwell presents his early involvement with imperialism as a learning process rather than a form of complicity with empire, and he portrays his later sufferings in the lower-class contexts of Paris, London, Wigan, and Catalonia as a heroic act of self-sacrifice in the interest of social justice and personal redemption. In his own words, traveling served him to pay penance for his earlier political "sins" and for his social background as a member of the bour-

geoisie. In this sense, then, Orwell's journeys were indeed—to invoke
Paul Fussell's insight—a form of "travail." [1] Rather than being exer-
cises in sadism, however, Orwell's self-imposed sufferings were meant
to be cathartic. He intended to purify himself of unsavory ideological
inclinations by undergoing purgatorial experiences, and to expose, by
proxy, the readers of his travel books to a similar experience of ideological reorientation.

Orwell's social and political convictions were greatly affected by
his involvement in the British imperial service. Already his father
had been an official in the British Empire (he served in the infamous
Opium Department of India, that branch of the imperial administration that sought to undermine China's social stability by soliciting its
population into opium addiction). In fact, Orwell (né Eric Blair) was
born in India in 1903. He moved to England with his mother one year
later and thereafter saw his father only at rare intervals. Due to his
father's regular income, though, both mother and son were able to
maintain a comfortable middle-class existence in Oxfordshire. Orwell
grew up to be a bright boy and his intellectual abilities earned him a
scholarship to the well-regarded Saint Cyprian's preparatory school.
Another scholarship paved the way to Eton College. It was at Eton that
Orwell's consciousness of class was intensified, since he was one of the
few students not from a fully upper-class background.

The painful memories of being a social misfit are invoked in Orwell's *Keep the Aspidistra Flying* (1936), his third novel, where the protagonist Gordon Comstock, Orwell's alter ego, argues that "probably
the greatest cruelty one can inflict on a child is to send it to school
among children richer than himself. A child conscious of poverty will
suffer snobbish agonies such as a grown-up person can scarcely even
imagine" (53). The idea that upward mobility can be obtained through
elitist education is seriously questioned in *Aspidistra,* as Gordon turns
into a poet manqué in spite of his family's sacrifices to secure him an
education.

In his own life, a botched academic career rather than social determinism were the causes of Orwell's modest professional aspirations
after college. Bernard Crick argues that "the idea of serving in India or
Burma would have come up quite naturally and from the family, especially with his maternal grandmother still in Mandalay. . . . Uncertain where he belonged, it was as if he wanted to go back to where he
was born, even before his memory" (73). So, quite "naturally," Orwell

joined the Imperial Police in Burma, where he served as headquarters assistant from 1922 to 1927. But while he fulfilled the practical side of this job with distinction, he was plagued by ever increasing moral and ideological doubts about his complicity with the system he served. Orwell came to realize more and more clearly that his work as a servant of the British Empire was incompatible with his moral outlook. Orwell's first novel, *Burmese Days* (1934), and several of his best short stories and essays (among them "Shooting an Elephant" and "A Hanging") are attempts to deal with this troubling experience. While on home leave in 1927, Orwell decided to quit the imperial service. But in choosing to comply with the dictate of his conscience, he also chose temporary poverty. Indeed, the decision left him penniless, and he refused to ask his family for financial assistance.

Instead of relying on others, he decided to fend for himself, renting a cheap room in London. It was in the same year that his fascination with tramp life began. Orwell would regularly exchange his clothes for beggar's rags and mingle with unemployed laborers, sailors, and tramps in London's harbor district. The reasons for Orwell's "slumming" can be found in his curiosity about and strong sympathy for the social underdog. Moreover, a profound desire to rebel against the patriarchal order of his own class prevailed. He would comment later that "failure seemed to me to be the only virtue. Every suspicion of self-advancement, even to 'succeed' in life to the extent of making a few hundreds a year, seemed to me spiritually ugly, a species of bullying" (*Wigan Pier*, 180).

Part of this attitude originated in the harsh and unloving environment of his five-year preparatory school. One of Orwell's biographers maintains that "St. Cyprian's had prejudiced him against success early in life because it had given him such a corrupt view of merit" (Shelden, 117). Once again, Gordon Comstock in *Keep the Aspidistra Flying* acts as Orwell's alter ego: "There are two ways to life, he decided. You can be rich, or you can deliberately refuse to be rich. You can possess money, or you can despise money; the one fatal thing is to worship money and fail to get it" (57). Faced with this choice, Comstock decides to opt out of capitalist means of self-advancement: "Already, at sixteen, [Comstock] knew which side he was on. He was *against* the money-god and all his swinish priesthood. He had declared war on money." (57). But Orwell's pristine anticapitalism was based on subjective impressions and, perhaps, on a certain amount of self-loathing,

rather than on abstract political theories. This is particularly evident
in *Down and Out in Paris and London* (1933), which Orwell wrote on
the rebound from his experience as an imperial officer.

• • •

Down and Out in Paris and London, Orwell's first published book,
was a travel book. In it Orwell chronicles his experiences at the very
bottom of the social scale in Paris and in London. Lacking an occupation more attractive than writing, he had moved to the French capital
in 1928 as a means to get into that profession. Paris was then the hub
of aspiring and established writers in the Western world, and it was
logical for a young author to try his luck there.

Most events described in *Down and Out* are autobiographical, but
there is some fictional elaboration and a good deal of rearrangement
to give the semblance of a continuous narrative. Orwell lumps together in the second half of the book events that happened to him in
London both before and after he went to Paris. The transition between
the Paris and the London sections of the book is particularly fictitious,
as the I-narrator of *Down and Out* escapes from menial kitchen work
in Paris only to find himself pitched into a tramp's life in London. In
reality, Orwell spent the Christmas of 1929 in the comfort of his paren-
tal home in Southwold. In sum, the story of *Down and Out* is a travel
experience in two senses: first, the Paris section describes a foreigner's
experience in the French capital; and second, the people Orwell mixed
with, both in Paris and in London, were so far removed from the world
of his middle-class context that his prolonged exposure to their way of
life can aptly be identified as a form of social exploration. In the words
of Averil Gardner, Orwell was "a courageous and truthful explorer of
areas of human experience known at first hand to few of his contemporaries" (19).

The opening sections of *Down and Out* demonstrate that Orwell's
concern with poverty was at that point intuitive rather than politically
programmatic. The picturesque and imaginatively estranged nature of
his descriptions overrides any particular social concern. For instance,
Orwell's living quarters in Paris are described as consisting of "a very
narrow street—a ravine of tall leprous houses, lurching towards one
another in queer attitudes, as though they had all been frozen in the
act of collapse" (6). This description, with its sensationalist appeal,
savors rather than laments the reality of social degradation. Its defam-

iliarization rests on the invocation of the ravine, a familiar topos of romantic poetry, which is now subverted to suit the almost surrealistic perspective of the "lurching" walls of decaying houses. Furthermore, Orwell's use of the journey motif in combination with the social descent suggests parallels with the picaresque tradition.

In keeping with this narrative convention, Orwell introduces a narrator whose adventures in unknown and socially degraded contexts serve both as social documentary and as entertaining story material. Accordingly, the two "protagonists" (Orwell himself and an exiled Russian named Boris) have distinctive Cervantian overtones. Orwell fills the role of the "tricky servant," comparable to Sancho Panza, as he steals victuals, jumps the rent, and does other mischief, while Boris, in the tradition of another stock character (i.e., the braggart soldier or *alazon*), is given to virtually boundless idealism: "After eating, Boris became more optimistic than I had ever known him. 'What did I tell you?' he said. 'The fortune of war! This morning with five sous, and now look at us, I have always said it, there is nothing easier to get than money'" (58). While such contrasts between realism and idealism add color to the story, they tend to detract from the political and economic causation of social inequity.

Orwell's quixotic temperament in *Down and Out* signals a low degree of ideological self-awareness. Indeed, when asked by Boris, "'Have you any political opinions?'" the character based on Orwell answers with a simple, "'No'" (61). It is important to see the implications of this denial. In the absence of a clear ideological commitment, Orwell merely fictionalizes his own immersion in the working-class context of Paris. This makes the Paris section of *Down and Out* an entertaining, fantastical, unreliable, and not very enlightening analysis of a foreign cultural and social environment. The impulse to tell a good story practically annuls the subversive, socially corrective potential of the eyewitness's factual observations and analytical reflections. As a rhetorical achievement the text is superb; as an episodic story, the book has its bright moments (even though it is rather loosely plotted). But as a testimony to foreign living and working conditions, the text offers no more than pointers and subjectively filtered impressions.

• • •

From a decidedly unpolitical and only vaguely conceptualized working-class experience in Paris, Orwell goes on to describe life as a temporary member of London's tramp community. Interestingly, Orwell is more adversely affected by the conditions he finds at home than by the situation in Paris. In the London part, everything that is ugly and disgusting about poverty moves in much closer around Orwell. Indeed, in Paris the burrow-like structure of his Hotel X is vaguely fascinating and Madame F.'s seedy lodging house appears "homelike" (7). Moreover, in Paris it was the outside of houses that looked "leprous"; in London, metaphorical leprosy is found inside the dwellings: "The walls were leprous, and the sheets, three weeks from the wash, were almost raw umber" (178). Orwell's graphic descriptions of urban poverty, shocking in themselves, gain additional poignancy when compared with Jack London's grim account of the East End some thirty years earlier. In fact, Orwell's scandalized remark, "I was going to wash, when I noticed that every basin was streaked with grime—solid, sticky filth as black as boot-blacking" (178) is directly reminiscent of passages in Jack London's *The People of the Abyss* (1903): "two by two, we entered the bathroom. There were two ordinary tubs, and this I know: the two men preceding had washed in that water, we washed in the same water, and it was not changed for the two men that followed us. This I know, but I am also certain that the twenty-two of us washed in the same water" (71). Obviously, the dehumanizing, unsanitary conditions at London's "spikes" and "doss-houses" (shelters and boardinghouses for the poor and unemployed) had remained exactly the same since Jack London's social explorations, a fact that lends further urgency to Orwell's calls for reform.

But even while Orwell literally followed in Jack London's footsteps, he also adopted his predecessor's basic method—a stark naturalism inspired by social compassion. As a consequence, the picaresque appeal that had dominated the first half of *Down and Out* begins to fade, with Orwell paying more attention to the specific sociopolitical causation of poverty: "A tramp tramps, not because he likes it, but for the same reason as a car keeps to the left; because there happens to be a law compelling him to do so. A destitute man, if he is not supported by the parish, can only get relief at the casual wards, and as each casual ward will only admit him for one night, he is automatically kept moving" (272).

Besides giving sound reasons for the phenomenon of tramping, Orwell also makes concerted efforts to better the moral image of tramps: "The English are a conscience-ridden race, with a strong sense of the

sinfulness of poverty. One cannot imagine the average Englishman deliberately turning parasite, and this national character does not necessarily change because a man is thrown out of work. Indeed, if one
remembers that a tramp is only an Englishman out of work, forced by
law to live as a vagabond, then the tramp-monster vanishes" (273).
Such sympathetic reflections are complemented by ideas for reform-
ing the ways in which tramps are treated. Even though Orwell does not
present a coherent proposal for the abolition of trampdom, he does
come up with a suggestion that might better their plight. Of course,
his idea to turn tramps into indentured farmers producing their own
food has a rather strong air of the impractical about it. Nevertheless,
Orwell's argument that tramps deserve to be treated respectfully gives
his narrative a socially revisionist appeal. The political significance of
Down and Out is thus enhanced in the same measure as its infatuation
with narrative diminishes to make room for a more pragmatic, documentary approach to travel writing as a form of social critique.

• • •

After the favorable reception of *Down and Out* and the moderate
success of Orwell's first two novels *(Burmese Days* and *A Clergyman's
Daughter)*, his publisher Victor Gollancz, one of the coeditors of the
Left Book Club, commissioned Orwell early in 1936 to investigate the
conditions of working-class life in England's industrial North. What
is more, he paid Orwell the considerable sum of £500 as an advance
on the project. The goal was to produce a "Condition of England"
book that could be used as an instrument for political change. Indeed,
earlier examples of this genre, such as Henry Mayhew's nineteenth-
century investigation into the living conditions in London's cholera
districts, had triggered a vast response, including parliamentary calls
for sanitary reforms. Gollancz was confident that Orwell's research
among coal miners and unemployed laborers would result in a treatise
as influential as Mayhew's series of articles published in the *Morning
Chronicle* between September 1849 and December 1850 (later issued
as a book under the title *London Labour and the London Poor*). After
all, just like Mayhew, Orwell could evoke vivid and detailed accounts
of lower-class living conditions, thereby engaging middle-class sympathies for the victims of capitalism. However, while Mayhew had
written exclusively about London's poorest metropolitan districts, Orwell went beyond London to report on rural and industrial poverty in

England's mining districts, thereby outlining a vaster and less manageable socioeconomic predicament.

There was another precursor to Orwell's book about the working and living conditions of the nation's poor—J. B. Priestley's *English Journey* (1934). By comparison with the book that Orwell produced, *English Journey* retains more of the travelogue. Indeed, along with his investigations into unemployment and socioeconomic hardship, Priestley included detailed descriptions of cathedrals, museums, and of the countryside. Orwell, on the other hand, carefully pruned his writing, cutting out the trappings of conventional travel books such as the pastoral, art criticism, and culinary samplings, in order to emphasize the social relevance of his journey. The few references to the natural environment that are included are merely extensions of the particular social milieu he investigated: "For quite a long time, perhaps another twenty minutes, the train was rolling through open country before the villa-civilisation began to close in upon us again, and then the outer-slums, and then the slag-heaps, belching chimneys, blast-furnaces, canals and gasometers of another industrial town" (20).

Tellingly, Orwell never zooms in on the "villa-civilisation," which may cause one to wonder whether his exclusive focus on poverty and destitution is actually the most effective way of critiquing the divisive mechanisms of capitalism. In fact, Priestley's more panoramic account, with its quaint villages and busy factories (beside slag heaps and closed mines), has the undeniable benefit of showing what is, after all, a predominant feature of capitalism: uneven development.[2] By limiting himself to one particular vista of the total socioeconomic spectrum of his time, Orwell followed his monistic inclination—a tendency that becomes even more pronounced in his later work. Methodologically, however, Orwell's critique of capitalism could have gained momentum by exposing the extreme disparity between the upscale residences of the well-to-do and the abject abodes of the poor. His avoidance of the sites of prosperity left him open to the charge of exaggeration—not a characteristic that would have been a recommendation for policymakers to take his message to heart.

When, some eleven months after returning from his tour, Orwell presented Gollancz with the fruit of his labors—a manuscript entitled *The Road to Wigan Pier* (1937)—the publisher's reaction was ambivalent. Indeed, parts of the manuscript appalled him, and he considered suppressing the offensive material. Although Gollancz liked part 1 of the book, with its gripping descriptions of poverty and unemployment among miners, he was bewildered by part 2, Orwell's idiosyncratic political manifesto and (partial) autobiography. There Orwell poses as devil's advocate, elaborating in trenchant manner his now famous views about Britain's socialists: "There is the horrible—the really disquieting—prevalence of cranks wherever Socialists are gathered together" (173). It is no wonder that Orwell's publisher feared the readers of the Left Book Club would be offended by such statements.

The whole journey through the region around Sheffield, Manchester, and Liverpool lasted only two months, but it had a profound influence on Orwell's political and artistic outlook. It was the period that contributed to the hardening of his unbending commitment to democratic socialism. In "Why I Write," he argues that "every line of serious work that I have written since 1936 has been written, directly or indirectly, against totalitarianism and for democratic Socialism as I understand it" (*Collected Essays* 424). The year mentioned, 1936, coincides with the date of his journey to Wigan. His encounter with coal miners, employed and unemployed, in one of England's main industrial zones convinced Orwell that art had an important function to play in the struggle against social, economic, and political injustice.

Some critics claim that the artistic impulse in Orwell's work led to idealization rather than to social realism. Bernard Crick argues that "the miners were not sociologically typical, only symbolically. They grew in his imagination as personifying both the fate and the hopes of the whole working class" (190). Indeed, there is a persistent tendency in Orwell's social reportage to turn figures of distress into bizarre fictional characters. In this, Orwell differs from Mayhew, whose reportage was based, first and foremost, on interviews and on eyewitness reporting. While Mayhew quoted his interviewees at length, Orwell in *Wigan Pier* hardly ever introduces any other voices than his own. Instead of quoting others, Orwell quotes himself to emphasize the authenticity of his observations: "As to what they are like and how they compare with the slum houses, I can best give an idea by transcribing two more extracts from my diary" (68). Statistics and stark pictures complement Orwell's appeal to truthfulness and authenticity, but they do not necessarily represent the perspective of the people whose life Orwell came to document. As a social observer in the industrial districts of North England, Orwell is as much an intruder from another world as the ethnologist among tribes in the Amazon.

The disaffection between Orwell and the objects of his inquiry is particularly noticeable at the beginning of *Wigan Pier*. Indeed, his grotesque descriptions of a working-class boardinghouse have been interpreted as evidence of Orwell's deep-seated bourgeois loathing of the lower classes. For instance, Frank Gloversmith stated that "the plethora of physical detail carries a load of apprehension, resentment" (111). Ironically though, it is precisely in his sensationalistic reflections on poverty that Orwell most closely approaches a popular register of style, whereas in his passages of detached analysis he reveals, though uneasily, his own moorings in the world of social and educational privilege. Except for the farcical opening chapter, however, this upper-class voice is clearly in the ascendant throughout the rest of *Wigan Pier*.

The transition between the two modes of discourse can be documented precisely in Orwell's description of the working conditions in the coal pit. There we notice a move beyond the level of visceral description to more deliberate sociopolitical commentary. Orwell starts the chapter with perceptual data: "The first impression of all, overmastering everything else for a while, is the frightful, deafening din from the conveyor belt which carries the coal away. You cannot see very far, because the fog of coal dust throws back the beam of your lamp, but you can see on either side of you the line of half-naked kneeling men. . . . Down this belt a glittering river of coal races constantly" (22). Soon, however, the prose slides into a more distant, objective style, with only a sprinkling of imaginative wording: "Coal lies in thin seams between enormous layers of rock, so that essentially the process of getting it out is like scooping the central layer from a Neapolitan ice" (30).

The experience of the pit is further conceptualized within the context of larger social issues, as the topic of coal production provides a vivid image of capitalist class divisions: "Watching coal-miners at work, you realize momentarily what different universes different people inhabit. Down there where the coal is dug it is a sort of world apart which one can quite easily go through life without ever hearing about" (33). The final analysis is purely ideological:

> For all the arts of peace coal is needed; if war breaks out it is
> needed all the more. In time of revolution the miner must go on
> working or the revolution must stop, for revolution as much as
> reaction needs coal. . . . In a way it is even humiliating to watch

coal-miners working. It raises in you a momentary doubt about
your own status as an "intellectual" and a superior person generally. For it is brought home to you, at least while you are watching, that it is only because miners sweat their guts out that superior persons can remain superior. (35–36)

This passage cleverly exposes the primary purpose of bourgeois ideology, which is to naturalize and render invisible the social contradictions that are at the basis of capitalist societies. Orwell's task as an ideologically conscious traveler is to "unearth" the layers of submerged or
repressed consciousness that are at the root of class divisions—a process that starts, appropriately, with the act of self-indictment.

After the coal-mining passages, Orwell goes on to detail a miner's
income, household budget, nutrition, health risks, and housing conditions, providing various statistics and citing official reports. In particular, he condemns the social injustice perpetuated by the so-called
Means Test.[3] From such specific political and economic issues, Orwell
moves on to more general matters of class ideology. For instance, he
elaborates on the ideological basis of the social stigma attached to
unemployment: "The middle classes were still talking about 'lazy idle
loafers on the dole' and saying that 'these men could all find work
if they wanted to,' and naturally these opinions percolated to the
working class themselves" (85). Significantly, this section of the book,
containing factual information and political rhetoric, is followed by
thirty-two starkly naturalistic photographs that corroborate Orwell's
eyewitness report about the inhumane conditions of working-class
life. Part 1 of *Wigan Pier*, then, follows the same pattern as *Down and
Out*, starting out with an imaginatively appealing prose style before
shifting into a more realistic documentary and analytical discourse.
For the bourgeois observer in Orwell, the strangeness of working-class
life, though appalling, also held a curious fascination. It was the next
best thing to exoticism, and Orwell regularly had to work through the
1930s intellectual's typical fascination with dirt and disease before he
could assume the factual tone and carry out the pragmatic analysis of
the sincere social explorer.

• • •

The theoretical and autobiographical part 2 of *Wigan Pier* is devoted to practically nothing but ideology, thereby further accentuating

the book's transition from a journey narrative to a political argument. Orwell's desire for ideological transformation is nowhere uttered more urgently than in this former colonial's confession that "I wanted to submerge myself, to get right down among the oppressed, to be one of them and on their side against their tyrants" (180). For Orwell, colonial duty abroad (a sort of travel in its own right) led to a quasi-revolutionary consciousness and generous sympathy with the suppressed. Orwell leaves no doubts about his attitude toward imperialism: "I hated the imperialism I was serving with a bitterness which I probably cannot make clear" (175).

Four years earlier, he had poured his aversion against imperialism and its executors into *Burmese Days* (1934), his first novel. This book, set in upper Burma, is a sustained argument against the dehumanizing and alienating potential of imperial rule. The protagonist, an officer named Flory, carries an ugly birthmark on his cheek, thereby symbolizing the self-disfiguring quality of being employed in the service of imperialism. Instead of associating the foreign country with a symbol that would define a repressed aspect of the imperialist's identity (as in *Heart of Darkness*), Orwell places the most prominent symbol of the novel on the face of imperialism's very agent. And for Flory, as for the British Empire, the disfiguring symbol is a bad omen.

Orwell shows in *Burmese Days* how imperialism morally corrupts both the local dignitaries and the British administrators because both conspire to destroy the reputation of a local intellectual, Dr. Veraswami, a skilled physician whose dream is to become a member of the European club at Kyauktada. Moreover, imperialism is undermining the very fiber of genuine selfhood, as exemplified in the protagonist's fate. Flory admires Burma's native culture and tries to adapt to the local standards of taste and judgment. At the same time, he is desperately in love with an Englishwoman who epitomizes all the racial and cultural snobbery of "mem-sahibdom." Torn between the impulses to "go native" and to be a useful member of the imperial organization, Flory ends up putting a bullet through his head. *Burmese Days* records Orwell's first major attempt to purge himself of the guilt of having participated in Britain's imperial endeavors. But the denunciation of imperialism in his novel was not enough. In part 2 of *Wigan Pier*, Orwell strives to overcome the very bourgeois ideology that had enabled the imperial project to flourish in the first place. In order to fulfill his sense of social justice, individual freedom, and fair economic relations between the classes (and races), Orwell realizes that he has to undergo an ideological transformation.

Orwell sums up his approach to travel by emphasizing its ideological component: "I have seen just enough of the working class to avoid idealizing them, but I do know that you can learn a great deal in a working-class home, if only you can get there. The essential point is that your middle-class ideals and prejudices are tested by contact with others which are not necessarily better but are certainly different" (147). To test one's ideological prejudices through social travel is but one thing, however; to transcend these class-based ideas is quite another matter, and Orwell is remarkably realistic about this: "Is it ever possible to be really intimate with the working class? . . . I will only say here that I do not think it is possible" (147). At the same time that he recognizes the importance of acknowledging ideological differences between divergent social and racial populations, Orwell also warns against the naive belief that such differences could easily be overcome by brief exposure to another social milieu. Thus, travel alone is not enough for the kind of self-transformation that would make one a true member of another social class. Such a transformation would take both ideological reorientation and the kind of self-alienation that would result from prolonged social displacement.

• • •

The beginning of the Spanish civil war in July 1936 intensified Orwell's political activism. The following December, immediately after finishing the *Wigan Pier* manuscript, Orwell began to cast about for the channels that would introduce him to the ranks of the Spanish Republican army. His aim was to support the fight against Franco and to write dispatches for the *New Statesman and Nation* about his experiences in the war. But the British Communist Party, wary of Orwell's critical attitude toward communism, refused to provide him with introductory letters to the leaders of the Spanish Popular Front. The ILP was more helpful. Although Orwell was not a member of the party at that time, they arranged contacts to the militia forces of POUM, the anarchist faction, or Partido Obrero de Unificación Marxista (The worker's party of Marxist unity) in Barcelona. By December 22, 1936, Orwell was on his way to Spain. Four days later, in Barcelona, he joined the ranks of the POUM militia.

The POUM faction was the political and military organization of

the anarchist trade union CNT (Confederación National de Trabajadores). Of the government forces, unified under the banner of the
Popular Front, the anarchist POUM was the smallest of various socialist and Marxist groups, greatly outnumbered by the communist trade
union and their political and military wing. Thus, by sheer coinci-
dence, Orwell seems to have joined the one faction on the Republican
side that most closely corresponded to his political and social views.
But even though he denied associations with so-called Trotskyism, it
is clear that he was part of a political movement that remained faithful
to the maxims of Trotsky, as evidenced in their emphasis on permanent revolution and on achieving world communism.

Orwell's involvement with Spain undoubtedly brought about the
most fundamental ideological adaptation he had yet achieved in his
life, quite eclipsing his social journeys in England. Before this trip, his
dress, dialect, and complexion had often given him away as an "intruder" from another social sphere. During his six months in Spain,
however, he blended almost completely with the disparate lot of militiamen. Part of Orwell's unadorned narrative style in *Homage to Catalonia* (1938) and the clarity of his prose are related to that intimate
social connection. His participation in the war enabled him to render,
instead of strangeness (the ability to record strangeness is in fact
caused by separation) a social and political context as if it were his
natural milieu. Indeed, Orwell had metamorphosed from an observer
to a participant.

Homage is a rather untypical specimen of travel writing, however,
because it so studiously avoids the temptation of hyperbole or the
spinning of tall tales. Instead, we are soberly told that "twenty or thirty
hours' sleep in a week was quite a normal amount. The effects of this
were not so bad as might be expected" (41); or we learn that "the tem-
perature was not exceptionally low, on many nights it did not even
freeze, and the wintry sun often shone for an hour in the middle of the
day; but even if it was not really cold, I assure you that it seemed so"
(29); and finally, "in March there was heavy fighting round Huesca,
but I personally played only a minor part in it" (23). The cool tone of
detachment corresponds to Orwell's deliberate refusal to assume a
dominant, authoritarian point of view (but it also buys into a new,
tough-minded sort of heroic understatement, à la Hemingway). And
the caveats about his authority as a narrator are even more emphasized here than similar reservations mentioned in *Wigan Pier:* "I have

recorded some of the outward events, but I cannot record the feeling they have left me with. It is all mixed up with sights, smells, and sounds that cannot be conveyed in writing" (*Homage* 230). After all, this is the nature of experience—it is determined as much by external sociopolitical events as by purely personal impressions. Hence, any rendering of experience, be it in a domestic context or abroad, has its limitations, and Orwell is aware of them.

Accordingly, when Orwell approaches a topic as controversial as the existence of cultural differences or national types, he does so cautiously. One difference he records tends in fact to reflect on the habits of northerners, rather than documenting a sense of English superiority. Orwell remarks that "the Spaniards are good at many things, but not at making war" (12). This statement appears to be corroborated by the fact that "all foreigners alike are appalled by their inefficiency, above all their maddening unpunctuality" (12). However, the effect of this "maddening unpunctuality" is tempered by Orwell's admission that "in theory I rather admire the Spaniards for not sharing our Northern time-neurosis; but unfortunately I share it myself" (13). Thus, Orwell distributes his pejorative attributes evenly: first censoring the Spaniards for their unpunctuality, but then censoring northerners for censoring the Spaniards about this. But Orwell rarely indulges in useless stereotyping: what interests him more than considerations of "national character" are the specific conditions of the sociopolitical situation in which he is implicated.

• • •

Orwell's Spanish sojourn was a journey of initiation in several ways. One initiation concerned his reception into the world of proletarian soldiery. A second initiation was the experience of ideological and political betrayal. Even during Orwell's first stay at the front, the Catalan bourgeoisie had gradually emerged from their hiding places and started to reclaim their privileges. When he returned to Barcelona in late April 1937, it was no longer a "worker's city": "The change in the aspect of the crowds was startling. The militia uniform and the blue overalls had almost disappeared; everyone seemed to be wearing the smart summer suits in which Spanish tailors specialize. Fat prosperous men, elegant women, and sleek cars were everywhere" (106–7).

Moreover, the party of the communists had greatly increased its influence in the National Front, declaring that military victory had to be given absolute priority over social revolution. With this policy, the communists had antagonized the anarchists, for whom social revolution was inseparable from military victory. So Orwell, instead of enjoying his reprieve from the front, experienced the beginning of street fighting in Barcelona, as the different factions on the Republican side began vying for power. He was ordered by the POUM to stand guard on the rooftop of the organization's Barcelona headquarters.

Orwell's description of the in-fighting between different antifascist groups in Barcelona constitutes the most politically enlightening section of *Homage*. But Orwell significantly points out the ideological contingency of his representation of the conflict. Mystification is thus largely absent from his account of the Spanish struggle. After having thoroughly investigated the ideological and historical aspects of the situation in Barcelona, he cautions the reader about the reliability of his own point of view: "It is difficult to be certain about anything except what you have seen with your own eyes, and consciously or unconsciously everyone writes as a partisan. . . . Beware of my partisanship, my mistakes of fact and the distortion inevitably caused by my having seen only one corner of events. And beware of exactly the same things when you read any other book on this period of the Spanish war" (231). Orwell's caveat is not a mere rhetorical flourish. Indeed, some of his own representations have turned out to be less than accurate. Historians such as Hugh Thomas have challenged Orwell's version of the Barcelona events. Another critic, Murray Sperber, contends that Orwell's depiction of the anarchist POUM is "historically untrue. . . . After all, the POUM belonged to Trotsky's Fourth International, and nowhere in their literature did they ever indicate a tendency toward Orwell's very English sense of 'liberty and justice' " (227).

Nevertheless, Orwell's account of the political struggle in Spain deserves to be called exceptional because he is quite aware of the tricky nature of any attempt to render this conflict discursively. For example, he dedicates the entirety of chapter 11 to the issue of how a situation he had witnessed first-hand (the war-within-the-war in Barcelona) is represented both in Spain and abroad. He concludes that "a tremendous dust was kicked up in the foreign anti-Fascist press, but, as usual, only one side of the case has had anything like a hearing. As a result the Barcelona fighting has been represented as an insurrection by disloyal anarchists and Trotskyists who were 'stabbing the Spanish Government in the back,' and so forth" (157). Orwell, who had gone to

Spain with the intention to fight Fascism, sees himself suddenly portrayed as belonging to a group of fascist infiltrators, not only in the communist press in Spain but in major socialist publications abroad, such as the British *Daily Worker*.

This instance exemplifies the power of ideologically controlled discourses. Usually, the British subject is accustomed to be on the emitting end of such practices, to dish it out, not take it. In Catalonia, however, Orwell experienced how it felt to be defined by others, to be made the subject of a discourse that denies or distorts one's identity. That he recorded such an experience and traced the political basis of its influence makes for an interesting variety on the topic of an English traveler's discursive subject position.

• • •

After a few tense weeks in Barcelona, Orwell returned again to the front near Huesca. This stay brought about Orwell's third initiation; namely, his encounter with death. Orwell, who had made a name for himself by various feats of daring (such as harvesting potatoes within reach of enemy fire), almost paid with his life for his disposition toward recklessness. Ten days after his return to the front, he spoke to a comrade without taking the precaution of keeping his head below the parapet. He was instantly hit in the throat by a sniper bullet, suffering a near fatal wound: "The doctors told him that if the bullet had been but a millimetre to the left he would have been dead" (Crick, 224). His recovery took several weeks, and in June 1937 he decided to quit the army. As it turned out, his injury can be seen as providential: the POUM forces were soon afterward ground up in Franco's offensive, and those who survived were attacked by the communists.

In order to get his discharge from the army, Orwell had to travel to the POUM headquarters at Sietamo. It is interesting to note the discursive transformation that occurs at that stage. Indeed, the country looks different to him now that he no longer sees it through the eyes of a militiaman: "It was queer how for nearly six months past I had had no eyes for such things. With my discharge papers in my pocket I felt like a human being again, and also a little like a tourist. For almost the first time I felt that I was really in Spain, in a country that I had longed all my life to visit. In the quiet back streets of Lerida and Barbastro I seemed to catch a momentary glimpse, a sort of far-off rumour of the Spain that dwells in everyone's imagination. White sierras, goatherds, dungeons of the Inquisition, Moorish palaces, black winding trains of mules, grey olive trees" (203). Orwell's catalog of "archetypal" Spanish sights rumbles on and on, but it does not get more interesting. The things that dwell in "everyone's imagination" constitute, of course, the myth of Spain, a concoction of actual features and constructed cultural symbols that equates the myth of "dark" Africa or the legend of China, the "land of smiles." Ironically, although Orwell claims that, for the most part, he "was really in Spain" only after becoming an unpolitical traveler, his most piercing, evocative passages about the country are written from the perspective of the partisan activist—a strange instance of self-deception.

When Orwell returned to Barcelona to recover from his injury, the communists were firmly entrenched in all key political functions, and they made it their first order of business to outlaw the POUM. What had begun in euphoria for a good cause ended in persecution and humiliation: "There was a particular evil feeling in the air—an atmosphere of suspicion, fear, uncertainty, and veiled hatred" (186). In fact, a warrant was out for Orwell's arrest, and only thanks to a quick warning by his wife Eileen, who had been waiting for him at the hotel entrance, was he able to escape capture by the communists. Subsequently, Orwell had to dodge communist henchmen night and day, sleeping outdoors and shifting positions during the day.

At the end of the month—it was still June 1937—Orwell managed to leave the country secretly, accompanied by his wife and two other English volunteers, McNair and Cotman. Taking the train from Barcelona to Port Bou, they had the good fortune not to be stopped by the Republican police at the border. Pursued by the very people they had gone to help in the fight against fascism, they had escaped into France. Now they were running from a disease more widespread than fascism—the disease of political violence and ideological tyranny. Orwell's Spanish experience left him deeply scarred, both literally and mentally. He had risked everything for a cause that was now self-destructing. Thus *Homage* is a testimony both of personal triumph in the face of adversity and of the defeat of a political ideal.

What distinguishes the book above all is its skillful interweaving of political analysis and personal memoir. Contrary to *Down and Out*, where Orwell had discussed socioeconomic matters intuitively and in a structurally awkward manner (often the social analyses were simply tagged on at the end of a narrative section), and in contradistinction

to *Wigan Pier*, where he had still maintained some separation between reporting and politics, *Homage* brings the two aspects together.
The representation of physical and spiritual experience and their ideological contextualization substantially fuse. Ultimately, the journey recorded in *Homage* comprises both a personal level of engagement with
the ideals of socialism and a larger political investigation into the
workings of social revolution. *Homage* is a superior achievement of
political travel writing: it expresses the dignity of an individual's struggle for freedom and social justice. It also, however, confirms the view
that political travel is doomed in the era of totalitarianism.

Travel writing was Orwell's vehicle of choice to propound his views
of revolutionary change. In that respect, he was perhaps the most emblematic leftist traveler of the 1930s. He traveled in order to further the
cause of social justice and to dismantle damaging stereotypes about
"inferior" classes and nonwhite races. He was convinced that a journey can be considered to have value only if the traveler emerged from
his journey with a fuller understanding of social justice and racial
equality. This was already evident in *Down and Out;* it was to become
much more pronounced in the confessional urgency of *Wigan Pier*,
and in *Homage,* the pinnacle of Orwell's confessional and political
travel writing, personal perception and ideological self-consciousness
are closely interwoven.

Orwell's travel writing, thus, moves from intuitively socialist concerns to the documentary investigation of social conditions, and
thence to direct political participation. His travels were clearly an attempt to move beyond the social and cultural boundaries that he felt
were erected around him by the parameters of bourgeois ideology.

2 EVELYN WAUGH

EVELYN WAUGH was an exceptional figure among the 1930s travelers insofar as he produced more travel books than anybody else and because he endowed them with a harder core of rightist ideology than most other 1930s English travel writers. Unlike Orwell, Waugh did not face the task of reconciling his bourgeois sensibility with the tenets of radical thought; instead, he simply professed his straightforward conservatism. While his books about the Mediterranean and British Guiana (respectively, *Labels, a Mediterranean Journal* [1930] and *Ninety-two Days* [1934]) are only implicitly political, his travel books about Africa (*Remote People* [1931] and *Waugh in Abyssinia* [1936]) and Mexico (*Robbery under Law* [1939]) contain explicit conservative opinions as well as a large dose of cultural pessimism, that hallmark of conservative thought.

In fact, social decay and cultural decline formed the mainstay of Waugh's imaginative resources during the late 1920s and early 1930s. His first novel, *Decline and Fall* (1928), immediately established him as the enfant terrible of London's literary circles. The novel displayed his talents for capturing a decadent world that had abandoned traditional values, a world whose degeneracy and recklessness undermined the very fabric of liberal humanism and of the gentlemanly ideology. *Decline and Fall* made Waugh many admirers as well as many enemies. His often ludicrous rendering of thinly disguised real personalities caused a good deal of offense and helped establish Waugh's reputation as a misanthropist. Of course, to London's Bright Young Things, misanthropy was a rather flattering attribute, and Waugh became the self-styled spokesperson for this social phenomenon of the Roaring Twenties.

In the introductory note to his second novel, *Vile Bodies* (1930), Waugh characterizes the Bright Young Things as being "totally unlike the various, publicized groups of modern youth, being mostly of good family and education and sharp intelligence, but they were equally anarchic and short-lived" (vii). *Vile Bodies* draws strongly on Waugh's experience among these ultrafashionable but morally unprincipled people (one incident in the novel involves the novelist manqué Adam Fenwick-Symes selling off his fiancée to a rival, the dissipated Ginger Littlejohn, for a modest sum).

But Waugh's identification with the unruly Bright Young Things did not diminish his concern for the authority of age, aristocracy, and law. Donat Gallagher comments: "Within the 'ultra-modern' young man in a modern and liberal era there was a conservative rebel on his way to Rome" (Waugh, *Essays, Articles, and Reviews*, 40). While Waugh's conversion to Roman Catholicism in 1930 marked the end of his ambivalent relationship with the Bright Young Things, it also deepened his political conservatism. Indeed, what Waugh called Catholicism's "competent organization and discipline" (*Essays, Articles, and Reviews*, 104) appealed to his reverence for authority and order.

But the sociocultural appeal of Roman Catholicism was equally important. In an article for the *Daily Express*, Waugh defended his conversion to Catholicism—a conversion that was widely publicized—as follows: "In the present phase of European history the essential issue is no longer between Catholicism, on one side, and Protestantism, on the other, but between Christianity and Chaos. . . . [Civilization] came into being through Christianity, and without it has no significance or power to command allegiance. . . . Christianity exists in its most complete and vital form in the Roman Catholic Church" (*Essays, Articles, and Reviews*, 104). These ideas mirror the views expressed by Hilaire Belloc in *Europe and the Faith* (1920). Belloc, a Roman Catholic apologist, insisted that European civilization had survived the onslaught of barbarism during the Dark Ages only because the seed of civilization had been preserved by Catholics. In conjunction with this argument, Belloc claimed that the foundations of civilization in Europe were laid by the Roman Empire.[1] The Bellocian basis of Waugh's argument in the *Daily Express* article demonstrates how receptive he was to Catholicism's Rome-centered cultural paradigm.

The racial implications of this paradigm caused Waugh to place Ethiopia squarely in the column of abject savagery, although the country had a long tradition of orthodox Christianity. In an article written for the *Times* shortly after his conversion, Waugh proclaims that "it is absurd to pretend that Ethiopia is a civilized nation in any western sense of the word," and he follows this assertion with a list of "barbarities and anomalies" (*Essays, Articles, and Reviews,* 121–22) that characterize life in Ethiopia. If anything, Catholicism confirmed Waugh in his social and cultural snobbery. But there is also a specifically political implication in his attack on Ethiopia, as Donat Gallagher points out: "The undesirability of Abyssinia's being imagined a 'civilized' state by the world at large reflects British Colonial Office thinking" (Waugh, *Essays, Articles, and Reviews,* 111).

• • •

But if Waugh's religious conversion strengthened his inherent conservatism, it did not abate his cynical and deeply antihumanist outlook. In fact, after the publication of his African novel *Black Mischief* (1932), several prominent Catholics attempted to disgrace Waugh as not being a true follower of the creed. In an open letter published in the *Tablet,* a Roman Catholic periodical, twelve dignitaries complained about obscenity, blasphemy, and, not surprisingly, Waugh's mocking representation of two "humanitarian" ladies in his book. Indeed, since *Black Mischief* exposes to ridicule not only the supposed savagery of a foreign nation (fictionalized Ethiopia) but also the humanistic tradition of the West, Waugh's satire may appear to cut both ways.

A similar sense of double-edged satire emerges from a passage in the book about British Guiana, *Ninety-two Days,* Waugh's third travel book. Here Waugh's conventional attitude toward barbarism is compounded by cynical attacks against the forces of modernity: "Not here those firm, confident tentacles of modernity that extend to greet the traveller, no tractors making their own roads as they advance, no progressive young managers projecting more advanced stations of commerce, opening up new districts, pushing forward new settlements and new markets, no uniformed law asserting itself in chaos. Instead we had overtaken civilization in its retreat" (172). But although Waugh jibes at the agents of modernity, his proimperial sentiments also cause him to believe in the necessity to civilize those left behind by progress. In an article for the *Evening Standard*, written in 1935, Waugh draws a political conclusion from the juxtaposition of two unequally developed cultures:

> It is one of the facts of history that it is impossible for two peoples of widely different culture to live peaceably side by side. Sooner or later one must absorb the other. It is not necessarily the higher culture which survives. It is the more virile. Early history is full of the records of advanced and fine cultures being absorbed by barbarians. Lately—but only very lately, in the last two centuries—the tale has been reversed and we have seen, one by one, the lower civilizations falling to the higher. . . . But it is in the nature of civilization that it must be in constant conflict with barbarism. (*Essays, Articles, and Reviews,* 163)

This, then, is no laughing matter. While the struggle between civilization and barbarism in British Guiana is presented in an ironic light, Waugh later took a more serious approach to the matter. This is expressed in the way he applied his polarity between barbarism and civilization to the conflicting impulses within every individual. Waugh suspects a core of barbarism in every person, a tendency that is merely suspended by the trappings of "civilization." In his last 1930s travel book, *Robbery under Law* (1939), Waugh exclaims: "We are all potential recruits for anarchy" (162). This view corresponds to Freud's insistence in *Civilization and Its Discontents* that "the development of civilization has . . . a far-reaching similarity to the development of the individual" (144).

Waugh, who can reasonably be expected to have read Freud's essay in the early 1930s, would have emphatically agreed with Freud's assertion that because of man's "inclination to aggression . . . civilized society is perpetually threatened with disintegration. The interest of work in common would not hold it together; instinctual passions are stronger than reasonable interests" (112). The political implications of Waugh's Freudian outlook on civilization were largely confirmed in his encounters with non-Western cultures, whose "barbarism" he considered a manifestation of inner drives and anarchic impulses that lurk in everyone. But Waugh parts company with Freud in evaluating the tension between "barbarism" and "civilization." While Freud claims that "what we call our civilization is largely responsible for our misery"

(86), Waugh sees a clear hierarchy of values between the civilized West and its "barbarous" fringes. For Waugh, barbarism is an inherently dangerous human capacity, and its counterpart, civilization, though beset with its own problems and neuroses, offers an infinitely more desirable rule to live by.

But such cultural pessimism is not Waugh's only way of attacking the ideology of humanism. In *Ninety-two Days*, Waugh debunks what he lists as humanist convictions regarding travel: "that one felt free . . . that one was untrammeled by convention . . . that one eats with a gay appetite and sleeps with the imperturbable ease of infancy" (118–19), and generally "that the greatest physical and mental well-being can be attained only in the wild parts of the world" (118). Waugh calls all these ideas a "bluff," arguing elsewhere in the book that "general skepticism" remains "one of the more valuable fruits of travel" (140).

In this assessment, Waugh not only contradicts the enthusiasm of primitivist travelers, he also destabilizes the humanist ethos according to which an individual's heroic struggle with his environment entails *Bildung*, or profound insights: "[my journey] makes no claim to being a spiritual odyssey" (179), a markedly anticlimactic statement, and one designed to discredit both escapist and humanist motives for travel.

•   •   •

In terms of the ideological subtext of Waugh's travel writing, nothing is more irksome than the systematic racial bias embodied in his work. Waugh's racial attitudes are evidenced in a variety of ways. For instance, in an essay entitled "The Tourist's Manual" (1935) Waugh advises travelers to strike an arrogant pose in encounters with natives and to altercate with them in English rather than trying to understand what they are saying in their own language. In another article, Waugh generously concedes that "there are always honourable exceptions in any general racial condemnation." Nevertheless, he maintains that "it is not too much to say that in general character the descendants of the Negro slaves in the British Empire are a thriftless and dissolute lot. . . . They have proved quite unfit for retail trade: they are clumsy mechanics, a superstitious and excitable riff-raff hanging round the rum shops and staring listlessly at the Chinese, Madeiran and East Indian immigrants, who outstrip them in every branch of life" (*Essays, Articles, and Reviews*, 135).

Waugh's condemnation of people of color often hinges on their economic performance. Consequently, slavery is not such a bad institution for those who are inherently "lazy" or improvident: "I have seen slave-owning communities in Abyssinia and Arabia and got the impression that the slaves are far better off than wage-earners in those countries" (*Essays, Articles, and Reviews,* 135). The efforts of abolitionists such as William Wilberforce are ridiculed as "fallacies that are being abandoned today: the idea of a perfectible evolutionary man, of a responsible democratic voter, of the beneficial effect of mechanization, and, above all, of sentimental belief in the basic sweetness of human nature" (*Essays, Articles, and Reviews,* 135). Once again, antihumanism is tightly knit into the fabric of Waugh's racist pronouncements, so much so that Waugh's antihumanism makes humanism appear to be a vastly more agreeable ideology.[2]

Considering his elitist political ideas, Waugh was undeniably one of the most conservative authors of the 1930s. James Carens concludes that Waugh is actually "tied to an older ideology which moves, to be sure, in the same direction as Fascist racism and often bears similar fruit. In *Remote People* and *Waugh in Abyssinia* he is reactionary in that, evoking once again the attitude of such writers of the late nineteenth century as Rudyard Kipling and W. H. Hudson, he argues that the European is entitled to carry civilization, by force if necessary, to the 'lesser breeds without the law'" (133). In fact, Waugh is harking back to an aristocratic social model where political legitimacy is carried in the bloodline and the burden of government is founded upon values of loyalty and honor. This makes not only modern, impersonal forms of democracy suspect to Waugh, but also nationalist liberation movements that lack an aristocratic pedigree.

• • •

Interestingly, however, Waugh was not impressed by the dynastic tradition of Ethiopia's ruling aristocracy, the Amharas. Although he was intrigued by the supposed anomaly of an African state that was governed by an indigenous aristocracy and, moreover, claimed the status of an empire, he never viewed Ethiopia as anything less than a cultural backwater, ready to tip over into anarchy. A look at the historical record casts doubts over Waugh's derogatory opinions, however, and before returning to Waugh it will be worth examining that history in some detail.

Historians such as Richard Pankhurst and Harold Marcus have argued that Ethiopia's claim to an independent, continuous form of nationhood is older than that of most European nations. Although Ethiopia is an ethnically heterogeneous state (comprising many separate tribes such as the Tigray, Amhara, Shewa, and Oromo), Harold Marcus says that "Ethiopia's history contained an analytical truth. . . . From time to time, the nation had disintegrated into component parts, but it had never disappeared as an idea and always reappeared in fact" (xiii). Moreover, the main factors that contributed to the development of Ethiopia's unique culture—namely, the concept of statehood, the acceptance of Christianity, the importance of trade, and a tightly organized military class—align this nation far more closely with European standards than Waugh makes us believe.

The ancient empire of Axum marks the beginning of Ethiopia's long-lasting tradition of nationhood. Holding its own against the Roman Empire, the Axumite state existed from 100 to 1100 A.D., controlling vital trading routes from Egypt to Arabia and India and thereby establishing a network of wealthy ports and trading towns within its territory. In the fourth century A.D., Christianity (then the official state religion of the eastern Roman Empire) spread into Ethiopia in the wake of very active trading relations between the two empires. From then onward, Ethiopia often played the role of a defender of Christianity in Africa, first holding its own against Judaism and then forming a bulwark against the spread of Islam. Over the centuries, the area extending in a wide semicircle inland from the African side of the Red Sea was controlled and administered by successive Ethiopian dynasties. After the decline of the once powerful Axumite empire, the rule passed to the house of Zagwe, whose kings controlled an area largely congruous with the previous state of Axum. Their reign lasted until 1270, when a Shewa ruler, Yekuno Amlak, killed the reigning emperor and proclaimed himself his legitimate successor. Amlak, an Orthodox Christian like his predecessor, sought to legitimize his conquest by fabricating and circulating the most persistent of fables surrounding the history of Ethiopia. He claimed to be a direct descendant from Menilek I, son of King Solomon and Makeda, the queen of Sheba. The Solomonic dynasty, as it has been called ever since, ruled Ethiopia for roughly 250 years before it went into decline in the sixteenth century due to the rise of Muslim rulers in that region.

Shortly before his death in 1540, the Christian emperor of Ethiopia,

Lebna Dengel, asked Portugal for support against the incursions of Islam. The call was heeded, and in April 1541 a company of several hundred musketeers defeated Imam Ahmad's army, thereby consolidating Ethiopia's reputation as the vanguard of Christianity in Africa. But Portugal, wanting to make sure that the right kind of Christianity would prevail in Ethiopia, sent Jesuit missionaries to Ethiopia in order to convert the local Orthodox Christians to Roman Catholicism. Indeed, the Ethiopian church had, during the centuries of isolation, developed a highly idiosyncratic form of Christianity, shot through with pagan and Judaic elements such as sacrifices, circumcision rituals, and the avoidance of unclean animals. But the Jesuits were too eager in trying to teach Ethiopia the "true" creed of Christianity. In 1632, the ruler of Ethiopia, Susenyos, decided to expel all Jesuits from his country for meddling in the country's internal affairs, persecuting and killing many of them in the process.[3]

With the Portuguese support gone, the formerly unified, tightly ruled political entity was further weakened by ongoing wars against Muslim forces and by strife among Ethiopia's different ethnic groups. The period of weakness and national dissolution was reversed in the nineteenth century when Menilek II ascended the throne. He was a particularly capable, courageous, and intelligent leader, and he inflicted one of the most smarting defeats to European imperialism. Indeed, Italy, a belated player in the scramble for Africa, had made it clear in the 1890s that it coveted Ethiopia, then the only place left to be scrambled for, partly because the other European nations had implicitly accepted the nation's sovereignty. After years of political maneuvers and military skirmishes, the Italian armies were poised in 1896 to attack and conquer Ethiopia. War between Italy and Ethiopia was declared after Menilek II annulled a peace treaty between the two countries. He had discovered that the Italian copy of the treaty contained a clause that virtually signed away Ethiopia's independence to the Italians, whereas the same clause was phrased entirely differently (referring only to voluntary cooperation) in the Ethiopian copy of the agreement. Then, a half-starved army under the command of Menilek II managed to hand the Italian army at Adwa a crushing defeat. This exploit "gave the country a status similar to that of Afghanistan, Persia, Japan, and Thailand as accepted anomalies in the imperialist world order" (Marcus, 100).

When Menilek's rule ended there followed a period of wars of succession, which threatened to undermine both Ethiopia's national unity and the international prestige it had gained. But with the rise of Ras Tafari in the 1920s, first as regent to empress Zawditu, then as king, and finally as Emperor Haile Selassie, the country had once again a skilled diplomat and capable political leader: "Haile Selassie centralized the state and expanded Ethiopia's civil society as a counterweight to ethnic forces. He fostered unity through the development of a national army, a pan-Ethiopian economy, modern communications, and an official culture." (Marcus, xiii).

But Haile Selassie faced great odds at the beginning of his reign. Italy's defeat at Adwa had rankled for a long time, and Mussolini vowed to get even with Ethiopia by breaking its resistance to colonization once and for all. In a series of flagrant violations of international law and national sovereignty, Mussolini marched his troops against Ethiopia, determined to conquer this nation come what may. No means were too noxious to achieve this end. Although Haile Selassie had ordered his forces to take their positions thirty kilometers behind the Ethiopian border to avoid any pretext for warfare, Mussolini's forces capitalized on this strategic advantage. With the help of poison gas, dumped in big quantities on the Ethiopian front lines, he managed to take Ethiopia in 1936.

The League of Nations, meanwhile, had looked on passively, although Ethiopia had been a member state, thereby discrediting the whole purpose and legitimacy of the international body. But the Italian hold on the country was tenuous at best. Much of the territory remained unconquered, and incessant guerrilla warfare made an effective administration almost impossible. Only five years later, in January 1941, joint British and Ethiopian forces succeeded in driving the Italians out of the country. Haile Selassie was restored to his position as emperor of Ethiopia, entering World War II on the side of the Allies. It is against this background that Waugh's attitudes toward Ethiopia in general and his depiction of Haile Selassie in particular need to be assessed.

• • •

During the 1930s, Waugh maintained a more intense relationship with Ethiopia than with any other nation outside England. Although he despised the country for its supposed "barbarity," he must have felt a certain fascination for it: he returned there twice. Waugh first traveled to Ethiopia in 1930 to cover Haile Selassie's coronation for the *Times* and the *Daily Express*. He then returned to Ethiopia in 1935 as a war correspondent for the *Daily Mail* and, in 1936, toured a portion of the country as an official guest of the Italian occupation force. Throughout this period, he wrote not only two travel books about the country (*Remote People* and *Waugh in Abyssinia*),[4] but also based two novels (*Black Mischief* and *Scoop*) on his experience as a traveler and journalist there. Each successive book in this quartet voices more explicitly rightist, proimperial opinions. Although the political motivation for his first journey to Ethiopia in 1930 may have been rather vague, the comparative design of *Remote People* (where a section entitled "Ethiopian Empire" is followed by one entitled "British Empire"), fosters a highly unfavorable opinion of native rule in Ethiopia, compared with conditions in the European colonies.

Although an element of curiosity and wonder prevents *Remote People* from sliding into open bigotry, Waugh's approach to Ethiopia is sarcastic enough to give a distorting image of the country and its people. For instance, Waugh speculates about the reasons for "this sudden convergence on Abyssinia of the envoys of the civilized world. . . . Honest colonists all over Africa grumbled at this absurd display of courtesy towards a mere native. At the legations themselves there was some restlessness; all this would still further complicate the task of impressing on the Abyssinians their real unimportance in the greater world" (8). Such words—"civilized world," "honest colonists," "a mere native"—could be considered as tokens of irony, even as a potential form of self-criticism. Indeed, Waugh states confidently "that a prig is someone who judges people by his own, rather than by their standards" (40). But Waugh's systematic use of demeaning terms in referring to Ethiopia—he describes the country as "a tangle of modernism and barbarity" (42) whose leader lived in "a great jumble of buildings" (29) in order to "impress on his European visitors that Ethiopia was no mere agglomeration of barbarous tribes" (23)—shows that he rarely himself followed his own standard of what would not be priggish. Even initially appreciative comments such as the assessment that "Somalis are a race of exceptional beauty" (12) do not go unmodified, as when in a later passage he refers to the "monkey-like faces and sooty complexions" (86) of the Somalis.

The foregoing quotations are all elliptical, for Waugh is a master in couching stereotypical or arrogant statements in a web of reasonable-sounding, inoffensive language. By writing thus, Waugh eludes the charge of outright racism or ethnocentrism. For instance, the comment on Ethiopia's "tangle of modernism and barbarity" is tucked away as a subordinate clause in a longer passage of an ostensibly "neutral" character: "After all, there really was something there to report that was quite new to the European public; a succession of events of startling spectacular character, and a system of life, in a tangle of modernism and barbarity, European, African, and American, of definite, individual character. It seemed to me that here, at least, the truth was stranger than the newspaper reports" (42). Moreover, the statement about Haile Selassie's supposed attempt "to impress on his European visitors that Ethiopia was no mere agglomeration of barbarous tribes," is ostensibly formulated as a negation, although it conveys the opposite meaning; namely, an affirmation of Ethiopia's barbarism.

The manipulative potential of such language is further heightened by Waugh's skillful use of the stylistic ambivalence between reported speech and authorial elocutions. Consider the following example:

> The coronation festivities were thus the final move in a long and well-planned strategy. Still maintaining his double ruff of trumping at home with prestige abroad, abroad with his prestige at home, Tafari had two main motives behind the display. He wished to impress on his European visitors that Ethiopia was no mere agglomeration of barbarous tribes open to foreign exploitation, but a powerful, organized, modern state. He wanted to impress on his own countrymen that he was no paramount chief of a dozen independent communities, but an absolute monarch recognized on equal terms by the monarchies and governments of the great world. (23)

It appears as though Waugh were actually rendering in indirect speech Haile Selassie's own thoughts or words on the matter. In this manner, he gives the impression of neutral reporting, while actually conveying subtly disguised opinions that argue the general underdevelopment, mimicry, and depravity of Ethiopia (and of other African societies).

• • •

For Waugh, fiction was the continuation of travel writing with different means. In *Black Mischief*, Waugh even strengthens the racist subtext that had percolated through *Remote People*. Although his personal encounter with Haile Selassie had left Waugh with a modicum of respect for the ruler (*Remote People*, 54–55), in *Black Mischief* Haile Selassie is transformed into the buffoon emperor Seth, whose whimsical ideas produce one political disaster after another.

Although Waugh's fictional country of Azania is a (nonexistent) island off the coast of Somalia in the Indian Ocean, the parallels between Azania and Ethiopia are unequivocal: Azania's capital is called Debra Dowa, clearly after the railway junction Dirre Dowa in which Waugh spent three very boring days, and the Armenian businessman Youkoumian is a direct portrait of Mr. Bergebedgian, that "ultimate cosmopolitan" described in *Remote People.* Most importantly, Seth is intent on "modernizing" his country just as was Haile Selassie. But Seth not only incorporates characteristics of Haile Selassie, he is also in part based on Selassie's predecessor, Menilek II. Indeed, Seth's initial struggle with Prince Seyid over the imperial throne recalls Menilek II's power struggle with his rival, the former emperor of Ethiopia, Yohannes. In the last quarter of the nineteenth century, King Menilek had engaged in a long and intense rivalry over the throne. When the Mahdists attacked Ethiopia in 1888, Yohannes was killed in battle and Menilek II immediately ascended his throne.

Waugh's idea to have a young English adventurer become Seth's adviser in *Black Mischief* is in all likelihood based on a historical figure, too. Indeed, Menilek II had hired "Alfred Ilg, a young Swiss engineer who would remain in the king's employ until 1908, serving as architect, builder, plumber, medical adviser, concessionaire, and, finally, foreign affairs advisor" (Marcus, 77–78). The profile of this jack-of-all-trades as Menilek's adviser fits the description of Waugh's Basil Seal in *Black Mischief.* Seal, a debauched Londoner turned would-be journalist, travels to Azania for no better reason than to escape the dreary "hell" of London's fashionable life. Upon his arrival in Azania, Seth recruits him directly to the head of the Ministry of Modernization, overseeing such projects as the issuing of boots to the Azanian army, the introduction of birth control, and the distribution of paper money. Thus, Waugh appears to have relied on historical records for the construction of his setting and for his characters, although he also distorted the historical facts to suit his political thesis.

Throughout *Black Mischief,* Waugh pokes merciless fun at the emperor's doomed attempts to introduce his people to the benefits of Western civilization. In one scene, Seth finds himself left behind in a train carriage, after the locomotive (that quintessential emblem of modernity) has steamed off by itself; the scene ironically comments on Seth's own breakaway reforms. In this predicament Seth exclaims: "'My people are a worthless people. I give orders; there is none to obey me. I am like a great musician without an instrument" (128). But instead of admitting the uselessness of modernization in his country, Seth pines for "a man of culture, a modern man . . . a representative of Progress and the New Age" (129) who could assist him in his programs. As it turns out, neither the "modern man" (i.e., Basil Seal) nor Seth himself can advance the country beyond the state of primitive squalor and political anarchy. The entire assignment of boots for the army is served up as stew to the soldiers, the birth-control campaign is interpreted by the native population as an incentive to have more children, and the money bills are worth less than the paper they are printed on. These failures herald the country's return to complete anarchy, and the novel ends with a bloody uprising that claims Seth's life.

Only a military intervention by combined French and British forces can restore peace to this troubled country: "Among the dhows and nondescript craft in the harbour lay two smart launches manned by British and French sailors, for Azania had lately been mandated by the League of Nations as a joint protectorate" (235). This scenario is actually a cynical foreshadowing of the infamous Hoare-Laval plan, developed jointly by French and British diplomats in 1935 to appease Mussolini. But the novel's ending is also reminiscent of Italy's decision in 1889 to turn Ethiopia into a protectorate. Within the bounds of such thinly disguised historical references, *Black Mischief* actually contains a reactionary wish-fulfillment fantasy. At the same time it serves as a form of political propaganda. Indeed, the racist premises of the book (whose title contains a racial slur) correspond almost exactly to the Italian position vis-à-vis Ethiopia at the outset of Italy's imperialist venture at the Horn of Africa: "With great internal logic but with complete ignorance of the facts, Crispi and Baratieri regarded Menilek as the barbarian leader of primitive African peoples" (Marcus, 97). Of course, the Western forces in Waugh's fictionalized Azania are spared the humiliating defeat that the Italians, "blinded by racism and cultural arrogance " (Marcus, 97), suffered in Adwa.

Waugh, equally blinded, descends to the ultimate depths of Western racial prejudice about Africa at the end of *Black Mischief*: the mystery of a white woman's disappearance is solved when human bones turn up in a large communal cook pot. Faced with such barbarism, the impressions of calm and order at the end of the novel ("The streets were empty save for an occasional muffled figure slipping by them silently with a lantern" [240]), are clearly associated with the benefits of the foreign military intervention. The waves have literally calmed ("the water lapping very gently on the sea-wall" [239]) while the "English and French police patrol the water-front" (239). Imperialism as innocuous as this, accompanied by tunes of Gilbert and Sullivan, is a civilizing mission indeed.

• • •

The direction of Waugh's sociopolitical thought took a further swing toward the extreme right with the approach of World War II. When Italy decided to attack Ethiopia in 1935, Waugh was ready to embrace an explicitly fascist form of imperialism. Italy's aggression against Ethiopia marked the first instance ever of a war fought under fascist banners. Accordingly, world opinion was outraged and public interest peaked when it became apparent in the fall of 1935 that Italy was going into the offensive against Ethiopia.

From the beginning of the conflict, it was clear where Waugh stood politically. In fact, he had caused a small stir by openly supporting Mussolini at an early stage of the crisis. Disregarding the outpourings of public sympathy for Ethiopia, he published an article in the *Evening Standard* under the inflammatory title "We Can Applaud Italy." In it, he reiterated his evaluation of Ethiopia as "a barbarous country. By this I [mean] . . . that it is capriciously and violently governed and that its own governmental machinery is not sufficient to cope with its own lawless elements" (*Essays, Articles, and Reviews*, 163). He goes on to predict that "the conquest of Abyssinia . . . is an object which any patriotic European can applaud. Its accomplishment will be of service to the world, and, fortunately, the world may be allowed to play the part of spectator" (*Essays, Articles, and Reviews*, 164).

When Waugh declared his interest in revisiting Ethiopia, the editors of the rightist *Daily Mail* were well disposed toward his proposition. In addition to being paid for his journalistic field work, Waugh obtained an advance of £950 from Longmans for a book about the trip. The book that came out of his journey, *Waugh in Abyssinia* (1936),[5] consists of three parts. The first part is a defense of imperialism and a historical explanation of Italy's right to invade Ethiopia. The large middle part deals with the trials and tribulations of the foreign press corps in Addis Ababa during the early days of the conflict. And the third part is an eyewitness report about conditions in Ethiopia after the Italian conquest. Consequently, *Waugh in Abyssinia* has been called a "Fascist tract" by reviewers such as Rose Macaulay. Indeed, Waugh's justification of Italy's aggression is of a different order than were his impressionistic evaluations of Ethiopian cultural backwardness and his rather naive portrayal of benevolent imperialistic intervention in *Black Mischief.*

Strangely, Waugh's proimperialist argument is grafted upon a conditional rejection of imperialism's vilest aspects. In the introduction to *Waugh in Abyssinia,* he condemns the "avarice, treachery, hypocrisy and brutality" (5) that characterize the imperial powers' arbitrary drawing of boundaries. He also brands the duplicity of disguising "the shady business [of colonialism] with pious expressions of principle" (6). But such reservations against the work of empire appear to be little more than lip-service aimed at more progressive readers. Indeed, Waugh shows his true colors a little further on: "In Africa, the result [of colonialism] has been, in the main, beneficial, for there are more good men than bad in Europe and there is a predisposition towards justice and charity in European culture; a bias, so that it cannot for long run free without inclining to good; things which have begun wickedly have turned out well" (25). Such views acquire a bitter significance when read in conjunction with Waugh's lauding Italy's conquest of Ethiopia toward the end of the book.

• • •

Waugh's fortunes as a war correspondent in Ethiopia were anything but good. He repeatedly found himself in the wrong place at the wrong time. Even when he did have the chance to get a scoop, he lost his chance through a lack of professional experience. Indeed, when the Italian ambassador in Addis Ababa told Waugh in private conversation that he planned to withdraw from Ethiopia, Waugh sent the cable containing the story in Latin, trying to keep competitors from preying on the news. Unfortunately for Waugh, the editors at the *Daily Mail* thought it was a joke and dismissed the cable—until the news became official the next day.

Waugh made good for such disappointments in his fourth novel, *Scoop* (1937). In theme, setting, characters, and style, *Scoop* closely

corresponds to the middle part of *Waugh in Abyssinia,* with the difference that it reverses the disappointing trajectory of the real events and
turns them into a success story. Like most of Waugh's 1930s fiction,
Scoop is essentially a roman-à-clef. The protagonist, John Courtenay
Boot, is a rather thinly disguised version of Waugh himself (the book
opens with a eulogy of Boot's successes as a novelist). There is the
owner of the newspaper, the *Beast* (the *Daily Mail*), Lord Copper (Lord
Northcliffe), the leftist war correspondent Corker (Stewart Emeny),
and the wealthy English businessman Baldwin (F. W. Rickett). In
Scoop, these characters play roles similar to those of people in *Waugh
in Abyssinia:* Copper pesters Boot to deliver "spot news" ex nihilo, as it
were; Corker makes a nuisance of himself by his meddling, yet vastly
superior, professional expertise; Baldwin puts a cash price on the
whole of Ethiopia. Among these characters, Baldwin and Boot rise,
phoenix-like, from the shambles of the political turmoil. They experience a degree of success that outstrips by far the actual achievements
of Rickett and Waugh in the late months of 1935.

Indeed, Waugh's novel completely turns the scales. In reality, he
was faced with interminable delays, bureaucratic restrictions, and logistic impasses during his entire stay in Ethiopia. He certainly had no
reason to enjoy his assignment. Waugh not only resented the manner-
isms of African officials, he also loathed the company of the boisterous
and aggressive press people thronging the local hotels. He hated most
of all the general atmosphere of suspended animation. In fact, the
entire period of hectic international coverage of Ethiopia on the eve
of the Italian invasion was marked by an almost complete absence of
newsworthy events. The longest chapter in *Waugh in Abyssinia* is accordingly entitled "Anticlimax."

In *Scoop,* however, Waugh has the entire crowd of journalists de-
part from Addis Ababa (named Jacksontown in the novel) in search of
war action. Boot, Waugh's alter ego, is the only correspondent to stay
behind in the capital. Because the rest of the press corps had been led
astray by trumped up reports about the beginning of the war in a distant corner of the country, Boot has the huge scoop of a socialist over-
throw of the regime all to himself. In the meantime, the wealthy British
industrialist Baldwin (i.e., Rickett), succeeds in the midst of the political crisis to buy up the whole country for cash down, cutting short the
political existence of the "Soviet Union of Ishmaelia" to one day.

In reality, the Rickett affair largely contributed to Waugh's journalistic disgrace in Ethiopia. While Waugh was following up a rather uninteresting spy story in Harar, Rickett (who had repeatedly warned Waugh that something was in the offing) sprang his scheme of purchasing mining rights from Haile Selassie in exchange for (unsubstantiated) promises of protection by the U.S. government. The deal was later called off, and Rickett departed Addis Ababa rather ingloriously. But the story had kicked up dust, and Waugh had missed out on it, a blunder that made Waugh the laughingstock of the whole crowd of journalists in Addis Ababa.

All this is negated and inverted in the novel, which shifts the focus of the satire to the native population as the butt of a rather nasty racial and political comedy. Indeed, when Baldwin "buys" Ishmaelia, he not only subjects the country to British economic interests, but also denies Ishmaelia's population any political say in the matter. Throughout this episode, Waugh insists on the fickle, politically immature nature of the Ishmaelites. Waugh's narrator comments that "the temper of the people was apathetic. They liked to see the place lit up. Oratory pleased them, whatever its subject" (175). It is the story of the childlike native all over again. The only fully individualized characters in this political drama are Boot, Baldwin, and a perpetually intoxicated Swede who single-handedly breaks up a ridiculous political rally, causing the native orators to plunge "over the rail on to the woolly pates below" (176). The racist vocabulary ("woolly pates," "rolling eyes," and "flashing white teeth") complements Waugh's customary use of "darky" or "nigger" in referring to black people. Thus *Scoop* is based on the same set of imperialist and racist presumptions that also characterize *Black Mischief*. Moreover, like the former novel, *Scoop* is essentially a wish-fulfillment fantasy, both personally and politically.

Throughout the book, the fictional equivalent of Ethiopia, Ishmaelia, appears as a ruthless, culturally backward nation that can only benefit from foreign intervention. The natives of Ishmaelia are seen as "an inhospitable race of squireens [who] cultivate the highlands and pass their days in the perfect leisure which those people alone enjoy who are untroubled by the speculative or artistic itch" (*Scoop*, 105). The business of government in Ishmaelia is equivalent to banditry: "Towards the end of each financial year the General's flying columns would lumber out into the surrounding country on the heels of the fugitive population and return in time for budget day laden with the spoils of the less nimble" (*Scoop*, 107–8). That such views are not restricted to the imaginatively constructed world of fiction is proven by passages in *Waugh in Abyssinia* that abound in similar impressions: "They had no crafts. It was extraordinary to find a people with an ancient and continuous habit of life who had produced so little" (64).

Scoop closes with a description of Boot's return from Ethiopia. Back in London, he is knighted and feted like a hero of the trade. Thus *Scoop* is the mirror image of Waugh's actual experience in Ethiopia, an image that conveys the depth of Waugh's wishful thinking.

• • •

After the Italians had conquered Ethiopia's major cities in the spring of 1936, Waugh went back to Ethiopia to witness the new conditions. He was the only foreign journalist allowed to enter the country, a privilege he had "earned" with his pro-Italian essays in the English press. In Addis Ababa, Waugh met with the fascist Field Marshal Graziani: "He gave me twenty minutes. I have seldom enjoyed an official audience more" (228). Of course, he does not mention that Graziani, in Waugh's judgment "one of the most amiable and sensible men I had met for a long time" (230), had won his viceroyship in Ethiopia at the cost of heinous poison-gas attacks and large-scale slaughters. Subsequently, Waugh goes on a tour of the northern part of the country to witness the wonders of Italian engineering. The last few pages of the book, detailing this third trip, have been described by critics otherwise well disposed toward Waugh as "silly" (Fussell), as "facile and naive" (Sykes), and "absurd" (Stannard). It is here that Waugh's rightist ideology is delineated most glaringly: "The collapse of the Shoan system of government . . . was a triumph in Rome. . . . But it was the beginning of an enormous work in Africa and of work which had to be postponed through tedious months of rain. . . . It was a severe test of morale and they stood up to it in a way which should dispel any doubts which still survive of the character of the new Italy. . . . The new régime is going to succeed" (240–41).

Waugh's advocacy of the Roman/Italian conquest of Ethiopia echoes Belloc's apologia for the Roman Empire in its function as the progenitor of Roman Catholicism. Both views emphasize the cultural and religious righteousness of conquest if carried out by a nation that subscribes to the right creed. By this logic, the "barbarian" nature of places such as Ethiopia calls for imperial interventions, in the interest both of the countries thus brought into the Roman Catholic fold and of the nations at the heart of European civilization.

• • •

Paul Fussell has associated *Waugh in Abyssinia* with "the gradual corruption of the genre [of travel writing] as the '30s begin to gear themselves for war. . . . It abandons subtlety and irony; it grows political, strident, sentimental, and self-righteous" (197). To me, the sharp distinction between the political or corrupted and the unpolitical or authentic travel book does not hold. In fact, the difference between *Remote People* and *Waugh in Abyssinia* is one of degree, not of kind. Certainly, travel still provides the backbone of *Waugh in Abyssinia,* and there is as much "anomaly" (the marker par excellence of travel writing according to Fussell) in it as in his less politically explicit travel accounts. In fact, the middle part, with its satirical portrayals of Ethiopia, can serve to demonstrate the continuity between political argument and seemingly "unpolitical" observations. For instance, Waugh's tendentious comparison of Ethiopian culture (captured for him in "the artificial silk and painted petrol cans of Addis Ababa" [141]) with the splendors of a Gothic cathedral ("the avenues of fluted columns, branching high overhead into groined and painted roof, each boss and capital a triumph of delicate sculpture" [140]) is as biased as his insistence on the Ethiopian taste for raw beef. Both instances of "barbarism" occur within pages from Waugh's political assertion that "an unconquered Abyssinia would never accept effective reform" (132).

The question of a generic distinction between travel book and political treatise does pose itself, however, with regard to Waugh's last 1930s travel book, *Robbery under Law.* This book, which is based on Waugh's visit to Mexico in 1938, after the oil expropriation crisis, contains a programmatic manifesto in favor of political conservatism at the very outset. In remarkably candid manner, Waugh declares that one should "dispense [with] the humbug of being unbiased" (15) when traveling to another country. But unlike Orwell's similar caveat in *Homage,* Waugh's statement is not so much a disclaimer of propaganda as a prelude to it.

Let me, then, warn the reader that I was a Conservative when I went to Mexico and that everything I saw there strengthened my opinions. I believe that man is, by nature, an exile and will never be self-sufficient or complete on this earth, that his chances of happiness and virtue, here, remain more or less constant through the centuries and, generally speaking, are not much affected by the political and economic conditions in which he lives. . . . I believe . . . that the anarchic elements in society are so strong that it is a whole-time task to keep the peace. I believe that inequalities of wealth and position are inevitable and that it is therefore meaningless to discuss the advantages of their elimination; that men naturally arrange themselves in a system of classes. . . . I believe that war and conquest are inevitable. (15–16)

This is a neat summary of Waugh's antihumanist views and conservative ideology. He not only rejects the idea of progress, a central theorem of modernity, but also expresses his religious conviction that happiness has no place "on this earth," thereby implicitly acknowledging the only place wherein peace can be achieved: the realm of spiritual salvation.

The assertion that no political system can dramatically improve the lot of man is in keeping with Waugh's misanthropist bent, but it jars oddly with the proclaimed intention of his book, which is to restore the material happiness of wealthy people like the Cowdrays. This inconsistency is typical for Waugh, whose spiritual aspirations never stood in the way of his materialistic concerns. Indeed, his acquisition in 1937 of Piers Court, a country estate, fulfilled his ambition to become a country gentleman. He delighted in wealth and reputation, an enjoyment that stood in a strange relationship to his declared contempt for progress and improvement, including self-improvement.

Compared with *Waugh in Abyssinia,* however, the Mexican book is almost completely devoid of travel lore, except for a few farcical episodes at the beginning. This is not, really, very surprising, since Waugh traveled in the company of his second wife, with an all-expenses-paid tourist arrangement. There was none of the daring, the exhaustion, and the danger that he had sought (and found) on his earlier trips. It appears that after the elimination of hardship and risk, the only thing that remained for Waugh to write about was politics. The explicitly political content of *Robbery under Law* accounts for more than 80 percent of the book's bulk, which features separate chapters on the oil expropriation, President Cárdenas's socialist six-year plan, American-

Mexican relations, and church-state relations in Mexico. Thus the focus is no longer on personal experience and its ideological inflections (or political usages) but on supposedly factual information in the service of a narrowly defined political goal. Consequently, the tone of *Robbery under Law* is monologic and didactic. Instead of grotesque social tableaux or blundering characters, we get passages like this: "Now there is monotony in the judicial decisions. They go on purely ideological grounds. The proletarian is always right; between proletarians the one who is nearest the CTM boss; between bourgeois the one who is nearest to the governing gang. . . . It is no exaggeration to say that to be an employer in Mexico is to outlaw oneself" (64). The rhetorical panache is still in evidence, but the complete lack of irony makes for generally dull reading.

Although one may resent Waugh's biased constructions of foreign cultures, at least he is entertaining as a satirist. But as a writer of didactic political literature, he cannot hold the reader's interest in the fashion that George Orwell can. In chapter after chapter, Waugh dishes out lengthy comparisons of claims and counterclaims between British companies and the Mexican workers and provides historical surveys and political analyses. But all these explanations are too blatantly interested and one-sided to elicit anybody's interest except those who already share Waugh's opinions. Christopher Sykes points to this deficiency when he notes that Waugh "had abundantly the gift of describing, albeit as a caricaturist, the times in which he lived, but, for all his intelligent respect of the past, he could never be a historian except of a peripheral kind" (187).

The immediate cause for Waugh's trip to Mexico was an offer by Clive Pearson, son of the oil magnate Lord Cowdray, who was willing to pay him handsomely for a book that would take issue with the nationalization of foreign oil companies in Mexico.[6] At the time, public opinion in England was dominated by leftist views, which depicted the Cowdrays as ruthless capitalist exploiters and the Mexican government as a benevolent Marxist institution that had a right to expel its blood-sucking parasites.

But there was also another implication. Like Graham Greene, Waugh was fascinated by the persecution of Roman Catholics under Mexico's socialist regime. In *Robbery under Law*, Waugh places the church-state conflict in an analogy with the oil expropriation. The church, too, Waugh insists, had been robbed by arbitrary political powers for the benefit of a few. It is true that the Mexican constitution of 1917 had provided for a strict separation of church and state, but many of the constitution's anticlerical provisions were not implemented at first. Only when the church publicly repudiated the constitution in 1927 did President Calles begin to confiscate ecclesiastical property, kill or exile the priests, and enforce the constitutional provisions that curtailed the church's function in education and religious services. But the measures were unpopular, as Mexico's population was (and still is) predominently Roman Catholic. Many peasants stood up for the church, unleashing the bloody Cristero war (*Cristero,* short for *Cristo Rey,* translates as Christ the king). Relations between the church and the government gradually relaxed in the second half of the 1930s, and by 1938, when Waugh (and Greene) traveled in Mexico, the church had in most places almost recovered its former functions, if not all of its property assets.

The oil expropriation was an entirely different matter. It had its roots in Cárdenas's election as Mexican president in 1934. Indeed, Cárdenas had built his political power on the basis of workers and peasants. He had founded Mexico's largest trade union, the Confederación de Trabajadores. Moreover, he had invited workers and peasants to share political power in the official party, the Partido Revolucionario Institucional (PRI). During his six-year term, Cárdenas was an immensely popular president. Under his auspices, more than 43 million acres of land were redistributed to peasants and communal cooperatives *(ejidos).* The strength of the labor movement made itself felt on the economic plane by frequent strikes that especially targeted foreign-owned enterprises. Already in 1937, the foreign railway companies had become involved in labor conflicts and were promptly expropriated. In 1938, the labor crisis erupted in the oil industry, then almost exclusively in the hands of a few British and American concerns. Workers demanded higher wages and representative power in the management. When these demands were uniformly rejected, Cárdenas proceeded to expropriate the foreign businesses and put Petróleas Mexicanos (Pemex), a government agency, in charge of running the plants. Neither diplomatic protests, propaganda, nor economic boycotts could prevent the transfer of these companies into Mexican hands. All the companies involved in the expropriation were eventually paid off, but at terms that were set largely by the Mexicans. American oil interests were paid compensation until 1950; the British concerns received awards for the liquidations until 1963.

Robbery under Law did not succeed in affecting public opinion regarding the oil-expropriation issue. Part of the book's rapid obsolescence was, of course, due to the outbreak of World War II, which gave people other things to worry about. But even Waugh himself decided to expunge the book from the canon of his travel writings. In the introduction to an anthology of his travel writing, *When the Going Was Good* (1946), Waugh wrote that he was "content to leave [it] in oblivion" (7). This should not detract from a selective appreciation of the book. In fact, toward the end of *Robbery under Law*, more universal concerns begin to supersede Waugh's particular quarrels with the Mexican government. It gradually becomes apparent that the specific material claims surrounding the oil expropriation are less important to Waugh than the "world wide significance" of the Mexican "condition" (273). This "condition" is identified as a symptom of "the universal, deliberately fostered anarchy of public relations and private opinions that is rapidly making the world uninhabitable. The succeeding pages are notes on anarchy" (3).

The anarchy he observed (or thought he observed) in Mexico represented to Waugh the ideal breeding ground for a fascist movement. Of course, Waugh was patently wrong in his prediction that "judged by recent European standards Mexico seems to be in the condition where a Fascist party is due to rise and conquer" (74). Statements like these sound embarrassing when judged with hindsight.[7] After all, Waugh openly supported fascism in his pronouncements about Ethiopia, and he said in *Robbery under Law* that he considered himself "a partisan of Franco" (44). In all fairness, though, it must be said that Waugh only courted fascism as a "cure" for chaotic sociopolitical conditions abroad, not as a viable political alternative to the English democratic system. What all his imperialist, racist, and aristocratic views added up to was the solemn invocation of a bygone way of English life where social stratification was not questioned and the values of tradition, soil, and social rank commanded greater respect.

That Waugh regularly dwelled on the "barbarian" implications in distant countries, rather than focusing on the appalling conditions in England's mining districts or on the atrocities committed in Hitler's Germany, shows to what degree his rightist ideology guided his choice of travel destination. Although Waugh knew that the crisis of civilization also manifested itself in Britain in decaying moral values and revolutionary agitation, this crisis seemed to him a foreign importation. Consequently, what Waugh found during his travels was likelier to corroborate rather than to undermine his disparaging views about foreign societies. Ethiopia and Mexico were thus politically important to Waugh because they were the sites where he could demonstrate the inferiority and perniciousness of native leadership or socialist government, compared with the appeal of authoritarian, rightist rule.

With the exception of *Ninety-two Days,* every travel book after *Labels, a Mediterranean Journal* contains more frequent and longer political digressions, a fact that reflects the growing importance of political issues at home rather than any inherent need to politicize foreign places. And *Robbery under Law* epitomizes the political anchoring of 1930s travel books in the domestic context. Although most 1930s travel books were written specifically for a British audience and were meant to influence the reader's political thinking about relevant domestic issues, no book was more bluntly "about" British interests and concerns than Waugh's Mexican book. In that respect, *Robbery under Law* epitomizes, rather than subverts, a general trend of 1930s English travel writing.

3 GRAHAM GREENE

ANY ATTEMPT TO draw Graham Greene's ideological pro-
file is fraught with difficulties. Indeed, Greene's ideology changed not
only over the course of time but also depending on his spatial location.
Before he joined the Independent Labour Party in 1933, he had supported both the Conservative Party and the communists for a while.
During Britain's general strike in 1926, Greene's conservative instincts
dominated his response to the crisis, and he did, in fact, serve as a
special constable, helping to quell the labor unrest. From 1930 onward, Greene became a leftist liberal (though strongly anticommunist) [1] whose fiction showed unmistakable sympathies for the lower
classes. Anthony Mockler describes Greene's early novels as "decidedly left-wing, anti-Fascist, in tone and sympathy" (127). *It's a Battlefield* (1934) displays an intense awareness of class struggle and attacks
the dehumanizing effects of industrial work. For instance, Greene satirizes the self-deceiving complacency of the factory-owner character:
"A finger sliced off so cleanly at the knuckle that it might never have
been, a foot crushed between opposed revolving wheels. 'It never
hurt her. She suffered nothing. Fainted at the sight of the blood. So
brave' " (24). In *England Made Me* (1935), Greene thematizes the corruption and "seediness" at the highest levels of corporate politics, as
evidenced in the unscrupulous dealings of the multinational industrialist Erik Krogh and his associates. The complexities of Greene's ideological views are further compounded by his conversion to Roman Catholicism in 1926. Grahame Smith comments that "a Catholic convert

with left-wing sympathies was bound to be something of an outsider in the England of the 1930s" (5).

By general consent, the six novels Greene wrote between 1938 and 1951 are considered explicitly Catholic in content and philosophy. These books focus on various psychological and religious aspects of the human struggle between salvation and damnation and on the mystery of divine grace. Except for *The Power and the Glory* (1939) which is set in an environment of religious persecution, most of the Catholic novels (*Brighton Rock* [1938] through *The End of the Affair* [1951]) exclude specific political issues to concentrate on moral and spiritual phenomena.

At first, however, Greene was only a reluctant believer. Nine years after his conversion (ostensibly in order to marry a Roman Catholic woman), he still claimed that "I am a Catholic with an intellectual if not an emotional belief in Catholic dogma" (*Journey without Maps* [1936], 17). Richard Johnstone offers an enlightening comment on the separation between emotional and intellectual facets of faith during the 1930s, claiming that the distinction

> is an artificial one in the sense that purely emotional or purely intellectual belief are impossibilities, but at the same time the implications of both terms are clear. Intellectual belief denies or substantially reduces the importance of the individual's background and personality and circumstances in the decision to believe. It is a logical, and by implication unimpeachable process, by which any rational human being might become convinced of the validity of Catholicism or indeed of Marxism. Emotional belief, by contrast, emphasizes the personal need for faith, the willingness to accept belief without a rigorous understanding of premises or dogma. It carries implications of weakness or immaturity. (63)

By 1938, Greene was ready to admit to the emotional, irrational promptings of his faith as well as to its intellectual appeal. Indeed, he traveled to Mexico with Catholicism as the one thing on his mind. Greene later described his religious metamorphosis in these terms: "I think it was under those two influences [the Socialist persecution of religion in Mexico and General Franco's attack on Republican Spain]— and the backward and forward sway of my sympathies—that I began to examine more closely the effect of faith on action. Catholicism was no longer primarily symbolic, a ceremony at an altar with the correct canonical number of candles. . . . It was closer now to death in the afternoon" (*Ways of Escape* [1980], 79). By the late 1930s, the former Protestant and quasi atheist had become a Roman Catholic fundamentalist, an ideological transformation that can be seen, at least in part, as a reaction to the materialism, pessimism, and the spiritual emptiness that was rife among the members of his generation. The conversion was, however, also a response to the deep despair registered in Greene's early novels, as well as an escape from the stifling sense of boredom that had led him to play suicidal games during his early adulthood. It is said that between the ages of nineteen and twenty Greene resorted to Russian roulette as a means of emotional stimulation, pulling the trigger on six separate occasions.

The basic conservatism inherent in Catholicism seems to have fallen on fertile ground when Greene converted to Rome. Even though he and many fellow intellectuals declared themselves to be liberal leftists, their ideological convictions seldom translated into a sustained revolutionary practice. In the case of Greene, for instance, his middle-class social background seems to have generally overruled the writer's expressly leftist viewpoints as incorporated in such novels as *It's a Battlefield*. Greene's social distance from working-class contexts is emphasized by Smith, who argues that Greene's "working-class characters are frankly unbelievable . . . [which] is in striking contrast to Greene's sureness of touch in handling the idioms of a slightly seedy middle-class slang" (121–22). Indeed, Greene unabashedly numbered among his social ambitions the goal "to make a lot of money." Greene's bourgeois sensibility is also evidenced in his abhorrence of disorder, dirt, and unchecked emotions. Moreover, the boredom he so intensely experienced during all of his travels can be seen as the quintessential middle-class syndrome of a (relatively) well-to-do individual whose need to be entertained claimed a higher priority than the bare needs of sustenance.

Of course, Greene was also steeped in the cultural heritage of Joseph Conrad, Rider Haggard, and G. A. Henty (all of whom he mentions in an early part of *Journey without Maps*), who transmitted to him Victorian primitivist notions about alien cultures. S. E. Ogude therefore calls Greene "a Victorian at heart and like the Victorians, he sees the existence of 'the child races of the world' as the greatest proof of the civilization of the whiteman" (54). This judgment is only partly right, though. Indeed, as an admitted disciple of Conrad, Greene also recognized the necessity of questioning the moral foundations of imperialism and to critique the outright plundering of colonized realms. Moreover, his outspoken sympathy for the social underdog determined at first also his attitude toward the exploited victims of colonialism.

• • •

When Greene approached his publisher, Heinemann, in 1934 with the plan to travel to Liberia, he not only found favor with them, but secured an immediate advance for the promised travel book. Liberia had acquired notoriety in the late 1920s through allegations that the country's governing elite (descended from former slaves in the United States) had itself encouraged slavery and forced labor.[2] When Liberia was founded in 1822 (under the aegis of the American Colonization Society) hundreds of freed slaves were repatriated to West Africa. Ironically, however, these former slaves (referred to as Americo-Liberians) made sure that ethnic discrimination against the country's indigenous tribes was written directly into the Liberian Code of Law. The Americo-Liberian elite thus enjoyed a status of supremacy similar to that of colonial overlords elsewhere in Africa. In fact, the way in which the colony was founded differed little from European colonial practice.[3] The continuity between Liberia and its colonized neighbors is also evidenced in the country's administrative system, which "was patterned along the lines of the British colonial philosophy of 'indirect rule': the utilization of traditional tribal authorities as instruments of the central government in the maintenance of law and order at the local level" (Liebenow, 54).

The conflict between the indigenous tribes and the black settlers reached a climax in 1930, when a League of Nations commission published the report of its investigation into the slavery allegations. The report cited evidence that workers at the Spanish plantations on Fernando Po had been recruited "'under conditions of criminal compulsion scarcely distinguishable from slave raiding and slave trading'" (quoted by Anderson, 106). The report caused the immediate resignation of the Liberian president, Charles King. His successor, Edwin Barclay, promised to make the eradication of forced labor and other ills cited in the report his primary goal. Nevertheless, suspicions that the African Republic of Liberia had enslaved the native population were hard to root out. Moreover, new reports about the bloody suppression of tribal minorities, especially the Kru, kept issuing from the country.

Greene was clearly intrigued by Liberia's political predicament, and it is very likely that he intended to write an investigative report about the country's political troubles. In *Journey without Maps*, his account of the trip, he refers specifically to his plan to talk to Chief Nimley, the leader of the Kru rebellion that had been brutally suppressed in the wake of the League investigations. The Kru, a large tribe in the southeast of Liberia, had repeatedly rebelled against the Americo-Liberian supremacy. In the early 1930s, they tried to capitalize on the momentary weakness of the central government as a result of the League investigation. Chief Nimley wanted to carve out an independent political status for the Kru, the most modernized of Liberian native tribes. But his rebellion was crushed by Liberia's notorious Frontier Force.

Greene admits that his intention to talk to the Kru leader was "another plan which came to nothing through lack of money and exhaustion" (47). Further evidence for a political mission to Liberia can be inferred from Greene's contacts with Sir John Harris, parliamentary secretary to the Anti-Slavery Society in London, prior to his departure for Liberia. Accordingly, Norman Sherry speculates that "it appears . . . Greene would be seeking information about present oppressions, including slavery, for the Anti-Slavery Society" (511). Such an engagement would not have been far-fetched in the context of the 1930s, when, according to Greene's foreword to *England Made Me*, "it was impossible . . . not to be committed" (vii). Thus, Greene's later claim that his account of the trip through Liberia was "not a political book in the sense that Gide's *Voyage au Congo* was political" (*Ways of Escape*, 50) cannot convince. Indeed, critics such as Smith conclude that "Greene's engagement with public events is . . . an important strand in his life; if nothing else, it has prompted him to travel the world, acquiring in the process an enviably wide knowledge of international politics" (5). In light of his lifelong preoccupation with political matters, Greene's denial of any political intentions in *Journey without Maps* has a defensive ring about it.

Notwithstanding Greene's assertions to the contrary, *Journey without Maps* has a politically relevant core, although it is an ambivalent and unstable one. I will focus here primarily on the book's manifest political message, reserving a discussion of the covert and contradictory implications of Greene's ideology to chapters 5 and 6.

Greene's antiimperial views are clearly foregrounded at the begin-

ning and again at the end of the book. This coincides with his description of two towns that historically had played an important part in
the fight against slavery. Both of Greene's two destinations in West Africa—first, Freetown, in Sierra Leone, and then Monrovia, the capital
of Liberia—had been originally settled by freed slaves. Freetown was
also an important port from which antislavery operations (such as
raids on slave-carrying ships) were conducted and where the recap-
tured slaves were released.

But although Freetown had originally been established in the 1780s
by British philanthropists, when Greene visited the place the spirit
of philanthropy was no longer visible. In fact, Freetown, now the capital of a British colony, offered Greene first and foremost a shocking
glimpse into the strange and hybrid world of colonialism. His first reaction upon arrival was a romantic impulse to embrace native culture
and to reject the markers of European presence there: "Everything
ugly in Freetown was European. . . . if there was anything beautiful in
the place it was native: the little stalls of the fruit-sellers which went
up after dark at the street corners, lit by candles" (38). But Greene's
sympathy for Freetown's African heritage did not extend to the Creoles—that is, the Westernized descendants of Freetown's original
population of liberated Africans. As we learn from Oliver and Fage,

> many of these freed slaves became assimilated to European ways,
> especially as a result of the educational work of the Protestant
> missions, who deliberately chose Sierra Leone for their first foot-
> ing in West Africa. Some of the liberated Africans became consid-
> erable traders along the coast, while others augmented British re-
> sources by becoming priests, doctors, lawyers, administrations,
> and clerks in the service of the British mission, trading compa-
> nies, or government. (159)

Greene, however, in scorning the assimilationist achievement of these
Africans, throws out the child with the bathwater. Although he condemns the effects of imperialism on indigenous cultures, he has no
sympathy for those Africans who succeeded in turning the instrument
of their oppression into a means of social betterment. Instead of sid-
ing with these "products" of imperialism, Greene ridicules Freetown's
Creole population as mere puppets, hollow men who belong wholly
neither to Africa nor to Europe:

The men . . . had been educated to understand how they had
been swindled, how they had been given the worst of two worlds,
and they had enough power to express themselves in a soured of-
ficious way; they had died, in so far as they had once been men,
inside their European clothes. . . . these men had been given their
tin shacks, their cathedral, their votes and city councils, their
shadow of self-government; they were expected to play the part
like white men. (39)

To Greene, these "mimic men" are lost in a cultural limbo; they are the
results of the simultaneous erosion of their indigenous way of life and
of the imperfect adaptation to the colonizer's culture.

In contradistinction to Homi Bhabha's contention that "the *men-
ace* of mimicry is its *double* vision which in disclosing the ambivalence of colonial discourse also disrupts its authority" (88), Greene
does not see any subversive potential in being "almost the same but
not quite." Rather, he ridicules the weakness of this hybrid population: "and the more [the Creoles] copied white men, the more funny
it was to the prefects. They were withered by laughter; the more desperately [the Creoles] tried to regain their dignity the funnier they became" (39). Instead of undermining the colonizer's authority through
mimicry, "the Creole's painful attempt at playing the white man [is]
funny; it is rather like the chimpanzee's tea-party, the joke is all on
one side" (41).

The self-debasing nature of mimicry extends even to the white
colonizers. The joke of hybridity, as it were, is not only on the side of
the Creoles, it is also on the side of the displaced, infrastructural seg-
ments of the white colonial society. Indeed, Greene reports that the
"prospectors, shipping agents, merchants, engineers had to reproduce
English conditions if they were to be happy at all" (43). These middling
colonials had been trapped in the same paranoid economy of mimicry
and self-denial as the Creoles. But in contrast to them, they still had
dignity: "they were not guilty of these meannesses; they were only
guilty of the shabbiness of Freetown" (44); moreover, they held on to
a "fidelity, a kind of patriotism: (44). Greene concludes that "if one
must condemn, one should condemn not the outposts but the headquarters of Empire, the country which has given them only this: a feeling of respectability and a sense of fairness withering in the heat" (44).

At this point, Greene's critique of empire aligns itself with the imperial center/margin paradigm, although he ironically inverts the conventional moral implications of that model. According to his logic, the center—that is, the imperial headquarters—is the most corrupt part of the organization. And Greene is intensely critical of their mission:

> It was these men who had so much to answer for: the wages, for example, of the platelayers on the little narrow-gauge line which runs up to Pendembu near the French and Liberian borders. These men were paid sixpence a day and had to buy their own food, and yet in the days of the depression they were docked one day's pay a month. This was perhaps the meanest economy among the many mean economies which assisted Sierra Leone through the depression. (43–44)

Next on the scale of condemnation come the "real rulers" (43) who carry out the dictates of the system in coastal towns like Freetown. The colonials living at the margin of Greene's inverted center/margin paradigm are clearly the least corrupted. In Greene's view, they "were of a finer, subtler type than on the Coast; they were patriots in the sense that they cared for something in their country other than its externals; they couldn't build their English corner with a few tin roofs and peeling posters and drinks at the bar" (54).

This discourse of authenticity, implying that the Englishmen who were stripped of the ability to mimic their home culture were more authentically British than their counterparts on the coast, is reinforced by a primitivist valuation of "the real native [who] was someone to love and admire. One didn't have to condescend; one knew more about some things, but they knew more about others" (54). Mary Louise Pratt has called this discourse of authenticity, which claims innocence for the work of empire at the "contact zone," the practice of "counter conquest." But the assumption of innocence for the work of exploitation and dispossession is as soon invoked by Greene as it is undercut by the traveler's keen awareness of the injustices and social contradictions effected by these very same colonials. At Kailahun, in Sierra Leone's furthest reaches, Greene realized that the social conditions fostered under the "finer, subtler" colonial rulers was even worse than the debasing situation he had encountered on the coast ("what impressed me at the time was the dirt and disease" [60]). And he concludes that "civilization as far as Sierra Leone was concerned was the railway to Pendembu, the increased export of palm-nuts; civilization, too, was Lever Brothers and the price they controlled" (61). He goes on to ask: "Why should we pretend to talk in terms of the world when we mean only Europe or the white races?" (61).

At this point, Greene appears to question the mystifications implied in the center/margin model and to reject the claims of innocent conquest. But his moral indignation about the degree of poverty and exploitation he encountered in Sierra Leone's hinterland also raised a problem of ideological self-definition. Obviously, in the African context it was race and not class that determined the individual's social status: "neither ILP nor Communist Party urges a strike in England because the platelayers in Sierra Leone are paid sixpence a day without their food." (61). Here Greene recognizes the racial imbalance of much socialist theorizing, as oppressed Africans were obviously not considered worthy objects of working-class solidarity by many European socialists. But, as it turns out, Greene seems to share rather than to critique this lack of sympathy for the nonwhite victims of capitalism.

Indeed, Greene's radical ideological impulses compete with an ever increasing sense of his own racial and cultural superiority in Africa. For instance, Greene glories in his power as an expedition leader at whose command two dozen native carriers could be set in motion "like a long mechanical toy" (68), although he admits that his "carriers were disgracefully underpaid" (148). Faced with this dilemma, Greene resorts to irony to smooth over the ripples of an ideological contradiction. For instance, he says about a British district commissioner in Sierra Leone's hinterland that his work "was to a great extent the protection of the native from the civilization he represented" (61). Such ironic statements also determine the tone of his encounter with Liberia's President Barclay: "It was not easy to stem the rolling tide of the President's hopes, the roads, the aeroplanes, the motor-cars. It was a paradoxical situation; a black preaching progress to a skeptical white [who] had come out of the busy bustling progressive scene" (108).

Under Barclay's rule, Greene concludes, the native tribes in the interior "weren't interfered with as they would certainly have been interfered with in a white colony, and one was thankful for their lack of education, when one compared them as they were in Buzie country, striding along the narrow forest paths, the straight back, the sword with an ivory handle swinging against the long native robe, with the anglicized 'educated' blacks of Sierra Leone, the drill suits and the striped shirts and the dirty sun-helmets" (108). In such passages, the primitivist in Greene conflicts with the social realist in him. The former values underdevelopment as a more authentic mode of existence, while the latter asserts that "the 'noble savage' no longer exists; perhaps he never existed" (61). It is hard to recognize a coherent leftist argument in such ironically undercut and contradictory views. Only at the beginning and at the end of his trip, at Freetown and Monrovia, is Greene quite explicit in his condemnation of imperialism and its exploitative and dehumanizing motives. But in the interior, he is at a loss as to sort out his political principles. Here Greene truly travels "without maps," both in the literal and in the ideological sense.

• • •

Greene recovered from the hardships of his five-week trek, which had brought him to the brink of death in an attack of fever, in Monrovia, Liberia's capital. There he met with the former president, Charles King, and with a member of the currently ruling cabinet. The portrait of King is one of resignation and mild corruption. Although the former president had enriched himself throughout his tenure, now, as a sick and defeated man, he no longer aims to play a role in politics: "He was quite ready, he said, if he was elected to accept the League of Nations plan of assistance, tie his finances to European advisers, put white Commissioners in charge of the interior, give away Liberian sovereignty altogether, but he knew quite well he wasn't going to be elected" (241). Notably, the irony of this passage is double-edged, as it not only satirizes the Liberian politician's lack of self-confidence, but also the European attempts to turn this independent nation into yet another colony.

Greene's differentiated perspective is further elaborated by a pragmatic approach to the political situation in Liberia: "No one can pretend they have made much of their country. Colonel Davis's conduct of the Kru campaign is only one example of the horrors of their history, but to me it seems remarkable that they have retained their independence at all: a kind of patriotism has emerged from the graft and the privation" (231). This rather discriminating treatment of Liberian politics merges with an explicit criticism of a type of economic intervention that creates a neocolonial type of dependency: "England and France in the last century robbed them of territory; America has done worse, for she has lent them money. . . . Nor can you wonder at their hatred and suspicion of the white man. The last loan and the last concession to the Firestone Company of Ohio all but surrendered their sovereignty to a commercial company with no interests in Liberia but rubber and dividends" (231–32).

The critical rhetoric of such passages can be seen as an indication that Greene was aiming to strengthen the book's radical backbone. The explicit criticism of corporate designs on Liberia's national sovereignty, linked with the criticism of the Americo-Liberian power monopoly, carries a distinctly leftist political agenda. This contrasts with Greene's muddled attitudes voiced in the country's interior, where he conceals his reactionary politics behind ironic statements or just plainly states colonialist ideas. *Journey without Maps* is, thus, a deeply political book that does not yield a clear political argument. Its ideological weight is carried in the subtext of tropes, phrases, and perspectives that establish a conservative counterweight to the book's liberal, democratic rhetoric.

• • •

No account of *Journey without Maps* would be complete without mention of the "companion piece" to this book; namely, *Land Benighted* (1938), the account written by his traveling companion. Greene was accompanied during the whole journey by his twenty-three-year-old cousin Barbara Greene, although he barely mentions her presence in *Journey without Maps*.[4] During the entire trip, Graham Greene was the guide and leader of the expedition, while his cousin trotted along as an invited but rather redundant companion. She was, however, useful to Greene as a nurse during his serious illness toward the end of the trip. But even that service, crucial as it may have been for his survival, is not recorded in *Journey without Maps*, a book that, as we have seen, is almost obsessively self-centered.

So elusive was Barbara Greene's presence during the journey that Greene did not even notice that she took copious notes along the way. His surprise must have been considerable when she brought out her own account of their journey. Her book, originally entitled *Land Benighted* (it was reissued in 1981 under the title *Too Late to Turn Back*), was obviously an afterthought, as she explains in her preface: "When a few years after our return to England, my father became seriously ill, I rewrote the notes I had recorded (keeping strictly to the truth) and made them into something I could read to him every morning to amuse him and keep his mind off his troubles" (xvi).

In a sense, Barbara Greene gives a less gloomy account of the Liberian trek. As if in direct defiance of her cousin's emphasis on dirt and disease, the younger writer often emphasizes the joy of traveling in Africa: "It was a wonderful and exciting trek" (37), she exclaims, and adds at a later stage: "But the beauty of the village, the courtesy of the natives, the music, the dancing, the warm moonlit nights were things that gladdened the heart anew every day" (99). In her cultural construction of Africa and in her ideological view of the country's inhabitants, however, she is in agreement with Graham Greene on all major points. In fact, she borrowed rather liberally from *Journey without Maps*, a book she must have read closely before composing her own account.[5] Even during the journey, Barbara Greene's attitude toward her cousin had been one of admiration and consent. She states that "Graham took all the decisions and made all the plans. I merely followed" (xiv); she emphasizes that they "never quarrelled, not once" (61). Among their topics for conversation, "politics was the first thing to go" (61).

But surely, the implied politics of Graham's approach to Africa were there to stay. Indeed, *Land Benighted* is a good example of the ideological hegemony of ethnocentric myths about racial and cultural "others" that pervaded both male and female travelers' descriptions of Africa. Especially the myth that African adults are mere children: this one is flogged even more excessively by Barbara Greene than by her cousin.[6] In fact, she is so wrapped up in this myth that she does not notice the contradiction between saying that Graham "from the beginning treated them exactly as if they were white men from our own country" (68) and asserting simultaneously that "he, like a benevolent father, would smile kindly upon them. . . . But with child-like simplicity they handed all responsibilities over to my cousin" (68). Like a self-fulfilling prophecy, however, the myth of the childlike African depends wholly on the attitude of the foreign visitor. For instance, when one of the carriers needs a bandage for a cut toe, Barbara "tore up a handkerchief and tied up his toe with a big bow on the top. He was pleased as Punch, and showed it with the utmost pride to every one" (71). Here Barbara Greene first imposed her expectation on the man, based on the assumption that the carrier's psychology was childlike, and then notes with satisfaction that the carrier played by her script.

Compared with Graham's book, however, the politics of *Land Be-*

nighted are wholly immanent. In what appears to be a well-rehearsed gesture, Barbara explains early on that she was "more interested always in the natives than in the politics of an adolescent government. It was the little everyday things that pleased me most" (44). This plays into the hands of conventional gender roles, which confined the woman's sphere of interests to matters of domestic and private experience.[7] In keeping with this model, Barbara includes more intimate perspectives in her account than Graham does in his book: "The village girls crowded into my hut with me and watched with great interest while I changed my shirt and washed. . . . When I washed myself they could not understand what the soap was, but loved the way it made the water fluffy. They dipped the tips of their fingers into it when I had finished, and then gazed at the bubbles as they gradually disappeared" (58).

Such glimpses into the private lives of both the traveler and her native hosts are complemented by Barbara's description of her cousin as a private person. Indeed, *Land Benighted* is a treasure trove of biographical information for all those interested in Graham Greene.[8] But such discursive practices will not do as an example of disruptive female travel writing. It comes as no surprise, therefore, that Barbara Greene is not among the authors studied in *Penelope Voyages: Women and Travel in the British Literary Tradition*. Indeed, Karen Lawrence sets out to investigate how "travel writing reveals a set of alternative myths or models for women's place in society" (xi), and how women travelers tend to employ "the figure of movement to explore pressing issues of personal and historical agency, problems of (and opportunities for) women's cultural placements and displacements" (xi). There is very little, if any, sign of subversiveness in Barbara Greene's account of Africa, a circumstance that shows how gender need not be a determining factor in female travel writing.

In fact, *Land Benighted* stays well within the boundaries prescribed to the female traveler by patriarchal social conventions, and its (implicit) political framework is firmly rooted in imperial fantasies of domination. How this ideology of racial and cultural superiority works in detail, both in the male and the female accounts, is revealed in the strike scene that features importantly in both books. Faced with his carriers' demand for better pay, Graham declines any negotiation with them, although he admits that "the merits were all on their side" (149). Instead of renegotiating their contracts, he resorts to bluffing, specu-

lating that he and his cousin are as lost without their carriers as the
carriers are lost without their guidance in territory unfamiliar to them.
Pretending to dismiss them, he offers to pay them off on the spot. At
this point, the carriers drop their demands and fall back in line. After
claiming victory in the labor struggle ("But I had won" [150]), Graham
goes on to comment on how the carriers had taken their defeat: "They
were like children who have tried to get an extra holiday but bear no
grudge because they have never really believed they would succeed"
(150). The image of the child here serves to rationalize the carriers'
complete lack of political rights in this dispute. Like children, they are
disciplined, threatened, and then graciously forgiven when they come
to their senses.

Tellingly, Barbara's analysis is based on the exact same analogy:
"They were just a lot of children trying to get something out of us"
(88). Barbara makes sure that the message has got across by rein-
forcing her stereotypical characterization of Africans: "Like children,
they felt neither the future or the past. It was only the moment that
counted" (89). In *Journey without Maps* the corresponding passage is
formulated as follows: "The character of a carrier is childlike. He en-
joys the moment. He cannot connect cause and effect" (116). Such
condescending, demeaning attitudes are not uncommon, of course:
they form the moral bedrock for the colonial exploitation of Africa
(and elsewhere).

Barbara Greene's unquestioning acceptance of such supremacist
myths undercuts any general claims about the supposedly "gentler,"
counterdiscursive potential of female travel writing when compared
with the imperial voices of its male counterpart. Critics such as Alison Blunt and Wendy Mercer have distanced themselves from the
"implicit binarism in which man = coloniser and woman = coloni-
sed" (Mercer, 147), rejecting the romantic view that women feel a
"natural" solidarity with the plight of the exploited colonial "other"
because they are themselves exploited by men.[9] This seems to be a
relatively recent understanding, though, because a slightly older study
still argues that female explorers in Africa such as Mary Kingsley and
Florence Dixie "develop strategies of accommodation, not confrontation or domination, and write richly eclectic, loosely structured narratives of their discoveries about the continent, its peoples, and their
own psyches" (Stevenson, 160). Against this view, I agree with Mercer,
who concludes that the supposedly male models of exploitation and

cultural stereotyping are repeated with only minor variants in female travelogues.[10]

• • •

Graham Greene's second travel book, *The Lawless Roads* (1939), an account of his journey through Mexico in 1938, was originally intended to be a political manifesto against Mexico's atheistic regime— a project directly inspired by Greene's growing identification with Roman Catholicism. Having finished *Brighton Rock,* Greene felt ready to write a Catholic travel book.

In an authorial note at the beginning of the third edition of *The Lawless Roads,* Greene explains that he had been "commissioned to write a book on the religious situation" (5), thereby forestalling possible attacks on his admittedly biased presentation of Mexico. In *Ways of Escape,* his 1980 autobiography, Greene further claims that *The Lawless Roads* was based on "personal impressions of a small part of Mexico at a particular time, the spring of 1938, shortly after the country had suffered at the hands of President Calles . . . the fiercest persecution of religion anywhere since the reign of Elizabeth" (84). This statement makes doubtful claims. In fact, President Calles had resigned as president in 1929 (although he maintained a certain amount of informal political influence for several years thereafter). Moreover, President Cárdenas had started the country on a return to religious "normality" three years before Greene visited Mexico. As Bailey points out, "Cárdenas took steps to reduce the hostility between the revolutionary regime and the Church. In 1937 public worship resumed in Veracruz, long a hotbed of anticlericalism. . . . By 1938 the official thaw was evident everywhere, and that year the Mexican clergy patriotically supported Cárdenas's expropriation of foreign oil holdings" (297).

The questionable basis of Greene's partisan view of the Mexican situation carries over into other historical facts. What Greene describes as a one-sided religious persecution under President Calles was in fact a tripartite conflict in which the militant peasants who took up arms in defense of their religion (the so-called Cristeros) stood in opposition both to the state, which fought them, and to the church, "which condemned and excommunicated the Cristeros" (Meyer, 216). Historical sources even indicate that the peace agreement between the church and the government (the *arreglos* of 1929) was beneficial to both parties.[11] Moreover, the persecution of the Cristeros seems to have intensified rather than abated after the treatise: "Responsibility for the annihilation of the catholic militants following the 1929 agreement was never fixed. . . . Many Mexicans agreed with Leopoldo Lara y Torres that more Cristero chiefs perished after the surrender than died on the field of battle" (Bailey, 294). In a cynical twist of political fate, the so-called peace agreement would harm rather than protect the former Cristero fighters who had put their lives on the line in defence of their Catholic faith.

What appears in Greene's sketchy historical references as a relatively simple issue ("Mexico remained Catholic; it was only the governing class—politicians and pistoleros—which was anti-Catholic" [20]) was in fact a more complex and involved political situation. Indeed, the conflict between the state, the church, and its Catholic believers was as much a religious issue as a class struggle. The members of the Cristero movement were mostly recruited from the poor rural population. This set them apart both from the governing elites and from the representatives of the higher clergy. According to Camin, "It was a confrontation between two world visions and two plans for the country. The first one, which Calles represented, included the educated middle classes and the direct beneficiaries of the revolutionary political establishment; the second one included the faithful peasant masses that followed their saints and their multisecular customs, the regions and the towns where they lived, the local priests, the small holdings, and the subsistence agriculture" (87). The church, which claimed substantial holdings, represented the interests of a wealthier class.

Throughout its history, the Roman Catholic Church in Mexico was a state-within-the-state, fighting for its own privileges: "The Church always loomed politically powerful because its extensive properties alone provided more income than total government revenues" (Brandenburg, 185). By rejecting the constitution of 1917, the church was not only fighting for the freedom of religious practice, but also defending its own riches, which were threatened with being parceled out between landless *campesinos* and communal holdings or swallowed up by the country's political elite. In that context it is not surprising that the church turned a cold shoulder to the populist movement of the Cristeros while negotiating a pragmatic "solution" for the crisis with those in power.

In contradiction of these facts, Greene overlooked the political role played by the church in the conflict and collapsed both popular movement and clerical resistance into a single entity—the Cristero movement. This is evidenced in his portrayal of Father Pro's persecution in *The Lawless Roads:* "I thought of Father Pro coming into this country in disguise—the badly cut suit and the striped tie and the brown shoes; then the secret Masses, the confessions at street corners, the police hunts and the daring evasions—the long rainy season and afterwards the dry and then the rains again, and, when they cleared, arrest and death, unshaven, crying 'Hail Christ the King' " (34). A similar impression is given in the novel *The Power and the Glory* (1940), where the young priest Juan is described as a "new soldier of Christ" in the fight against "President Calles [who] was discussing the anti-Catholic laws in the Palace of Chapultepec" (50). According to historical sources, however, the clergy generally did not join the ranks of the Cristeros, because the church condemned the armed insurgence against the government forces (Meyer, 70, 72, 75–76).

By eliding the crucial difference between the peasant movement of the Cristeros and the elitist position of the church, Greene fashioned his political argument to suit his own needs. Indeed, he aimed to show that Mexican Catholics had put up a massive popular resistance against the godless state, a project that just could not be squared with the actual circumstances.

The Cárdenas presidency (1934–40) was characterized by an unprecedented degree of popular support, not least because Cárdenas took rigorous measures to assert Mexico's political and economic independence (the petroleum expropriation is but the most spectacular example), but also because his large-scale agrarian and economic reforms were committed to the needs of the peasants and working classes. In 1936, furthermore, Cárdenas decreed the opening of the churches throughout the country. As for the Cristeros, they were a quasi-anarchist movement with reactionary overtones. While they stood up for their religion, they simultaneously defied the goals of the Mexican Revolution—that is to say, modernization and secularization of the state. Claims that the Cristeros were a "proto-fascist" movement are easily refuted: their basis was the peasantry and they lacked a centralized structure of political power (Meyer, 213).

• • •

The whole question of taking sides in the Mexican conflict was so convoluted that Greene opted out of making the finer distinctions.

Instead, he reduced the multifaceted situation to a confrontation between faith and godlessness. Greene considered himself a socialist, but because of his commitment to Catholicism he could not sympathize with Mexico's socialist regime. Similarly, Greene did not make his position clear vis-à-vis the Spanish civil war. He was one of the few recipients of Nancy Cunard's questionnaire who did not respond to the invitation to "take sides" on the issue. While he rejected fascism unequivocally, he was unable to "side" with the Republicans, who were destroying churches and driving away the priests.

At the same time, however, Greene felt disconnected with Mexico's Roman Catholics. For one thing, he had obviously miscalculated the Mexican predilection for martyrdom. In Orizaba, where Greene heard about the killing of a child by a soldier, he resignedly comments that "the outburst of religious zeal all over Veracruz state" in the wake of that murder "was spent like an orgasm—sleep returned to Orizaba" (94). But Greene was not only disappointed over the lack of popular resistance against the government; he felt properly alienated from the very beliefs of his fellow Catholics there.

The gap that separated Greene from a full understanding of Mexico's Catholics (with their preference for loud, graphic, and dramatic displays) was largest in his encounters with the country's indigenous population. Indeed, Mexico's Indian population adhered to a form of religiosity that appeared to Greene as "a dark, tormented, magic cult" (170), that was dimly threatening. Contrary to his African journey, where Greene had taken something strange (African traditions) and turned it into something familiar ("childhood," "home," etc.), in Mexico the natives had taken something that was familiar to him (Roman Catholicism) and made it strange, a reversal that is registered with amazement: "And in the mountains, as I saw later, they have what the people of Yajalon do not possess—their crosses, their places of worship; Christianity existing like themselves wild and cut off and incomprehensible" (155). The implication seems clear: such wildflowers of Catholicism were not the authentic thing, thus they could not be considered the spiritual vessel whereby redemption might be granted. Only Greene's own religious habits could make sense of the desolation he encountered. This underlines once again the tendency of 1930s travel writers to interpret foreign conditions according to their own ideological and spiritual conceptions. Greene showed no anthropological interest in the "aberrant" religious practices of the Chiapas hill people. Their belief merely bewildered him.

• • •

In his derogatory attitude toward Mexican politics, Greene followed the lead of D. H. Lawrence, whom he quotes as saying that " 'Socialism here is a farce of farces, except very dangerous' " (91). Greene himself concludes that "the Mexican Revolution was phony from the start" (*Ways of Escape*, 85). Of course, no degree of land-reform and socialist labor reform can disguise the fact that, far into the 1930s, certain states (especially Tabasco and Chiapas) enforced drastic antidemocratic laws banning the freedom of speech and restricting religious practice. However, at the time of Greene's visit, all signs pointed in the direction of a gradual liberalization.

Greene's skewed historical and ideological presentations are designed to convey an impassioned critique of Mexico's socialist regime. Thus, by the time of his Mexican trip, Greene's latent conservatism had come to dominate his political views, overriding his earlier commitments to the political Left. In this respect, *The Lawless Roads* is a more straightforward, though not necessarily a more convincing, political book than *Journey without Maps*. Indeed, Greene's rejection of Mexico and its politics seems at times purely subjective, based on personal pique and irritation rather than on sound historical analysis or careful cultural observations. Of course, this attitude is not anomalous among travelers to "underdeveloped" countries, but it deserves mention here because Greene is ostensibly fulfilling a larger mission and should therefore be capable of mustering more detachment from his surroundings than he does.

4   REBECCA WEST

REBECCA WEST burst on the scene of Britain's political life in 1911 and she soon commanded a good deal of respect as a socialist feminist with an awesome rhetorical talent. Her polemical articles, written during the 1910s for the *Freewoman* and for the socialist *Clarion,* called for the inclusion of all social classes in the fight for woman's suffrage and pleaded for higher pay and better working conditions on behalf of the working classes.[1] There is, however, a critical consensus that West modified her youthful radicalism as she grew older.

Janet Montefiore associates West's political stance during the 1930s with "the perspective of English left-liberalism" (189), while Victoria Glendinning, because of West's anticommunist, pro-Labour sentiments at the end of World War II, defines her mature political position as that of a "democratic socialist" (165). This agrees with Carl Rollyson's analysis: "As the defender of true liberalism, she stood squarely between the Communists and the Right" (255). To me, however, she was primarily a confirmed liberationist, and *Black Lamb and Grey Falcon* (1941), West's only published travel book, confirms this finding. Indeed, her journeys in the Balkans furnished her with a host of arguments against every kind of oppression, in the public as well as in the private spheres. Consequently, *Black Lamb and Grey Falcon* is a monument to the ideologies of national self-rule, antiimperialism, and feminism.

To begin with feminism: this dimension of *Black Lamb and Grey Falcon* declares itself on almost every page. For instance, upon observing a woman in Prishtina who was "carrying on her back the better part of a plough . . . while [her husband] went free" (894–95), West is gripped by what she had earlier called "feminist rage" (488). She expostulates that "any area of unrestricted masculinism, where the women are made to do all the work and are refused the right to use their wills, is in fact disgusting" (895). In addition to such overt manifestations of her feminist commitment, other aspects of a gendered sensibility surface in West's travel book. For instance, Carl Rollyson states that "it is Rebecca's contention that what occurs on the world stage is connected with the private heart" and that "history must be brought home" (211). This view is consistent with Mary Louis Pratt's claim that "domestic settings have much more prominent presence in the women's travel accounts than in men's. . . . From these private seats of selfhood, [female travelers] depict themselves emerging to explore the world in circular expeditions that take them out into the public and new, then back to the familiar and enclosed" (159–60). Moreover, West's dialogic inclusion of her husband's opinions could be considered further evidence of a female approach to travel writing, one that contrasts with the masculine ethos of individual heroism, self-reliance, and monologue. Indeed, D. H. Lawrence, Evelyn Waugh, and Graham Greene wrote travel books that virtually ignored the presence of their female travel partners.[2]

However, as I have indicated in my discussion of Barbara Greene's travel book, a feminized form of travel writing need not imply a divergent or subversive ideological stance compared with the male discourse of travel. What gives a woman's travel account a disruptive, radical edge is not so much the gendered nature of her writing as the actual politics that motivate it, a politics based on specific views about social class, nationalism, and comparative anthropology.

In the case of Rebecca West, Karen Lawrence's argument that "women writers of travel have tended to mistrust the rhetoric of mastery, conquest, and quest that has funded a good deal of male fictional and nonfictional travel" (20) does not hold. West's discourse displays any number of "male" traits, specifically the "mastery" of foreign societies by appeal to discourses of history, politics, and anthropology, as well as an orientalist bias that could pass as a symptom of masculine cultural arrogance. In addition, West is not mistrustful of the quest motif at all. In fact, she is herself embarked on a significant quest; namely, the search for ultimate knowledge about what prompts man to seek death rather than pursue life. At the same time, however, West is one of the most outspoken critics of empire among all travel writers of her time, a fact that squares well with her feminist critique of patriarchal power structures. Moreover, her historical method is more sensitive toward women's issues and frequently invokes the private dimension of history, two elements that are consistently downplayed in contemporary academic histories. Thus, in West's case, the gendered nature of her discourse is ambivalent and hybrid, requiring an interpretive stance that, though gender sensitive, is not determined by ideological presuppositions about the progressive effects of gender on a woman's representation of foreign societies.

Besides feminism, West's other major political concern in *Black Lamb and Grey Falcon* is antiimperial nationalism. Her stance vis-à-vis these two kinds of liberationism is perhaps the strongest unifying feature of her enormously long, complicated book on Yugoslavia. It has frequently been held against *Black Lamb and Grey Falcon* that the book suffers from fragmentation and rampant digressiveness. At first (or even second) sight, the welter of historical narratives seems indeed to indicate a lack of structure. West's infatuation with history, together with her penchant for digressions on religious morality and aesthetics, has led critics to dismiss *Black Lamb and Grey Falcon* as "a collection of assorted ethical and historical essays" (Fussell, 206) or to call it "excessive, unbalanced" (Glendinning, 166). Yet, as I will demonstrate, there is more method in *Black Lamb and Grey Falcon* than meets the eye.

In fact, West consistently wove an ideological critique into her discussion of Yugoslav localities, turning places such as Split, Sarajevo, Belgrade, and Kosovo into sites whose history served her to exemplify different aspects of liberationism. In this way, West systematically elaborated her brief against patriarchy, against the Christian doctrine of atonement, and against imperialism, simply adapting the journey motif to the purpose of political rhetoric.

• • •

To West, Yugoslavia appeared to be a country where the forces of history were felt more directly and personally than in other places. West invokes a strong sense of historical determinism at the beginning of *Black Lamb and Grey Falcon* when she says: "I knew that the past has made the present, and I wanted to see how the process works"

(54). Her sense of a palpable history does not surprise, though, given that the Balkans were once again caught at the crossroads of history: even while the various parts of the newly formed Yugoslav nation were trying to coalesce during the 1930s, Nazi Germany to the north and Italy to the west posed military threats to the very existence of the country. The particular constellation of European power politics at that time, together with the region's long and painful history of imperial occupation and division, lent Yugoslavia virtually the significance of a symbol—a symbol for the wrongs of imperialism, but also an emblem of resistance and nationalism.[3]

Yugo-Slavia (or the "Kingdom of the South Slavs") was formed in 1919. During West's visits to the country it was ruled by Prince Paul Karageorgevic, a cousin of King Alexander I, whose assassination in Marseilles in 1934 forms the focus of West's introductory chapter. The Karageorgevic dynasty went back to Karageorge Petrovic, the Serb leader who had led the first large-scale revolt against Turkish rule since Serbia, four-and-a-half centuries before, had been integrated into the Turkish Empire. His rebellious spirit had kindled a new wave of nationalist insurgence in the region, leading first to Serbia's formal autonomy in 1815 and then, in 1878, to the creation of an independent nation. In an attempt to quell further nationalistic independence movements, Austria-Hungary occupied Bosnia and Herzegovina in 1878 and tightened its grip on Croatia. After the assassination of archduke Franz Ferdinand in Sarajevo on June 28, 1914, Austria-Hungary combined vicious punitive measures against Bosnia with an attack on the independent state of Serbia, which it annexed during World War I. However, even during the war, leaders of the various South Slav nations gathered in London to plan the political future of the Balkans. They agreed to found a union of South Slav states in the form of a constitutional monarchy, led by the Serbian Karageorgevic dynasty.

But Serb ambitions to be *primus inter pares* caused trouble from the start. When the country's new constitution was adopted by the parliament in 1921, it was on the strength of the Serbian parties and against the will of Croats and Bosnians, who saw themselves deprived of the autonomy they had hoped for. Thereafter, the centralized government in Belgrade (Serbia) was a constant source of dissatisfaction among non-Serb members of the kingdom. Antagonistic nationalist movements sprang up, both in Serbia and in Croatia, and vied for power in the state.

The tensions between Serbian supporters of a unified Yugoslavia and non-Serbian dissidents is felt throughout *Black Lamb and Grey Falcon*. Also felt is West's unwavering support of Serbia. Her pro-Serb stance is evidenced in the disproportionate importance she gives to Serbia's history (compared with Dalmatian, Bosnian, or Croatian histories), in her glorification of Serb heroism, and in her admiration of Serbia's Byzantine heritage. Like other commentators, Richard Tillinghast is rather perplexed by West's enthusiasm for Serbia: "Witnessing now the loathing that the South Slavic ethnic groups seem to feel toward each other, why was Rebecca West such a strong supporter of a Serbian-dominated united Yugoslavia?" (15). But Tillinghast offers two interesting answers to this question, arguing that West recognized the need for a strong centralizing power to hold the fledgling nation together: "[West] felt at home with the notion of a 'united kingdom' [since] she herself was a citizen of such a state" (15). Moreover, Tillinghast, writing in 1992, states that "West, though she would be horrified by the savagery of today's Yugoslavia, would still probably sympathize with the Serbs' sense that they have a right to dominate Croatia, Slovenia, Bosnia, and Macedonia. West often reminds us of the debt we owe the Serbs for having saved Europe from the Turks" (15). Indeed, West repeatedly states that the Balkan people "gave the bread out of their mouths to save us of Western Europe from Islam" (137), a feeling of gratitude that she directs particularly toward the Serbs, who had been the greatest shock absorbers of the Turkish drive toward Western Europe.

West never lost her interest in Yugoslavia, although after the 1930s she did not revisit the country. During most of World War II, West lobbied for a Serbian resistance movement against the Nazis, headed by General Mihailovic. She did not support Tito's communist forces, whom she linked with the detested image of the "'professional revolutionary . . . [who] seems to me to harmonise with no world, to work out at nothing but death and damnation. And surely Tito is the professional revolutionary'" (West quoted by Rosslyn, 113).

Although horrified by the internecine warfare between royalist and communist fellow Yugoslavs and gravely disappointed by the communist victory in 1945, West continued to keep a close eye on Yugoslav affairs. Her active support of Mihailovich and of the royalist Yugoslav expatriates in London caused many a controversy to flare around her. These controversies, according to Victoria Glendinning, "rumbled down the years, in books and articles and letters to the press, and Rebecca West never changed her ground, nor detached herself from Yugoslav issues" (165). But after the end of the war, her feelings for Yugoslavia were tinged with a degree of disappointment. In Rosslyn's view, West "did not merely love Yugoslavia . . . she believed in it—and she never forgave it for being other than she believed it was" (112). One can only speculate how West would have reacted to the disintegration of Yugoslavia and its ensuing ethnic warfare during the 1990s. Certainly, the violence attending these processes would have confirmed her in her pessimistic assessments "that the quality of Balkan history, and indeed of all history, is disgusting" (*Black Lamb and Grey Falcon*, 488).

• • •

During her three trips to Yugoslavia, West visited all the major towns and cities that bear the mark of Yugoslavia's convoluted and painful history. But she clearly privileged certain places in terms of the historical and political significance she attached to them. The passage on Split is a good example of West's interweaving of travel writing, history, and ideology.

West opens the section thus: "Split presents its peculiar circumstances to the traveller the minute he [*sic*] steps ashore. . . . And the history of the place was on our right and our left" (128). The most impressive historical site in Split is the ruined palace of Emperor Diocletian, destroyed in the seventh century by marauding Avars. The survivors of this raid settled in the ruins "against the day when there should be peace. They are still there. Peace never came" (139). This is the basic condition of the Balkans: dislocated people, poverty, and never-ending violence. From this bleak historical synopsis ("There is no use denying the horrible nature of our human destiny" [148]), West goes on to comment on the special significance that Dalmatia held for the crumbling Roman Empire: "Diocletian's palace commemorates . . . one of the prettiest of time's revenges. Rome destroyed, for perhaps no better reason than that she was an empire and could do it, the ancient civilization of Illyria. But when she later needed sound governors to defend her from barbarian invaders, Illyria gave her thirteen rulers and defenders, of whom only one was a failure" (144). The diversification in Rome's ruling stock came too late. In spite of very able rulers from Illyria, the empire's disintegration under "barbarian" pressure proceeded apace.

This not only demonstrates that the children of conquest may come back to haunt their conquerors, but also that any empire has only a limited lease. Indeed, as West argues, the destruction of the Roman Empire was, first of all, the consequence of internal problems rather than external pressures. Especially the oversize administrative apparatus and the social tensions between the increasingly rigid social classes contributed to the sapping of Rome's energy. Even Diocletian, though considered a *Restitutor Orbis* (restorer of the world) could not avert the empire's slow decay: "Order, it was said, was restored. But the greatest of the Illyrian emperors must have known that this was not true: that, on the contrary, disorder had been stabilized" (146). West concludes that "a society which is ruled by the sword can never be stable, if only because the sword is always passing from hand to hand, from the aging to the young" (147). This sums up West's essentially antiimperial stance, but it also expresses her strong concern with political stability.

While visiting Salonae, just outside Split, West elaborates her antiimperial views by attacking the Bellocian stance that takes Rome to be the sole foundation of European civilization. As indicated in chapter 2, Hilaire Belloc's doctrine that "the Catholic alone is in possession of the tradition of Europe" (7) had sparked a revival of conservative beliefs in the rightfulness of imperial rule during the 1920s and 1930s. In *Europe and the Faith* (1920), Belloc writes apologetically that the territories conquered by Rome "were occupied, taught, and as it were 'converted' into citizens of this now united Roman civilization" (29). The notion that Rome's legal system, its engineering genius, and military discipline redeemed the brute act of conquest had also been foisted upon West as a student:

> I regret that . . . my teachers should have found it necessary to
> instruct me, with far more emphasis than was justified by the
> facts in their or anybody else's possession, that the Roman Em-
> pire was a vast civilizing force which spread material and moral
> well-being all over the ancient world by its rule. I was taught that
> this was no mere accident: that the power to extend their rule by
> military means sprang from an intellectual and moral genius that

made them able to lay down the best way of living for the races they subdued. I find these assumptions firmly embedded in the mass of literature written by people who received a classical education. (164)

Almost everything West learns during her journey goes to show that such assumptions are very dubious.

While elaborating her critique of empire, West explicitly rejects the hegemony of the imperial center/margin dichotomy:

> We have no real evidence that the peoples on which the Roman Empire imposed its civilization had not pretty good civilizations of their own, better adapted to local conditions. The Romans said they had not; but posterity might doubt the existence of our contemporary French and English culture if the Nazis destroyed all records of them. . . . Yet neither I nor anybody else knows whether or not the conquest of Illyria by the Romans was not a major disaster, the very contrary to an extension of civilization." (165)

This passage not only subverts the imperial binary of the (supposedly) civilized center versus the barbarian margin, it is also a rejection of any meliorative imperial master-narrative, including the Bellocian view of spreading civilization on the wings of Christianity or Nazi Germany's (incomparably more noxious) program to establish the Third Reich. Thus, West's narrative goes beyond merely conveying historical data. Even though she starts out by describing the historical significance of an archaeological site (Diocletian's palace), her explanations resonate with contemporary political issues. By questioning the claim that Rome was a vast civilizing force, she implicitly undermines all imperial rationalizations of conquest (although, as we shall see later, she partly exempted the British Empire from such categorical criticism).

West's disbelief in the Bellocian model is of one piece with her rejection of Roman Catholicism and her consequent advocacy of Orthodox Christianity and Byzantine culture. Though West was not overtly religious, she regarded Orthodox Christianity as an authentic and venerable institution of Slav culture. Throughout the narrative, Roman Catholicism, partly through its linkage with Rome and partly through its association with the Habsburg dynasty, is presented as a limiting and oppressive religious system: "Now the Habsburgs are swept away you should see the Roman Catholic Church as it is: not at all democratic, not at all in favour of speculative thought, far more alarmed by the vaguest threat of social revolution than by any actual oppression, provided it is of monarchical or totalitarian origin, and wholly unsympathetic with any need for free expression but its own" (100). The Orthodox Church, on the other hand, is revered as a vehicle of authentic Serbian culture. Indeed, its priests function as proponents of the nationalist movement: "In a rich voice the Metropolitan announced that Christ had risen, and from the faces above the primrose flames came sharp cries of belief. Then he uttered a prayer or repeated a passage from the Gospels . . . and went on to deliver an address which compared the resurrection of Christ and the liberation of Christian Macedonia from the Turks by Serbia twenty-five years before. It was, in fact, straight Yugoslavian propaganda" (639–40).

Moreover, the Orthodox Church produced outstanding personalities such as Bishop Nikolai, whom West terms "the most remarkable human being I have ever met" (720). Nikolai is a "supreme magician" who "had full knowledge of what comfort men seek in magic, and how they long to learn that defeat is not defeat and that love is serviceable. He had a warm knowledge of how magic can prove this up to the hilt" (720). West's ecstatic language betrays her deep reverence for a Christian rite whose pagan sources are tinged with Byzantine "darkness" and mystery.[4]

• • •

The section that centers on Sarajevo takes up a different approach to what is basically the same cluster of issues surrounding notions of power, violence, and empire. No visitor to the capital of Bosnia (especially in the late 1930s!) could ignore the city's historical significance or casually pass over the fact that Franz Ferdinand looms large in the city's collective memory. And when the visitor is Rebecca West, one can reasonably expect a detailed historical recapitulation of the events that surrounded the archduke's assassination in 1914. Indeed, both the figures of Franz Ferdinand and his wife, Sophie Chotek, are described in the most vivid details.

But the lavishness of West's description is not self-serving. Richard Tillinghast comments that West "sees the assassination of Franz Ferdinand and Sophie less as a crime than as a symptom of the morbidity of empire" (18). In West's account of the events that preceded the *at-*

tentat, we learn about the intrigues that poisoned relationships at the Habsburg court, about the infamous *Schlamperei* (carelessness) of the administration, about Franz Joseph's senility, and about Franz Ferdinand's infatuation with mass-extinction-style hunting. "This capacity for butchery" West comments, "he used to express the hatred which he felt for nearly all the world" (334). The Freudian implications of this motif of displacement are extended in West's emphasis on Franz Ferdinand's compulsion to repeat the ritual slaughters and in the way these nightmares came to haunt him in his final hour. Indeed, the image of the hunter crops up again in West's use of the hunting metaphor to describe Franz Ferdinand's assassination. Only now the roles are inverted: Franz Ferdinand becomes the victim, while the "key batter in this battue" (345) is the only person that had any love for him: his wife. Because she suggested altering the course of their motor cavalcade through Sarajevo, she was instrumental in bringing her husband within range of Gavrilo Princip's loaded gun. Princip, who was a bad marksman, could take steady aim because Franz Ferdinand's vehicle stopped right in front of him, as the driver argued with an officer about what route to take.

What is unusual about the Sarajevo section is the intense scrutiny with which West analyses the motivations of the small band of Bosnian Serb nationalists who had planned and perpetrated the attack on Franz Ferdinand, as well as the sympathetic manner with which she portrays their fate after being captured by the Austrians. In West's telling, Gavrilo Princip and his fellow conspirators (Chabrinovitch, Chubrilovitch, and Popovitch, among others) become lively figures in a tragic tale of heroic nationalism.

One might speculate that West shows such a particular warmth and almost motherly care for "her" young heroes because she deeply identified with their struggle against patriarchal rule. In fact, her analysis of the Sarajevo assassination draws an explicit analogy between the domestic experience of one of the conspirators and his political deed: "It is the fashion now to sneer at Freud, but nobody could have predicted that in the mind of Chabrinovitch his revolt against his father and his revolt against the representative of the Habsburgs would seem one and the same, so that when a question was put to him in court that associated the two revolts, he answered not with the reason of an adult, but with the excuse of a defiant child" (425). West here refers to Chabrinovitch's treason trial, during which the assassin's father had complained about his son's ingratitude. To this the son replied: "'If I had been better brought up, I would not be seated on this bench'" (425). In accordance with a Freudian reading of political struggle, West sees the process of resistance against patriarchal rule in terms of a father-son conflict. Lesley Chamberlain comments that "the Freudian quality of her psychoanalytical analysis of Ferdinand and Sophie and indeed of much of the rebellion against Austrian power was supremely apt. Psychoanalysis was born in that Viennacentric world, and expressly designed to explain its maladies" (265).

At the same time as she denounces patriarchal rule, West speaks up in favor of Bosnian Serb nationalism. In fact, she clearly distinguishes between right-wing nationalism, as a rationale for conquest, and liberationist nationalism: "Nationalism is simply the determination of a people to cultivate its own soul, to follow the customs bequeathed to it by its ancestors, to develop its traditions according to its own instincts. It is the national equivalent of the individual's determination not to be a slave. The fulfillment of both those determinations is essentially a part of the left programme" (1101). West even goes so far as to designate the liberationist political struggle of the Bosnian Serbs as an "apt symbol of life" (381). Franz Ferdinand's assassination is, moreover, seen as nothing less than "a mystery"—West immediately continuing: "For that is the way the deed appears to me, and to all Westerners. But to those who look at it on the soil where it was committed, and to the lands east of that, it seems a holy act of liberation; and among such people are those whom the West would have to admit are wise and civilized" (381).

Here West acknowledges the paradoxical and morally ambivalent nature of nationalist liberation. Not only does the life wish of the Bosnians manifest itself in murder, the reverberations of this act cause harm to all of Europe: "When the Bosnians chose life, and murdered Franz Ferdinand, they chose death for the French and Germans and English, and if the French and Germans and English had been able to choose life they would have chosen death for the Bosnians. The sum will not add up" (382). West's anguish about the fact that the life wish and the death wish seem to be inextricably entangled with one another represents both her Manichaean sensibility and her perception of the current political climate in Europe, which was breeding wholesale anxiety and fear. But the dilemma does not suggest to her the preferability of stasis over active rebellion. On the contrary, West affirms that the oppressed have no choice but to rebel, no matter what the consequences are on a global scale. This prioritizing of the local over the universal, the ethnic over the imperial, the emotional over the pragmatic, constitutes the radical core of West's liberationist ideology.

• • •

The Belgrade section contains the longest historical digression in the entire book. Indeed, the story of Serbia's return to sovereignty in the nineteenth century takes up more than one hundred pages. In this book-within-a-book, however, there is an emotional and topical focus that demonstrates the peculiar quality of West's feminism.

Just as West focused her emotional energies on the young assassins of Sarajevo, her sympathies are now marshaled in defense of the Serbian queen Draga, who had become the victim of intrigues at the court and of malicious slander in the public sphere. Indeed, the queen "was hated as few women since the beginning of time, as no cruel mother, as no murderess, has ever been loathed" (549). Her reputation was tainted, not only because of her humble origins (she grew up in a small town, the second daughter of impoverished parents), but also because she had spent more than a year in dubious company in Belgrade after her husband's death. In this condition, Serbia's former queen Nathalie Obrenovic took her in as a chambermaid, because she had learned that Draga was in fact the granddaughter of a close friend of the former king Milosh Obrenovic, Nathalie's deceased husband. This is how Draga met Alexander Obrenovich, Nathalie's son and reigning king of Serbia. Alexander, a shy, awkward, sexually inhibited person (he reportedly suffered from genital deformations) fell madly in love with Draga, who was nine years his senior. Against the combined advice of his parents and his ministers and against the stiff resistance of the whole corps of army officers, Alexander vowed to marry his ill-reputed Draga. This marriage, contracted in July 1900, led to Serbia's international isolation, to the resignation of the entire cabinet and to the near desertion of the army corps (several officers had tried to dissuade Alexander from marrying Draga by claiming that they had "enjoyed" her previously).

But Draga's questionable moral character was not at the heart of the resentment against her, both in the high political echelons and among the common folk. Much more important was the suspicion that Draga exerted undue influence on the king's political decisions. By meddling in matters of the state, Draga unwittingly undermined Alexander's masculinity and thereby posed a threat to the patriarchal conception of Serb nationalism. As Margaret Beissinger pointed out, Serb nationalism was (and still is) a predominantly male ideology.[5] Consequently, any threat to the model of male leadership by a woman was perceived as a threat against the nation itself, a circumstance that is obliquely pointed out by Rebecca West: "The whole country was filled by the news of the approaching marriage by a black horror such as they would not have felt at a threat of invasion by the Turks" (553). West's figurative linking of the Turkish threat with the king's marriage to Draga basically squares with Margaret Beissinger more explicit statement of the matter: "if the centuries-long state of foreign domination (be it Ottoman or Austro-Hungarian) in the Balkans in the nineteenth century was viewed as a state of powerlessness, or by extension, femaleness, then the struggles for liberation were effectively struggles to gain or regain maleness (manhood) and power" (80). Draga flew in the face of this gendered model of nationalism, and her fate was sealed by the disproportionate contrast between her own assertiveness and her husband's pathetic weakness.

Although West had always been a keen interpreter of the symbolical roles attributed to women by social convention, she faltered somewhat in her analysis of Draga's tragic career. Her assertion that the whole affair "is a mystery. For Draga was insignificant" (565) is arguably a bad judgment call. Indeed, Draga was significant enough to influence her husband's political decisions and to impose her will on the court. There is evidence for what Gladt calls Alexander's "total compliance vis-à-vis Draga's advice" (359, my translation). She influenced his decision not to seek adoption of an aristocratic heir, a measure that might have saved his reign, as well as their lives (Gladt), and she persuaded him to indulge in flagrant forms of nepotism regarding her own family members, a fact that caused intense friction with the members of the national aristocracy and alienated the populace. She even tried to talk Alexander into appointing her own brother Nikodem Lunjevica, a dissipated, unprincipled character, as heir apparent to the Serbian throne. Although Draga most likely deserved little of the general opprobrium that was loaded upon her, she was surely less innocent than West makes her appear.

But West was surefooted in her interpretation of another element in the story; namely, the connection between Draga's tragic fate and her symbolical role as mother of the state. When news spread in 1901 that Draga was expecting an heir to the throne, the public seemed willing to bury their hatchets and look forward to the royal offspring. At last, Draga appeared to live up to her symbolical function. The importance of this function cannot be overstated in the context of nineteenth-century Serb nationalism. Indeed, in the nation's epic poetry, which had gained immense popularity during that time, women were "referred to in perhaps their most important role . . . as those who give birth to Serbian heroes. They are see as vessels that serve to bear male heroes" (Beissinger, 77). When it became known, however, that Draga had misled everyone, including her husband, and was not pregnant after all, the public hatred for Queen Draga intensified to near fever-pitch. Draga's enemies immediately capitalized on this embarrassment and fanned the propaganda about what became known as the "pregnancy comedy." But worse than accusing Draga of dissimulation, her enemies charged her now with treason.

Although failure to provide a dynastic heir was a serious enough matter, the "tasteless attacks by the international press were an insult to Serbia's national pride" (Gladt, my translation). Both West and Gladt agree that the charge of intentional deception on the part of Draga cannot be proved and that she may have suffered from a "malady [that] might easily have misled Draga into believing herself pregnant" (*Black Lamb and Grey Falcon*, 556). But nobody in Serbia, except for Alexander, were willing to give Draga the least benefit of the doubt. She was now confirmed to be the plague of the Serb family. West writes that "the people's mind was nursing an image that it always likes to hate and dandle in its hatred, the woman who is death, who is a whore and barren, They were moved to new folk-lore by this story, which troubled them by allusions to all sorts of dangers specially feared by the blood, to threats against kingship, to pollution of the race" (556). West correctly perceived the near mythical dimension of the incident, portraying the ensuing orgy of violence as an archetypal purging of the nation's sterile mother.

Indeed, the dissent between the army and Alexander, which had been fomenting since the beginning of his courtship with Draga, came to a head in the night of June 11, 1903. Under the leadership of Draga's brother-in-law, Colonel Mashin, several army regiments stationed in Belgrade rebelled and invaded the king's palace in an open attempt to kill the royal couple. Ironically, king Alexander, who had been put on his guard by repeated warnings about a possible coup, had carried with him a warning of the conspiracy. An unopened letter announcing the impending assault was later found in the dead king's trousers. Just before the horror struck home, the unsuspecting couple were sleeping in their bed. When marauding groups of half-drunken officers began searching the rooms of the royal residence, the king and queen, having awakened, were hiding in a concealed cabinet beside their bedroom. After several anxious hours in this cramped condition, Draga opened a window and, still believing in the loyalty of the palace guard, called out for help. She was immediately fired at by soldiers standing in the courtyard. Soon afterward, the door to the hidden closet was forced open and the king and the queen were dragged out. After an exchange of angry words, the royal couple was shot by as many as forty-eight bullets and maimed by the intruders' swords. They were then flung out of the window onto the lawn below. As a result of "guilt by association," the rioters also murdered two of Alexander's ministers and Draga's two brothers.

West's reluctance to lay the blame for these killings squarely at the feet of Serb nationalism could be seen as evidence that she gave priority to national over female liberation. Indeed, Loretta Stec has argued just that, maintaining that to West "the submission of women to men is a precondition to the resistance of one nation or people to the invasion, colonization or oppression of another" (151). I disagree with such a stern conclusion, for two reasons.

First, although West did not fancy the idea of compromising Serb nationalism (which she admired for its antiimperial potential), her narrative elaboration of the Draga story, complete with horrific details about the lynching of the royal couple, is far from abetting the masculine principle that was the engine behind the anti-Draga campaign. Despite her misrepresentation of Draga's character, West's graphic account of the violence directed against the queen constitutes an ugly blot on the record of Serb nationalism. Second, West actually alluded to the fact that the submission of women to men was of the same order as the betrayal of one nation by another. In a characteristic analogy, West illustrated the inequity visited upon Croatia by Austria-Hungary by drawing on sexual relations between a man and a woman: "And then, ultimately, they practised on them the supreme treachery. When the Dual Monarchy was framed to placate Hungary, the Croats were handed over to the Hungarians as their chattels. It has a kind of lowness that is sometimes exhibited in the sexual affairs of very vulgar and shameless people: a man leaves his wife and induces a girl to become his mistress, then is reconciled to his wife and to please her exposes the girl to some public humiliation" (54). In this view, the social status of women is linked to the political status of underdog nations seeking independence from the imperial yoke: both are trying to shake off ancient bonds of oppression and both are hampered by prejudice and scorn loaded upon them from the superior, patriarchal powers that rule their world.

There is also a biographical aspect involved in all this: West's willingness to rehabilitate Draga springs from a deep sympathy for the fate of the publicly maligned woman. Of course, West had first-hand experience with the sort of public slander that was heaped upon women who roused any kind of sexual suspicion. This long-time mistress of H. G. Wells and mother of an illegitimate child could identify with the pain caused by social censure based on masculine standards of sexual morality.[6]

By portraying Draga sympathetically as a tragic, if flawed, figure who was unluckily caught at the intersection of gender prejudice and political intrigue, West heightens rather than obscures the hateful character of the nationalist campaign conducted against her. In fact, she portrays Draga as a sacrificial victim, a ritual scapegoat who was killed in order for the community to regain its trust in the monarchy and its function as the nation's patriarchal symbol. This ties in the Draga story with the section about the Sheep's Field and with West's overall abhorrence of sacrifice. Indeed, Draga was a "black sheep" in the scheme of Serbia's dynasty, and she was sacrificed to the idea of national vitality, just like the black lamb is sacrificed on Saint George's Eve to ensure the "reproduction" of Macedonia's population.

Up to this point in her long narrative, West had been groping her way toward a realization of what prompts man to "please the bats at the back of his soul" (166); that is, what makes him prefer death to life. That she has not yet reached full realization on that count is demonstrated by her reference to Draga's killing as a "mystery" (565), much as the bloodletting following Bosnia's killing of Archduke Ferdinand had been a "mystery" to her. Only in Macedonia and Kosovo will West penetrate the "mystery" to resolve the puzzling meaning at its core. And the enlightenment will parallel her realization about the true meaning of the black lamb and its historical place-holders, among whom Draga looms as a shadowy figure that is partly obscured by the immense historical significance of the Tsar Lazar.

• • •

The section of *Black Lamb and Grey Falcon* that details West's experience in Kosovo unfolds her most deeply held political stance. In her view, the history of Europe hinges on events in the Balkans. She claims that had Stephen Dushan, the most illustrious of medieval Serbian rulers, not died prematurely, "he might have saved Europe from the Turks" (894). And further on she speculates "that the battle of Kossovo deducted as much from civilization as the sum of England after the Tudor age" (900).

But West is not only concerned with the central role that the Balkans played in the history of Western Europe. She also points out once again the inherent instability of empires: "I saw before me what an empire which spreads beyond its legitimate boundaries must do to its subjects. It cannot spread its own life over the conquered areas, for life cannot travel too far from its source, and it blights the life that is native to those parts. Therefore it imprisons all its subjects in a stale conservatism" (903). West reaches this conclusion after contemplating a group of impoverished Kosovo Albanians (she calls them "touts") who "looked incredibly fragile" (903) to her. West presents these people as a symbol of imperial self-destruction: "They stood wide, wide apart on the dark grass of Kossovo, for their flesh was too poor to feel the fleshy desire to draw together. A people that extends its empire too far from its base commits the sin of Onan and spills its seed upon the ground" (908). Significantly, the sexual reference, linking Turkey's imperial overextension to masturbation, is reminiscent of the way West thought about the political as both an extension and a symptom of the private, sexual aspect of life in the Draga section.

One reason why the Ottoman Empire became overextended, she concludes, was through their annexation of Serbia. At this point, West gives a differentiated, though clearly pro-Serb version of the famed battle of Kosovo in 1389. In her historical analysis, she rejects "the opinion of the anti-Serb historians [who] point out that within a short time [Stephen Dushan's] Empire had dissolved into its constituent parts, so that the Turks were faced not by a united people, but by a loose federation of feudal barons and their followers" (897). Although her Serb guide Constantine cautions her "that it was not treachery that

lost us Kossovo, it is that we were all divided among ourselves" (902),
West concludes "I knew it was nonsense" (897). In this way, West constructs a pro-Serb version of history and substantially aggrandizes the
nationalist myth in the process.

It is a myth that has served again and again to justify Serb aggression, however. For instance, during Serbia's campaign in Kosovo in the
spring of 1999 one could read statements such as these on Serb internet sites: "Over the centuries, historians have praised the sacrificial
courage of Prince Lazar and his army on that day in 1389-and, as we
enter a new century, that same courage is embodied by the spirit of all
the Serbian people." [7] Such statements show how intertwined history
and myth have become for the Serbs. (Is it, one asks, the business
of historians to praise quasi-mythical figures?) In the light of recent
events in the Balkans, it appears that West seriously miscalculated the
explosive potential inherent in such nationalist legends. Because of
her unconditional support of Serb nationalism, she did not question
the Kosovo myth as she had questioned and critiqued the myth surrounding Queen Draga.

Indeed, West goes so far as to base her central political argument
on a Serb ballad from the epic song cycle about Tsar Lazar entitled
"The Fall of the Serbian Empire." This song is printed (in abridged
version) twice in the book and provides the eponymous symbol of the
grey falcon. To West, this bird signifies the essence of self-sacrifice
and defeatism, because the leader of the Serb forces in the battle
of Kosovo, Prince Lazar, had followed the promptings of a heavenly
messenger (in the form of the grey falcon) to accept earthly defeat in
exchange for his entry into the heavenly kingdom. (For a detailed discussion of this ballad, see chapter 5.) Upon hearing Constantine recite
this poem aloud, West indignantly comments that " 'Lazar was wrong' "
(911), and she adds ironically that he "was a member of the Peace
Pledge Union" (911), a satirical reference to England's pacifist movement in the 1930s. Thus, West uses the myth of Kosovo as a case in
point to prove her thesis of the pervasive death wish implanted into
Western man by the Christian doctrine of atonement. This argument,
however, is not aimed primarily at the Yugoslavs but rather at her English compatriots. Indeed, West relentlessly attacked the national pa-
ralysis that had gripped the English people and its political leaders in
the period of appeasement policy.

The Kosovo section, then, served West as the ultimate backdrop against which to show that a spiritual basis for resistance was needed before action could ensue. The three previous sections skillfully established the ground for the climax at Kosovo: in Split, West investigated the corrupt nature of imperial domination, its infatuation with violence, and its tendency to impose cultural and historical hegemony. In Sarajevo, she focused on the liberationist potential of Balkan nationalism, which succeeded in mobilizing a strong resistance against imperial domination. In the Belgrade section, she expanded on the dark side of patriarchal nationalism, showing that national politics can entail a vicious backlash in the area of gender politics. And in Kosovo, finally, she demonstrated that the pacifist's urge to yield to force works against the fight for freedom. Her argument shows cumulatively the various facets of oppression and liberation, and it identifies the obstacles that must be overcome before liberal, democratic ideals of national self-rule and equitable gender relations can be achieved.

Given hindsight, however, it seems that West's liberationist argument may have outlived its usefulness at the end of the twentieth century. It is deeply ironic that *Black Lamb and Grey Falcon* was apparently revered by some of the militant Serb nationalists who wrought so much destruction in the Balkans during the 1990s. Coinciding with the start of Slobodan Milosevic's campaign to restore the glories of Greater Serbia in the late 1980s, a Serb intellectual by the name of Nikola Koljevic published an abbreviated Serbo-Croat translation of *Black Lamb and Grey Falcon* entitled *Crno Jagnje i Sivi Soko*.[8] This translation, which includes passages from all the main chapters of *Black Lamb and Grey Falcon*, went through four editions by the end of year 2000. Paradoxically, though, while Koljevic's foreword highlight's West's view on the morbidity of political expansionism, the translator himself did not put this knowledge into practice. As Bosnian-Serb vice president, Koljevic was one of the political leaders responsible for the bloody siege of Sarajevo in the mid-1990s. In one sense, then, Koljevic betrayed Rebecca West's high principles that he himself helped to popularize among his people, and yet at the same time he lent further credence to West's prophetic statement about the Shakespearean quality of Balkan history. (Koljevic was himself a Shakespearen scholar before he turned politician.)

Recent events in Serbia, however, have demonstrated that the era of Shakespearean politics in the Balkans may finally be over. The nonviolent revolution that overthrew Milosevic's government in October

2000 proved that Serbia still had some purchase on democratic liberationism and that its main political impetus need not exclusively be
derived from national myths and ethnic hatreds. The student movement Otpor (Resistance) that helped topple Milosevic was led by
young, forward-looking, democratic patriots who relied on modern information technology (cell phones and the Internet) rather than on
ancient legends and epic story cycles to achieve their political ends.
Although these protesters represent precisely the qualities West found
so endearing in the Serbs (i.e., intellectual vigor, courage, and a passion for democracy), it is very likely that they are unfamiliar with
West's book. This would be a "mystery" befitting West's perplexed realization that history is thoroughly unpredictable and that politics is
not an exact science but a welter of irrational impulses, chance, and
desire. How could travel writing possibly have any specific impact on
an amorphous, unstable, "moving target" such as Balkan politics? I
will return to this question in this book's conclusion.

PART TWO

**THE TROUBLE
WITH DUALISM**

Sites and Issues

THE INHERENTLY dualistic construction of national and international politics in the 1930s comes to the fore in the survey "Authors Take Sides" (1937), which was published, with writers' responses, in the *Left Review*. The questionnaire, which was addressed "To the Writers and Poets of England, Scotland, Ireland, and Wales," stated emphatically that "the equivocal attitude, the Ivory Tower, the paradoxical, the ironic, detachment, will no longer do," and it proceeded to pose the following questions: "Are you for, or against, the legal Government and the people of Republican Spain? Are you for, or against, Franco and Fascism?" Such dualisms not only undergirded the period's political discourse but also put their stamp on influential psychocultural reflections. Most prominently, Sigmund Freud stipulated in *Civilization and Its Discontents* (1930) that paired opposites such as Eros and Thanatos or individual and society were the two dominant aspects of human civilization:

> The two urges, the one towards personal happiness and the other towards union with other human beings, must struggle with each other in every individual; and so, also, the two processes of individual and of cultural development must stand in hostile opposition to each other and mutually dispute the ground. But this struggle between the individual and society is not a derivative of the contradiction—probably an irreconcilable one—between the primal instinct of Eros and death. It is a dispute within the eco-

nomic of the libido, comparable to the contest concerning the
distribution of libido between ego and objects. (141)

The sheer number of antithetical terms in this essay is astonishing.
Words such as *rift, conflict, contest, dispute, struggle,* and *opposition* are
strewn thickly throughout the tract.

Like many of his contemporaries, Freud was steeped in the rhetoric
of sociopolitical antagonism, and he recognized that the political conflict that was at the basis of this model could cause a catastrophe: "In
this respect precisely the present time deserves a special interest. Men
have gained control over the forces of nature to such an extent that
with their help they would have no difficulty in exterminating one another to the last man. They know this, and hence comes a large part
of their current unrest, their unhappiness and their mood of anxiety"
(vol. 14, 145). It was this unrest and anxiety that constituted a major
motivating force for English intellectuals of the 1930s to leave their
country, both in search of better socioeconomic conditions and, paradoxically, in pursuit of the worst that can be imagined—the zero point
of culture and society.

Although English travelers heeded Freud's universal pronouncements about the conflicted nature of the human condition, they were
also interested in the specifics of social and political processes, both
at home and abroad. In particular, they were obsessed by the rift between the upper and the lower classes, the conflict between right-wing
and left-wing politics, and the opposition between the older and the
younger generations. But in spite of these clear lines of demarcation
and antithetical patterns, dualisms in the 1930s had a way of becoming
either undermined by the mutual contamination of their oppositional
terms or to be subsumed under the monistic tendency of political totalitarianism. In this chapter, I will outline the ways in which 1930s
travel writing was predicated upon the dualistic principles that dominated the decade, while showing simultaneously how the travelers' experience of cultural and geographical displacement tended to unsettle
their antithetical conceptions.

One of the central arguments of this study—that 1930s travel books
explore cultural differences abroad from various positions that reflect
contemporary, English concerns—is but one aspect of the trouble
with dualism. For instance, Graham Greene's account of Mexico ends

with a description of air-raid precautions being taken in London. Evelyn Waugh delivered his famous "conservative manifesto" in his Mexican travel book, where he focused on the expropriation of the British
oil concerns by president Cárdenas. Furthermore, Orwell's account of
his antifascist fight in Spain is overshadowed by his concern with how
the English left-wing press would represent "his" side in the conflict.
And finally, Rebecca West discovered in Kosovo that the spiritual roots
of the British appeasement policy were somehow linked to the battle
of Kosovo in 1389. Thus, even when *abroad* was sought as an antithesis
to *home*, it often ended up reflecting (or inflecting) rather than con-
trasting "home." The whole dialectic of home and abroad was particularly vexed during the 1930s, of course, since the economic slump was
global; moreover, what was brewing was a *world* war, and decolonization seemed a vast, unstoppable development. Thus, what was going
on at home had its repercussions abroad, while some of the conditions in foreign places seemed eerily mirrored in England's own state
of affairs. As a result of such unsettling experiences (what Patricia
Yaeger termed evocatively the "strange effects of space"), travel often
complicated, rather than enabled, straightforward notions of political
commitment.

The task of taking sides, of lining up on one side of any given ideological or class divide was a tricky enough business at home, given the
conflicting social and political impulses arising from a simultaneous
desire for renewal and the fear of social and political instability. But
abroad, the business of placing oneself on one side or the other of
binary oppositions was an even more bedeviled task. Once leftist and
rightist intellectuals crossed literal, rather than metaphorical, boundaries, their predetermined, apparently unshakable political and cultural
dogmas became complicated, malleable, and confused.[1] A symptom
of this tendency is the way in which ideas about dystopian and utopian
modes of social organization would not be stabilized but had a tendency to become mutually imbricated with one another.

The purely imaginative dystopias captured in the work of Eliot,
Huxley, Zamiatin, and others had a counterpart in the period's travel
writing. The more overtly dystopian travel books of the 1930s were directly inspired by the political problems and socioeconomic crises that
dominated the contemporary climate. In their attempt to face the reality of violence, poverty, and oppression, politically minded travelers

of the 1930s shunned the sunny seaside resorts of Saint-Tropez and Capri. Indeed, the slum, the trench, the rat-infested African hut, and the decrepit Dalmatian village were the most typical loci of their investigations. One aspect of what Greene called "the fascination which worked on [travelers] in the dirt, the disease, the barbarity and the familiarity of Africa" (258) is the bourgeois intellectual's quarrel with the high degree of standardization and dehumanization at home. Mark Cocker speculates that "what some travellers are perhaps attempting is to fulfil the troglodyte and barbarian in themselves" (161).

Besides this psychological explanation, however, there is an even better historical one. After all, Waugh, Greene, Orwell, Fleming, Auden, Isherwood, and others all became "war correspondents" at one time or another, reporting on the nightmarish spread of fascism and other disheartening manifestations of totalitarianism. These travelers were not so much after a primitive reincarnation of themselves than attempting to feel the pulse of history, a history that seemed to be devolving into variants on the theme of dystopia.

Indeed, 1930s travelers could not resist the temptation of becoming chroniclers of the malaise of their time. George Orwell's writings about the poor were clearly motivated by a desire for complete and utter truthfulness about the current socioeconomic reality. The gloomy settings in books such as *Down and Out in Paris and London* or *The Road to Wigan Pier* depict a kind of underworld. As Jacques Rancière has pointed out, though, "horrible as the underworld may be, it is still a world. It is a place where you can find the disease of society, designate and touch it with your fingers. . . . The descent into hell is not simply a pitiful visit to the land of the poor—it is also a way of making sense, a procedure of meaning" (34).

But social revelations are not the only payoff from visits to dystopia—spiritual revelation can be procured from such trips as well. This brings us to the properly apocalyptic implication of journeys into depravity and corruption. Eric Rabkin comments that "in tales of the end of the world as we know it, crucial judgments arise by comparing the world destroyed with the world for which it makes room. The hope of the world under Noah's rainbow is brighter than that before the flood" ("Why Destroy the World?" ix). The revelatory aspect of apocalyptic writing is particularly stressed in Graham Greene's near biblical description of the Mexican town of Villahermosa. But even when the religious impulse is not paramount, as in Waugh's dystopias of cultural and social degradation, the representation of dystopian conditions abroad can have a relativistic and potentially reassuring implication regarding the contemporary sociopolitical situation at home.

Two opposed tendencies can be observed in the way English travel writers used the political potential implicit in the discourse of dystopia. Waugh, for instance, intended to strengthen his readers' reactionary sensibilities in his presentation of African and South American dystopias, arguing for authoritarian, imperialist interventions. Orwell, on the other hand, intended to strengthen his readers' progressive will and social solidarity by reporting on the awful conditions among the poor and oppressed of the world. Thus, handled by different travelers, the same motif can have radically opposed meanings.

Although the dystopian seems to be the overriding expression of comparative cultural observations in the 1930s, the period's travel writing contains occasional utopian glimpses as well. In fact, travel writing was perhaps the only contemporary discourses that offered a vehicle for conveying genuine utopian perspectives. Orwell's *Homage to Catalonia*, Greene's *Journey without Maps*, Waugh's *Remote People*, and even West's *Black Lamb and Grey Falcon* contain passages that have such a utopian appeal. They present intimations of societies or political systems that could serve as models for England's sociopolitical situation, be it the socialist brotherhood among Catalonia's militiamen, romantic Liberian natives, virile, freedom-loving Serbs, or paternal colonialists in Kenya. But it is usually the dystopian perspective that wins out in the end over any temporary assertion of utopia. Both Waugh's and Greene's hopes for finding the remnants of Latin American paradises turned into particularly haunting nightmares. Moreover, the betrayal of political idealism in Spain (Orwell) and the recognition of man's innate desire to kill and be killed (West) all went to show that traveling could not provide a radical and enduring escape from the socioeconomic and political awareness of crisis and decline that constituted the ruling spirit of England in the 1930s.

Hence, like so many other binary oppositions of the time, the dualism of utopia versus dystopia was only clear-cut on paper. As the 1930s progressed, it became increasingly obvious to the period's travelers that utopia and dystopia were not easily separable. The vexed potential for mutual contamination between utopia and dystopia undermined the travelers' trust in the viability or, indeed, the very existence of this, as well as other, oppositional conceptions in culture, society, and politics.

Although the opposition between utopia and dystopia proved increasingly deceptive, it did spawn a number of other dualisms, most importantly those of hope versus despair, life versus death, or redemption versus apocalypse. Moreover, Barbara Goodwin and Keith Taylor have stressed that the discourses of dystopia and utopia characterize two antithetical political attitudes as well. They argue that utopias represent a progressive political model, while dystopias are inherently conservative (27). This assessment conforms with Fredric Jameson's view that "Utopia is a transparent synonym for socialism itself, and the enemies of Utopia sooner or later turn out to be the enemies of socialism" (77).

But such a political typology seems to be problematic with regard to the period under discussion here, since it cannot account for the fact that the 1930s, or the Red Decade, as it was known among rightist contemporaries, did not produce utopias, but rather dystopias. Certainly, the claim that "dystopian warnings of future horrors, based on extrapolation and projection of current tendencies or ideas, serve to revalidate the present as the lesser evil, and to promote a 'decision' for no change" (Goodwin and Taylor, 27) does not hold with regard to Orwell's and Huxley's dystopias, which are based on a critique, not a quietist acceptance of present conditions. Bernard Bergonzi maintains correctly that in Orwell's *1984* "the future [is] little more than a pretext for writing about the present" (212). Indeed, apart from the aspect of optimism that, obviously enough, is lacking in dystopian scenarios, the proleptic quality of dystopias can be considered to have a constructive dynamic as well. After all, the extrapolation of current conditions is intended to avert negative developments by changing the course of history now and for the future.

Dystopia and Utopia in Africa

Although Evelyn Waugh did not use the term *dystopia* as such, his cultural perspective on foreign places was inherently dystopian. In his African books, Waugh singles out Ethiopia as the quintessential locus of a bad place (Greek: *dys-topos*) by virtue of its supposed lack of such civilizational amenities as law, order, technology, and good taste. I have already discussed Waugh's revulsion against what he considered the "barbarity" and the "sepulchral gloom" of Addis Ababa. Regarding Ethiopia's political system, Waugh equates it with humanity's worst vices: "Slavery and slave-raiding were universal; justice, when executed at all, was accompanied by torture and mutilation in a degree known nowhere else in the world; the central government was precarious and only rendered effective by repeated resort to armed force; disease was rampant" (32).

Given such a bleak perspective, Waugh must have considered the words *Ethiopia* and *Dystopia* as almost synonymous. But although Ethiopia presented to him a picture of the utmost human depravity, the way Waugh conceptualized this kind of dystopia is quite different from the significance of the period's fictional dystopias. For Waugh, Ethiopia was a "bad place" because modernity had *not yet* reached this part of the world, and because its ruling system was *not* capable of establishing a real power base and imposing central governmental control. Gorman Beauchamp claims that dystopia means "utopia plus technology" (56). But clearly, this formula does not apply to the kind of right-wing dystopia developed by Waugh. Indeed, for Waugh dystopia is constituted by a lack of, not by a surplus of, authority, standardization, and technology. By contrast, the period's leftist dystopias focus on the harmful consequences of combining science, technology, and efficient state bureaucracy. Thus, when reading leftist dystopias of the interwar period, we are faced with the mirror image of Waugh's description of Ethiopia. Especially when compared with the metropolitan tyrannies of *Brave New World* (and, later, of *1984*), Ethiopia seems positively quaint, although it is not so for Waugh.

Moreover, while fictional dystopias tend to be based on domestic places (one can recognize London in both *Brave New World* and *1984*), the travelers' dystopias are associated with places that are removed from the writer's home. There is also a temporal implication here: fictional dystopias are always set in a more or less clearly specified time in the future. For instance, *Brave New World, We,* and *1984* provide critical perspectives on contemporary society by showing potential future developments of science and technology in conjunction with totalitarian state power. But the "real" dystopias discovered by 1930s travelers were all of the present. Both the "real" and the fictive dystopias, however, effected a qualification of the cultural and political sys-

tem for whose public they are written—the fictional dystopias from
the perspective of temporal, the travel dystopias from that of spatial
distancing.

Waugh certainly did not detect any redeeming qualities in Ethiopia's almost total lack of technological and administrative sophistica-
tion. The precapitalist conditions he found there triggered a reactionary response that nothing in Huxley's or Wells's dystopias could equal.
These socialist writers mounted a critique of social conformity and
authoritarian rule that could be leveled against any totalitarian regime, both of fascist and communist persuasion. In contradistinction,
Waugh's critique has a different, properly conservative, ideological
spin. His revulsion from what he considered Ethiopia's technological backwardness, economic underdevelopment, and cultural banality
can indeed be read as a manifesto in favor of industrialization, tech-
nocratic functionalism, and centralized government. With his pejorative evaluation of Africa's only nation ruled by an indigenous elite,
Waugh may well have intended to show that the notion of dystopia
could be divorced from its implication in the leftist critique of industrial standardization and authoritative state power. Thus, Waugh's
rightist dystopia propagated precisely those attributes of political rule
that the period's leftist dystopias set out to demolish.

• • •

As much as political considerations conditioned Waugh's conception of Ethiopia as a premodern kind of dystopia, a different set of
ideological sensibilities and a different sociopolitical context caused
him to invoke utopian visions. When Waugh came across a state of
affairs that corresponded to his penchant for aristocratic and imperial
forms of government, he saw everything through rose-colored glasses.

This explains the salutary effect that Kenya's colonial life had on
Waugh's strained nerves. Indeed, upon entering Kenya, he lapsed into
a pastoral discourse that lacks the distancing sarcasm that otherwise
characterizes his tough-minded approach to foreign societies. In a
place where "colonization [was] carried out with so little ill-will between the immigrant and the indigenous races" (161), one can expect
the lay of the land to be as appealing as the sociopolitical context:
"The scenery is tremendous, finer than anything I saw in Abyssinia, all
round for immense distances successive crests of highland. . . . Bril-
liant sunshine quite unobscured, uninterrupted in its incidence; sun-

light clearer than daylight; there is something of the moon about it, the coolness seems so unsuitable" (168–69). Significantly, Waugh's celebration of the Kenyan "Happy Valley" (156) (an ironic reference to Samuel Johnson's utopia in *Rasselas,* which is set in Abyssinia) is preceded by the statement that "it is just worth considering the possibility that there may be something valuable behind the indefensible and inexplicable assumption of superiority by the Anglo-Saxon race" (167). In this sense, Waugh's "non-place" (utopia) is constructed as a real place, thereby illustrating a recent argument by Akhil Gupta and James Ferguson that places are ideal vehicles for collective ideological mobilization because it is so tempting to localize a particular political cause (41).

Waugh's identification of bad politics with badlands (Ethiopia) and of good politics with a pretty landscape (Kenya) accords well with the claim of the above mentioned critical anthropologists that "the experience of space is always socially constructed" (40). One may want to add, though, that in Waugh's case the experience of space was *ideologically* rather than socially constructed. Kenya was so beautiful to him because the spatialization of ideology could proceed unhindered there, turning the whole place into an arena for the enactment of a particular social order; namely, that of patriarchal colonialism.

Of course, Waugh is not the first colonial traveler to make the leap from satisfying exoticism to utopian polity: *The West Indies and the Spanish Main* (1859) by Trollope constructs the colony of Jamaica in much the same terms.[2] In this way, the landscape comes to symbolize no less than the triumph of a political idea. In the last consequence, Kenya offered Waugh the comforts of home, because the "others" living within its confines were as invisible to him as the dark Moroccans were invisible to Orwell.[3]

Such an identification between an ideological and a geographical entity is predicated upon an assumed identity of space and culture. For the very same reason, Waugh despised Zanzibar, whose multicultural makeup, with Arabs, Europeans, and Indians vying for influence in the same place, made it impossible for him to engage in cultural place making. As Gupta and Ferguson have pointed out, cultural migration has brought about the end of such easy collusions between place and culture.[4] As a consequence, identity constructions along the lines of clearly demarcated cultural locations can no longer be easily performed in a postcolonial age. Indeed, the dispersal of any particu-

lar "location of culture" has become the characteristic mark of what
Waugh called distressingly "a world of 'displaced persons'" (*When the
Going Was Good,* 9). What interested Waugh was the very opposite of
such a differentiated and complex understanding of cultural identity.
His cultural model was as compartmentalized as his idea of social belonging was hierarchical: the right "place" for a person was both on
the map and on the social scale. Imperialism seemed a valid tool to
enforce just such a concept of identity, rooted in place as much as in
class and race.

•   •   •

Interestingly, however, Waugh's dichotomy between dystopian
Ethiopia and utopian Kenya, and their parallel associations with
"strange" and "familiar," "there" and "here," could not be upheld to
the very end of *Remote People.* The forces of alienation would not stop
ante portas, as it were, in London. It appears that Waugh's defensive-
ness about Ethiopia's appalling otherness was as much based on cultural snobbery as on a real feeling of despair about the disintegration
of London as a cultural home and anchor of his own sense of identity.
Waugh's affiliation with London's Bright Young Things, a socially anarchic group, caused almost as big a threat to his conservatism as it
provided him with the subject matter for his novels of alienation and
cultural pessimism. Coming back from the outskirts of empire, though,
Waugh was startled into recognizing the intrinsic otherness of his own
social clique within the cultural milieu of bourgeois London.

A sequence of "nightmares" leads up to this troubling realization.
The "First Nightmare" in *Remote People* is devoted to the boredom
of a sophisticated traveler in Ethiopia; the "Second Nightmare" contained frightful as well as frustrating anecdotes from Waugh's passage
through the Congo; the "Third Nightmare," however, is set squarely
in London's decadent "underworld." In this sequence, there is even a
sense of growing rather than diminishing desperation from one nightmare to the next. In his "Second Nightmare," Waugh writes: "I thought
I had touched bottom at Kabalo, but Bukama has it heavily beaten. If
ever a place merited the epithet 'God-forsaken' in its literal sense, it
is that station" (203). As the dystopian perspective deepens, one ex-
pects a further twist of the screw in the "Third Nightmare." Although
the description of his London "Nightmare" takes up barely two pages,
Waugh has a few trenchant things to say about the way the African

dystopias he had witnessed compared with the "hell" of London's decadent society:

> Someone shrilled in my ear: "Why, Evelyn, where *have* you been? I haven't seen you about anywhere for days." My friends talked about the rupture of an engagement which I did not know was contracted. The wine tasted like salt and soda water. Mercifully a waiter whisked it away before we had time to drink it. "Time if you please." I was back in the centre of Empire, and in the spot where, at the moment, "everyone" was going. Next day the gossip-writers would chronicle the young MPs, peers, and financial magnates who were assembled in that rowdy cellar, hotter than Zanzibar, noisier than the market at Harar, more reckless of the decencies of hospitality than the taverns of Kabalo or Tabora. And a month later the wives of English officials would read about it, and stare out across the bush or jungle or desert or forest or golf links, and envy their sisters at home, and wish they had the money to marry rich men. Why go abroad? See England first. Just watch London knock spots off the Dark Continent.[5] (211)

In the global context, this particular locale figures rather below Kabalo instead of towering high above it. Although the sites of Waugh's African "nightmares" seem at first to be separated by a wide gap from Waugh's home society, the journey ultimately opened up a comparative dimension that undermined the classical center/margin model of cultural differentiation. Returning from Africa, Waugh realized that culture need not be tethered to a particular location—a thought that led to disturbing consequences. Indeed, English culture at its best seemed to be performed with greater success in Kenya than it was in England itself. The result is an inversion of values that might be funny were it not for the bitter aftertaste of cultural disillusionment.

In a world where cultural certainties were no longer stabilized within bounds, where England could settle in Kenya and African "barbarism" could suddenly colonize parts of London, the fear of erosion and contamination becomes virulent. Equally virulent is the fear that political ideals cannot be maintained in a world of transnational culture flows. Waugh's observation at the end of *Remote People* has a political implication similar to his disparaging comments about tourists in his first travel book, *Labels*. As Brian Musgrove observes, "rhetorical performance [carries] an immediate political point: a patrician revul-

sion at the clamorous order of mass modernity, and a class neurosis
over shifting, mobile lines of subjectivity. This is a crisis precipitated
by travel and contact within the western subject, whose low others are
not always defined in colonial terms" (33–34). Be it the silly tourists he
met in Ghize or the Bright Young Things in London's underground,
Waugh felt equally resentful against these "products" of modernity
as he was hostile against indigenous rulers abroad and colored immigrants at home. His satirical handling of these populations begins
therefore to look much more defensive than one may be inclined to
think if one reads his books out of context. Very often, too, satire
served Waugh to disguise his despair springing from a profound fear
of social change and cross-cultural adaptation. Social and cultural
politics are indeed joining hands in Waugh's conservative travel books.

• • •

It is consistent with the theory of place making as a social and
ideological operation that even Ethiopia can rise, phoenix-like, to the
status of a utopia, given an appropriate political context. This condition was fulfilled with Italy's invasion of Abyssinia in 1937. When
Waugh returned to the country to document the changes after the
Italian conquest, he could hardly recognize the land he had formerly
come to loathe. Commenting on Italy's building of roads, intended
primarily as a supply line and logistic precondition for the consoli-
dation of Italy's military conquest, Waugh waxed unusually grandil-
oquent:

> It was the beginning of the great trunk road that climbs from
> Massawa to Asmara and then runs through the mountains along
> the line of Badoglio's advance, through Adigrat, Makale, Kworam
> and Dessye; within a few weeks of the appearance of these words
> in print it will have reached Addis Ababa. . . . With its vast tribu-
> taries, of which Dessye is to be the point of confluence, it is at
> once the symbol and the supreme achievement of the Italian
> spirit. A main road in England is a foul and destructive thing. . . .
> Here in Africa it brings order and fertility. (*Waugh in Abyssinia,* 243)

The catalogue of place-names and the analogy between roads and riv-
ers lends this celebratory passage an epic tone. Given Waugh's predominantly ideological place making, it is only fitting that formerly
somber Ethiopia now appears as a land of pastoral beauty under fas-

cist rule. Waugh comments that the Italian roadworkers "employed their leisure in embellishing the road they had made with little gardens of saplings and wild flowers, ornamental devices of coloured pebbles, carved eagles and wolves, fasces and heads of Mussolini, inscriptions in the Roman fashion, recording the dates and details of their passage" (245). Here images of pastoral tranquillity jostle with symbols of fascist rule, as the fasces and busts are seen to be wholly innocuous, ornamental embellishments of this "monument of organized labor" (243).

Once again, Waugh's utopia of colonized Abyssinia is as anomalous as is his dystopian vision of the country when compared with the norms of fictional dystopias and utopias at his time. Although according to Rabkin "the utopian world is a pastoral one by virtue of the exclusion of technology" ("Atavism and Utopia," 3), in Waugh's Italo-Abyssinian utopia, pastoral beauty is linked with technological prowess and both are a function of efficient labor management. Hence, right-wing ideology and its military effects transformed Ethiopia into a place whose ideological coordinates coalesced with Waugh's political outlook. Now for the first time, Waugh did not get lost in that country, nor did he suffer from any nightmare of alienation, although what was brewing in Graziani's Ethiopia was in fact a humanitarian nightmare.

Hope and Despair in the Amazon

The opposite of Ethiopia's transformation from dystopia to utopia can be seen in the metamorphosis of a potential site for utopia into yet another dystopian nightmare in Waugh's third travel book, *Ninety-two Days* (1933). During the early stages of his trip through British Guiana, Waugh retraced the footsteps of previous fortune hunters, especially Sir Walter Raleigh, who believed to have found El Dorado in the lush setting of the Amazon.

Like his illustrious predecessor, Waugh nourished plainly romantic hopes during the early parts of his journey. But his carefully developed expectation that Boa Vista, literally and figuratively the turning point of his arduous trek, would prove a latter-day version of El Dorado is brutally subverted in his realization that the place is, in fact, no better than Ethiopia. Although Waugh was quite successful in constructing a utopia in Kenya, he could not sustain his utopian expectations in the depths of the South American jungle, far from the creature comforts offered through the mediation of British settler communities.

At first, it seems that the obstacles on the way to El Dorado only heightened the promise of commensurate rewards. At the British Guiana capital, Georgetown, Waugh had difficulties obtaining transportation to the trailhead. Next, his packhorses proved incapable of carrying heavy loads, forcing him to abandon his cherished stores of corned beef and tinned milk. Instead he had to eat farina, a local cassava preparation that tasted like sawdust, and *tasso,* dried beef with the texture of leather. Moreover, he was alternately soaked in torrential rains and roasted in blistering sunshine, as he slowly plodded through dense jungle and open savanna. At night, he slept in shacks teeming with spiders and during the daytime he sat on a bucking horse.

Throughout all these ordeals, however, Waugh looked forward to Boa Vista as a place of salvation: "Since the evening at Kurupukari when Mr. Bain had first mentioned its name, Boa Vista had come to assume greater and greater importance to me. . . . Everybody . . . had spoken of it as a town of dazzling attraction. Whatever I had looked for in vain at Figuirado's store was, he told me, procurable at 'Boa Vist'; Mr. Daguar had extolled its modernity and luxury" (85). The possibility that this wonderful town might be internally corrupted, though, is hinted at by Waugh's construction of the town as a fantasy of modernity, replete not only with "electric light, cafés, fine buildings, women," but also with "politics, murders" (85). This shows to what degree Waugh's elaboration of the utopian theme was already tainted by his cynical pessimism. Indeed, the darker side of "civilized" life has lodged the poison of decadence in the very heart of Waugh's imaginary utopia. Nevertheless, compared with the gray, economically depressed, unexciting London that Waugh had left behind (and also compared with the raw wilderness of the jungle), the Boa Vista of his imaginings promised to be a temporary resting place for the displaced, harassed, alienated intellectual of the 1930s.

But when Waugh finally reached the outskirts of the city he had looked forward to, it did not provide any of the "beautiful views" promised by its name: "On either side was a row of single-storied, white-washed mud houses with tiled roofs; at each doorstep sat one or more of the citizens staring at us with eyes that were insolent, hostile and apathetic; a few naked children rolled about at their feet. The remains of an overhead electric cable hung loose from a row of crazy posts, or lay in coils and loops about the gutter" (86–87). There is no room for the redeeming values of primitivism here, nor any sense of heroic discovery. What remains is the betrayal of a hopeful idea: "Already, in the few hours of my sojourn there, the Boa Vista of my imagination had come to grief. Gone; engulfed in an earthquake, uprooted by a tornado and tossed sky-high like chaff in the wind, scorched up with brimstone like Gomorrah, toppled over with trumpets like Jericho, ploughed like Carthage, bought, demolished and transported brick by brick to another continent . . . tall Troy was down" (88). The hyperbolical tone of this catalog not only heightens the naïveté of Waugh's previous expectations but also emphasizes the hollowness of the promise of modernity. To Waugh, Boa Vista epitomizes a modern urban decadence such as he recorded in *Decline and Fall* or *Vile Bodies.*

Confirmed in his cultural pessimism, Waugh sees no potential for reform in Boa Vista. He learns that, years ago, leaders of the Benedictine mission in Rio de Janeiro had hatched a scheme for sociopolitical improvements. A canning factory was to bring prosperity, health, and modern lifestyle to the town: "The monks saw that instead of its present position as a squalid camp of ramshackle cut-throats, it might be a thriving city, a beacon of culture illuminating the dark lands about it" (93–94). All these utopian plans, however, came to naught:

> From then onwards everything went against the Benedictines,
> who were insulted and boycotted. The canning factory proved a
> failure; no one would use the ice—an unnatural, impermanent
> substance, typical of everything foreign; dishonest stuff that had
> lost half its weight even before you got it home—they didn't want
> the hospital, much preferring to sicken and die in their ham-
> mocks in the decent manner traditional to the place; no one paid
> his electric light bill and the plant had to be stopped. The priests
> went down with fever and, one by one, had to be sent back to
> Manaos. "The Company" became bankrupt and all further work
> was stopped. (95)

This passage offers strong evidence for the argument that history and utopia are completely incompatible with one another. In fact, Waugh presses history into the service of debunking any hopes in a sustainable utopia, and in so doing he transforms the site of utopia into a dystopia.[6] The subversion of utopia under the impact of history is hastened by the traveler's realization that the only place of any utopia is in fiction, not in reality. After all, travelers dreaming of reaching a substantial utopia in space and time are necessarily compelled to compare the physical outlines of that place with their own fantasies, with the inevitable outcome that the place is found wanting.

But why then were the utopias of Kenya and Italo-Abyssinia sustainable in Waugh's view? The answer lies in the role played by ideology in these different places. Both in Kenya and in Italo-Abyssinia, Waugh's enthusiasm was sustained by an ideological infrastructure. Although Kenya's settlers and Italy's empire builders were beleaguered, they held the upper hand (if only temporarily) during Waugh's visit. In contrast, nobody seemed to be in charge in Boa Vista, and hence there was no overlap between the dominant ideology of the place (which seems to have thrived on a mild form of border-town anarchy) and Waugh's political ideas. Even the Benedictine monks, the only possible group with whom Waugh could have identified, were a desolate and, for all practical political purposes, a disempowered lot. They had fought a rearguard action against the forces of anarchy and the tropical climate, and lost.

For Waugh, then, utopia could not be built upon the foundations of modernity, anarchy, or even religion for that matter. It takes authoritarian, imperial, or aristocratic politics to achieve this end. Even the basic principles of Western civilization are too precarious to sustain any form of sociopolitical ideal in the Amazon. In fact, the failure of the monks in this place is symptomatic for the dubiousness of the very civilization they had relied upon to carry out their utopian aims. The implications of this stance are quite severe: if El Dorado is really El Dystopico, and if Western civilizational ideals have no power to reform a "bad place," then the whole notion of utopia has lost its cognitive and ideological value.

• • •

The feeling of absurdity that pervades *Ninety-two Days* has its counterpart in Waugh's novel *A Handful of Dust*,[7] where almost any form of optimism comes in for a heavy beating. The first disillusionment comes when Tony Last, the novel's protagonist, discovers that his marriage has been a sham and that his wife Brenda, after an affair with another man, has managed to lay an adultery charge against *him*. The divorce proceedings are unfavorable to Tony, and he fears to be shut out of his Gothic mansion, Hetton Hall. At this point, Tony decides to leave everything behind and join an exploratory expedition into the Amazon.

Significantly, the words Tony chooses to express his disappointment with the domestic predicament echo the terms used by Waugh to describe his own disappointment at Boa Vista: "A whole Gothic world had come to grief. . . . There was now no armour glittering through the forest glades, no embroidered feet on the green sward; the cream and dappled unicorns had fled" (173–74). In *Ninety-two Days,* Waugh had exclaimed that "the Boa Vista of my imagination had come to grief. Gone; engulfed in an earthquake" (88). The similarity between the two accounts of disillusionment extends to structural properties. In both cases, the statement of loss is supplemented by a whole catalog of what had been lost. Out of his disgust with the scheming, disingenuous, urban society, Tony decides to leave England in search of El Dorado.

The central chapter of the novel, tellingly headed "In Search of a City," describes Tony's ecstatic quest for self-fulfillment and spiritual renewal. This is the precondition for the second disillusionment that he has to face. Like Waugh, Tony Last travels to Georgetown to prepare his inland expedition in search of a mysterious city, a place roughly equivalent to Boa Vista. For Tony, as for Waugh, the notion of utopia has distinct aesthetic implications: "His mind was occupied with the City, the Shining, the Many Watered, the Bright Feathered, the Aromatic Jam. He had a clear picture of it in his mind. It was Gothic in character, all vanes and pinnacles, gargoyles, battlements, groining and tracery, pavilions and terraces, a transfigured Hetton, pennons and banners floating on the sweet breeze, everything luminous and translucent; a coral citadel" (184).

The same aesthetic standards that inform Tony's idealization of El Dorado also provide the rationale for Waugh's condemnation of Ethiopia's culture. As shown in my discussion of *Waugh in Abyssinia,* Waugh compares the "straggling, nondescript, tin and tarmac squalor of Addis Ababa" (89) with the splendors of a Gothic cathedral in order to discount Ethiopia's claim to have a civilization of its own. Thus, Waugh's understanding of utopia is both based on aristocratic social relations and on an aesthetic nostalgia for Gothic standards of taste. Places that neither correspond to authoritarian ideologies nor offer nostalgic aesthetic pleasures are either considered wholly insignificant or dystopian in nature.

Tony's trip in *A Handful of Dust,* however, follows a different trajectory compared with Waugh's African novels. Notably, it emphatically avoids the wish-fulfillment motif, as Tony does not reach even the vicinity of the famed city in the jungle. Already during the first weeks of his journey, he falls seriously ill, and his partner Dr. Messinger is drowned in an attempt to get help. Completely cut off from assistance or consolation and at the point of death, Tony is picked up by a mulatto farmer, Mr. Todd. This eccentric character is based on the religious fanatic named Christie whom Waugh had met during his journey in British Guiana. After having nursed Tony back to health, Mr. Todd forces him to read Dickens to him for the rest of his life. Tony's only hope of escape from the lunatic man is a search expedition from England that traces the steps taken by himself and Dr. Messinger two years earlier. When the searchers arrive at Todd's camp, however, Todd drugs Tony and hides him in a shed, claiming that he has already died. The book ends with a memorial service for Tony Last, believed to be dead, and the unveiling of a commemorative plaque at Hetton Hall. Thus, contrary to the two African novels, *Black Mischief* and *Scoop,* the burden of despair in *A Handful of Dust* is not lightened by the antics of a daredevil character (alias Waugh) who thrives on cultural depravity.

A Handful of Dust nicely demonstrates Valentine Cunningham's observation that "the '30s experience . . . was indeed a voyage—like so many voyages that happened in the '30s—out of Utopian notions of innocence into a kind of Christian awareness of sin" (467). Tony Last has also come down from his utopian search to be subjected to a special kind of purgatory at Mr. Todd's camp. Nevertheless, there is a satirical touch to his predicament that is absent in the more serious moralizing of the other Roman Catholic writer, Graham Greene. In fact, Greene's eschatological nightmare visions,[8] both in his fiction and his travel writing, are more reassuring than Waugh's bleak satires precisely because their apocalyptic dimension offers hope for renewal.

Apocalypse and Revelation in Mexico

In Mexico, Graham Greene underwent an experience that bears at first sight a striking resemblance to Waugh's disappointment in the Amazon. Indeed, *The Lawless Roads* records a frustrating journey from the Texan border down to the southern part of Mexico. But when his boat approached Villahermosa (trans.: beautiful city) in the state of Tabasco, Greene saw a glimmer of hope:

> And then suddenly, about eleven hours from Frontera, Villaher-
> mosa burst out at us round a bend. For twelve hours there had
> been nothing but trees on either side; one had moved forward
> only into darkness; and here with an effect of melodrama was a
> city—lights burning down into the river, a great crown outlined
> in electricity like a casino. All felt the shock—it was like coming
> to Venice through an uninhabited jungle—they called, trium-
> phantly, *"El puerto, el puerto!"* (111)

But the next morning brings a sobering correction of this image: "That effect of something sophisticated and gay in the heart of the swamp did not outlast the night—it was the swamp that lasted. I never, till the day I left, discovered what gilding had shone like a crown through the night—there certainly wasn't a casino, and the lights I had seen were not visible when once one was an inhabitant" (112). This is the quintessential recognition of the 1930s seekers after utopia: "once one was an inhabitant" of such an ideal world, all the glamour and attractiveness vanished in an instant. In the ensuing description of Villahermosa and its people, Greene develops an eschatological vision of human corruption and decline that outdoes even Waugh's grimmest descriptions. The vultures that "group themselves on the roofs like pigeons: tiny moron heads . . . peering this way and that attentively for a death" (124) are apt props for "the puritan as well as the Godless state" of Tabasco (113). The town's depravity is enhanced by the absence of churches (destroyed by the former governor of Tabasco Garrido Canabal), a fact that not only entails spiritual desolation but also physical discomfort: "Now in Villahermosa, in the blinding heat and the mosquito-noisy air, there is no escape at all for anyone" (123). In a place where "you gained an overwhelming sense of brutality and irresponsibility" (117) writes a disenchanted Greene, "cynicism, a distrust of men's motives, is the accepted ideology" (127).

In Greene's discourse, then, Villahermosa figures among the latter-day incarnations of the biblical Babylon. Christian morality and eschatological perspectives combine to form the bedrock of a discourse of human degradation (captured in Greene's trademark descriptions of "seediness") that seems at times almost morbidly attracted to places that represent "the abomination that makes desolate" (Dan. 11.31). Indeed, his cousin Barbara Greene stated in *Too Late to Turn Back* that Greene "clearly liked the idea of utter awfulness" (xxiv).

Of course, it is precisely the apocalyptic implication of Greene's vision that explains his paradoxical fascination with the place's awfulness. After all, the coming of the end, the apocalyptic crisis, suggests both the climax of desolation as well as the moment of divine redemption and ultimate knowledge. JoAnn James comments that "the Greek verb *[apocalyptein]* means to uncover, to disclose, to reveal. Neither classical Greek literature nor the Septuagint associate the term with cosmic upheavals. What is laid bare may provide a revelation—a new way of seeing, experiencing, knowing" (2). Moreover, there is a vital connection between apocalyptic writing and the sociopolitical status of the church, as evidenced in the book of Revelation: "The aim of John's revelation was to warn the churches against compromise with the religious, social, and economic values of a world heading for self-destruction because of its idolatry, and to encourage them in the witness to God and purity of life" (Metzger and Coogan, 652). In this context, Greene's apocalyptic perceptions in Mexico bear witness to his suspicion that the religious faith had been compromised in this country because of the church's weakness, an impression that is patently unhistorical, as demonstrated in chapter 3.

Overall, Greene's description of Villahermosa carries a more serious eschatological implication than Waugh's handling of Boa Vista's "barbarism." For Waugh, places like Boa Vista or Addis Ababa were both causes of concern and for merriment. For Greene, the entertainment value of dystopia was almost nonexistent compared with the spiritual threat that he felt it imposed on him and his religious belief. In the fallen world of Villahermosa, Greene saw a symbol for the spiritual disease that was threatening to plunge humanity into disaster. Before his Mexican trip, he had elaborated a social dystopia set in the nasty crime milieu of *Brighton Rock* (1938). But his obsession with sin and corruption had not been satisfied with treatments of the domestic context. His imagination thrived in a country where churches lay in ruins, where vultures peered from rooftops, and where *pistoleros* roamed the streets. What he found in southern Mexico seemed to him the quintessence of a fallen world hovering on the brink of social self-destruction. The political attacks Greene mounts against Mexico's socialist regime appear feeble in comparison with his gloomy, almost prophetic-sounding account of the human condition at large.[9]

• • •

Greene's Mexican novel, *The Power and the Glory*, presents a different spiritual scenario compared with his travel book. Certainly, *The Power and the Glory* owes much of its vividness to Greene's own nightmarish journey in Tabasco. Even small details such as the creaking of the police chief's revolver holster or the noise of cockroaches crushed under a bare foot enhance the novel's descriptive texture. Other elements that have made their way from *The Lawless Roads* into *The Power and the Glory* are the grove of huge wooden crosses located in Chiapas, suggesting an aberrant religious sensibility, and the omnipresent vultures, determining the atmosphere of gloom and decay in the capital of Tabasco. Most importantly, all the major characters of the novel appear already in *The Lawless Roads*, either as the real people Greene had met during his trip (the Coral and Lehr families, for example) or as figures of legend, as is the case with the whisky priest.

Similar to Waugh's invention of wishful alter egos in *Black Mischief* and *Scoop*, Greene's protagonist in *The Power and the Glory* also exceeds his "original" (i.e., Greene himself) in terms of his spiritual significance. While the whisky priest comes across as a symbol of resistance and redemption, Greene as the "protagonist" of *The Lawless Roads* remains an unheroic, peeved, irritable character. At one point, Greene even avows that his "growing depression, the almost pathological hatred . . . for Mexico" was due to "strained eyes" (145) after the loss of his sunglasses in Chiapas. As if sensing the incongruity of this claim, he continues: "Indeed, when I try to think back to those days, they lie under the entrancing light of chance encounters, small endurances, unfamiliarity, and I cannot remember why at the time they seemed so grim and hopeless" (145). Thus, for Greene the step from the travel book to the novel entailed, interestingly, a renewal of optimism and faith.

The whisky priest, who provides the novel's primary vehicle for hope, was not a figment of Greene's imagination. This character is based on a clergyman who was rumored to have held out for years in the swamps of Tabasco. His epithet derives from his inclination to tipple wine meant for the Mass, a predilection that had broadened into addiction during the grim years of persecution, loneliness, and fear in the late 1920s. Greene had heard different reports about this fugitive priest who played cat and mouse with his pursuers until an anticlerical posse finally apprehended and killed him in 1930.[10] Greene makes repeated reference to this figure in *The Lawless Roads:* "Every priest was hunted down or shot, except one who existed for ten years in the forest and the swamps, venturing out only at night; his few letters, I was told, recorded an awful sense of impotence—to live in constant danger and yet be able to do so little, it hardly seemed worth the horror" (106). The traits of this persevering though flawed religious fugitive are combined with the martyr qualities of another real-life person, Father Pro, the Mexican priest whose killing at the beginning of Mexico's religious persecution in 1926 had made such a deep impression on Greene.

The Power and the Glory, by many critics considered Greene's finest achievement in fiction, portrays the whisky priest's allegorical passion and progress through stages of evasion, endurance, betrayal, trial, and self-sacrifice. As befits a religious allegory, most of the book's characters are two-dimensional types. According to Greene, they represent "vice, pride, purity, etc." (*The Other Man,* 136). The protagonist, however, presents a psychological complexity that lends the book its ultimate interest. Although he is convinced of his worthlessness ("the whole globe was blanketed with his own sin" [29]), he goes on dispensing the Sacrament in secret. What redeems him are his lack of self-deceit, his fellow feeling, and, most importantly, his active resistance against the forces of godlessness. Although the priest himself does not believe that his soul will be saved through the benevolent intervention of divine grace, Greene suggests that it will be. Indeed, the novel's end is pervaded by signs of hope and revival. In spite of his shortcomings, the whisky priest is revered as a martyr (a handkerchief soaked in his blood becomes a cherished relic). Moreover, his death gives new impetus to the popular resistance (symbolized in a little boy's spitting on the police lieutenant). Directly following the whisky priest's execution, a new father enters the scene, ready to continue the struggle.

The hopeful glimmer that lights up *The Power and the Glory* lifts this book out of the dystopian tradition and marks it as a specimen of apocalyptic writing. The "appalling mystery of God's grace," as Greene called it, enables him to envision a world in which salvation is still possible, thanks to the offices of the church and the perseverance of faithful Christians. In contradistinction to Waugh's overriding pessimism, Greene's liberal humanism enabled him to hold on to the optimistic prospects of a religious struggle amid dystopian conditions. For Greene, the ambivalence inherent in apocalyptic visions was instrumental in his belief that even the worst social nightmare could be the beginning of a new world order that, if not utopian, might at least contain a modicum of respect for individual and religious freedom.

The whisky priest's psychological profile (both good and bad, humble and corrupted, "coast" and "interior") demonstrates that his Mexican journey had taught Greene to overcome the dualistic morality that had dominated *Journey without Maps* and *Brighton Rock*. Indeed, the stark moral contrast between the corrupt Pinkie and the innocent Rose in *Brighton Rock* (1938) is dissolved into the complementary moral and religious complexity of the whisky priest. A world in which dystopian conditions of godlessness and general corruption seemed to be all-pervasive could not harbor a sense of melodrama. Indeed, Greene points out at the end of his Mexican travelogue that the depraved condition of Mexico was typical rather than exceptional in a world teetering at the brink of another global war.

In lamenting the lack of distinctive features between the foreign dystopia and the domestic context, Greene resorts to a common topos of 1930s travel writing; namely, the I-thought-I-had-touched-bottom-at-X attitude, followed by the realization that the more one travels the worse things get. Frequently, this tendency did not stop once the travelers returned to England. Thus Greene exclaims sarcastically at the end of *The Lawless Roads*, "*This* was home" (223), a comment that is echoed in Waugh's rhetorical question "Why go abroad? See England first" (*Remote People*, 212), and in Orwell's gloomy assessment in the middle of *Down and Out* that "This was England" (118). These travelers realized that geopolitical and cultural dichotomies such as center/margin, civilized/uncivilized, virtuous/corrupted, superior/inferior, and so on, could no longer be sustained with England invariably occupying the privileged term of the binary opposition. Increasingly, England was seen as contaminated by the very dynamics that had heretofore been assigned to the second terms of these ethnocentric, imperialist, and chauvinistic dichotomies.

Revolution and Reaction in Spain

For George Orwell, the matter of taking sides, going over, and meeting the lower classes was vexed by his dualistic temperament, which caused him to embrace subaltern social and cultural orders while simultaneously distancing himself from them. One symptom of this dualistic temperament was his tendency sometimes to denigrate, sometimes to idealize the conditions of the oppressed. It is an ambivalence that made it impossible for Orwell to depict the conditions of the oppressed as plainly dystopian, although they seemed so to most other social observers. Even the trenches in Catalonia did not have the hellish implications of the battlefields of Flanders during World War I, although conditions seem bad enough:

> Sometimes there were shrieking winds that tore your cap off and twisted your hair in all directions, sometimes there were mists that poured into the trench like a liquid and seemed to penetrate your bones; frequently it rained, and even a quarter of an hour's rain was enough to make conditions intolerable. . . . The position stank abominably, and outside the little enclosure of the barricade there was excrement everywhere. Some of the militiamen habitually defecated in the trench, a disgusting thing when one had to walk round it in the darkness. (*Homage to Catalonia*, 31–33)

But the camaraderie of the militia men and their commitment to a classless society offered a compensation for the material discomfort in the trenches. In fact, one could even see utopian glimmerings in a passage that describes the social equality among Orwell's fellow soldiers:

> Up here in Aragon one was among tens of thousands of people, mainly though not entirely of working-class origin, all living at the same level and mingling on terms of equality. In theory it was perfect equality, and even in practice it was not far from it. There is a sense in which it would be true to say that one was experiencing a foretaste of Socialism, by which I mean that the prevailing mental atmosphere was that of Socialism. Many of the normal motives of civilized life—snobbishness, money-grubbing, fear of the boss, etc.—had simply ceased to exist. The ordinary class-division of society had disappeared to an extent that is almost unthinkable in the money-tainted air of England; there was no one there except the peasants and ourselves, and no one owned anyone else as his master. (101–2)

This feeling of ideological identification with the prevailing social order is the predominant feature of Orwell's brief acquaintance with utopia.

The very same impression had already taken hold of him upon his arrival in Barcelona in late December 1936. Although Orwell's assessment of the worker's utopia there also includes dimly troubling references, such as to the fact that "almost every church had been gutted and its images burnt" (8), he concludes that "there was a belief in the revolution and the future, a feeling of having suddenly emerged into an era of equality and freedom. Human beings were trying to behave as human beings and not as cogs in the capitalist machine" (9). Hence, although Barcelona was at that stage merely an imperfect social model, Orwell believed that it could be improved and stabilized. But this optimism did not last very long.

In fact, Orwell's description of social equality among the population and the militiamen of Aragon, quoted above, anticipates the swing toward disillusionment and dystopia that dominates the latter half of the book. Directly following the statement that "no one owned anyone else as his master," Orwell continues: "Of course such a state of affairs could not last" (102). This in itself is not surprising. Rabkin comments that "if a true utopia had ever existed, it would still exist today and we would be reading travelogues instead of fictions" ("Atavism and Utopia," 1). Since ideal social arrangements are conventionally perceived as projections into the future, any present utopia must by definition be a chimera. What is surprising, however, is the fact that it took Orwell a couple of months (or half the book) to come around to the conclusion that utopia has no place in the present (although dystopia *does*). Obviously, the Spanish struggle had focused powerful hopes, and it was hard not to believe in the redemptive potential of an egalitarian alternative to the status quo of bourgeois capitalism or totalitarian fascism. Orwell goes on to say that the situation he had witnessed in Aragon "was simply a temporary and local phase in an enormous game that is being played over the whole surface of the earth" (102). But even that statement, in its dualistic formulation of an antagonistic struggle between the worker's movement and reactionary forces, did not present an adequate model for describing the subsequent fragmentation of the political forces in the leftist camp.

The in-fighting between the communist and anarchist factions caused the worldwide struggle (the "game" earlier referred to by Orwell) to move beyond the stage of a clearly defined binary opposition to a more complex and no longer dualistically coded situation. To ask "Are you for, or against, the legal Government and the people of Republican Spain? Are you for, or against, Franco and Fascism?" would have been quite meaningless after the beginning of the communist purges in Barcelona. Once the persecution of anarchists and their allies (such as members of the International Brigade) by the communists had begun, brutal disregard of human rights and totalitarian tendencies spread in both camps of the conflict. Tellingly, it was the mounting tension between the Moscow-oriented communists, who put priority on military victory, and the anarchists, who put priority on genuine social revolution, that primarily caused Orwell's utopian beliefs to dwindle. In fact, during the last of his several stays in Barcelona, and after the suppression of the POUM, Orwell shuddered at the "autonomy of the lower ranks of the police. Many of the arrests were admittedly illegal, and various people whose release had been ordered by the Chief of Police were re-arrested at the jail gate and carried off to 'secret prisons'" (198). This scenario could be attributed to any right-wing tyranny.

Within half a year of Orwell's arrival, Barcelona had metamorphosed from a socialist ideal into "a reign of terror" (201). This workers' paradise had come to grief just like so many other utopian visions during the 1930s. "Everything had changed" (217), muses a disconsolate Orwell en route to France. "Only six months ago, when the anarchists still reigned, it was looking like a proletarian that made you respectable. . . . Now it was the other way about; to look bourgeois was the one salvation" (217). Although this sounds cynical, Orwell is in fact wary of cynicism. At the end of *Homage,* he states that the result of his sojourn in Spain "is not necessarily disillusionment and cynicism. Curiously enough the whole experience has left me with not less but more belief in the decency of human beings" (220).

This is a strange and somewhat forced conclusion after a narrative that ended with the "appalling disaster" (220) of torture, persecution, and extralegal executions in Barcelona. But it makes sense if one considers Richard Johnstone's thesis that Orwell's writing is pervaded by a division "between the instinctive conviction that reality is oppressive and threatening, and the contradictory conviction that within that reality may be discovered positive values which will reconcile the individual to his environment, defining his function within it. This division, so described, recurs throughout the fiction of the thirties generation" (126–27). Indeed, the distinction between Orwell's acute awareness of the destructive potential inherent in the political process and his hope for the integrity of the individual is only one (large) facet in Orwell's essentially dualistic outlook on social life. In his essays of the period, Orwell insistently dichotomizes: between the political movement of the 1920s and that of the 1930s, between left and right, between activism and resignation, and so on. But rather than confirming the political, social, and epistemological usefulness of such dualisms, Orwell is actually sounding their death knell. At the end of both *Homage* and "Inside the Whale" (1940), the monistic, dystopian perspective gains the upper hand against any dualistic conception.

In that light, Orwell's admission in the middle of *Homage* that he had joined the militia " 'To fight against Fascism' " and *for* " 'Common decency' " (46) marks precisely the transitional moment in which Orwell moves from a binary model of political thought to a nonbinary one. Indeed, the distinction he makes is a false binary, as "Common decency" is not the logical antithesis of "Fascism": the most likely candidate for a binary partner of fascism would have to be communism or socialism. Of course, Orwell cannot invoke this polarity, given his strong anticommunism and his resentment against organized socialism. Thus, the belief in "the decency of human beings" (220) is an attempt to state a nondualistic social principle.

In his famous essay "Inside the Whale," Orwell writes that "almost certainly we are moving into an age of totalitarian dictatorships—an age in which freedom of thought will be at first a deadly sin and later a meaningless abstraction. The autonomous individual is going to be stamped out of existence" (157). In this assessment, dystopia becomes monolithic. The destruction of the utopia/dystopia dualism that attended the conclusion of Orwell's experience in Spain has disabled his sense of balancing evil developments with a more optimistic political outlook: "Progress and reaction have both turned out to be swindles," he gloomily concludes in "Inside the Whale" (158). As Richard Johnstone rightly observed, there was in Orwell an abiding will to believe, in spite of his disillusionment with any organized political movement. But this belief manifested itself in the form of a distinctly unpolarized concept; namely, the simple notion of individual integrity. In Orwell's particular use of the term, *individual integrity* is not dualistically linked to any antithetical term, just as totalitarianism as a general trend of contemporary history could no longer be seen as opposed to anything in particular. At the end of the 1930s, both *common decency* and *totalitarianism* assumed monolithic qualities for Orwell. In fact, he mocks the appeal to dualistic formulations in communist propaganda: "God—Stalin. The devil—Hitler. Heaven—Moscow, Hell—Berlin. All the gaps were filled up" ("Inside the Whale," 145).

Only later, after the war, did Orwell once again revive the dualism of freedom versus oppression or utopia versus dystopia. In "Why I Write" (1947) he maintains that all of his work since 1936 was written *"against* totalitarianism and *for* democratic socialism" (424). Compared with the false opposition between fascism and common decency invoked in *Homage,* the dichotomy between totalitarianism and democratic socialism is a valid one. It took the conclusion of World War II, with the Allied victory and the beginning of the Cold War, to revive Orwell's confidence in the adequacy of dualistic political formulations. Although Orwell would probably have agreed that hope could be maintained only in the knowledge of despair, his trust in the viability of dualistic political conceptions had taken a heavy beating during his stay in Spain, to be only partially revived after the war. But, as his last two works of fiction *(Animal Farm* and *1984)* were to demonstrate, the dystopian impulse had been in the ascendant ever since the late 1930s, never to be matched by any corresponding utopian inclination.

Resistance and Defeatism in the Balkans

Black Lamb and Grey Falcon rests on a strong Manichaean foundation, an ideological structure that dominates practically all of West's pronouncements on morality, politics, and culture. West acknowledges her indebtedness to Manichaeanism from the beginning: "Mani created a myth that would show the universe as a field for moral effort" in which "all men who were on the side of the light . . . [had] to recover the particles of light that have become imprisoned in the substance of darkness" (172). This she considers "an extremely useful conception of life" (172), which caused Richard Tillinghast to speculate that "had Rebecca West lived in an age of theological heresies, she would have been a Manichaean—she admits to seeing history as a conflict between light and darkness" (16). And Yugoslavia was indeed her privileged "field for moral effort," as evidenced in the moral significance that she attaches to almost all of her observations. For instance, she says that "here on the Sheep's Field it could be seen where the cleavage lies that can be apprehended to run through art and life: on one side are the people who are accomplices of the [death wish] and on the other those who are its enemy. It appeared also where the cleavage lay in our human nature which makes us broken and futile" (831).

Yugoslavia presented itself to West as a scenario at large for this opposition between life and death, or Eros and Thanatos: "Yugoslavia is always telling me about one death or another . . . yet this country is full of life. I feel that we Westerners should come here to learn to live. But perhaps we are ignorant about life in the West because we avoid thinking about death" (917). Rather than being exclusive of one another, the dualisms in West's thinking are always dialectically involved. Especially West's master dichotomy, that between life and death, invokes the paradoxical relationship between utopia and dystopia.

In West's thinking, Eros is aligned with freedom and felicitous social arrangements bordering on utopia, while Thanatos is always associated with defeatism and destruction, and ultimately with dystopian gloom. While each of these two tendencies seems to be operating side by side for long stretches of her narrative, the liberationist perspective is eventually undermined by the defeatist implications of her observations, leading to ever darker speculations about the power of the destructive element in the human psyche and in history at large. The mutual contamination between liberationism and defeatism is directly inscribed into West's ambivalent interpretation of Serbia's heroic poetry, especially in her reading of the song about the grey falcon. Indeed, Serbia's oral balladry appears to be a pivotal dramatization of the *agon* between the forces of life and those of death.

At first, West considered Serbia's bardic tradition as an expression of the spirit of nationalist liberation. This stance was corroborated in conversations with Serbs and from historical evidence she gathered along the way. The defeatist reading that West arrived at later in the book, however, depended on her preconceived philosophical and political thesis, which she then applied to Serbia's heroic poetry. This thesis is based on her conviction that Christianity harbors a powerful death drive because it implants in every pious individual a desire to be subdued in hopes of a better afterlife. According to West, the Christian obsession with the doctrine of sin and atonement informs both the Serbian poem of the grey falcon and the ideology of pacifism and appeasement policy in England. My discussion of West's approach to Serbia's balladry follows the development of her own argument in *Black Lamb and Grey Falcon*, which moves from a liberationist to a defeatist and, by implication, from a utopian to a dystopian interpretation of this heroic poetry.

During a visit to the monastery of Vrdnik in Frushka Gora, where Prince Lazar's mummified body is being preserved, West insists optimistically on the possibility of turning a memory of defeat into an impulse toward liberation. Although the figure of Tsar Lazar reminds her "that the lot of man is pitiful, since the odds are against him" (516), West's pessimistic mood is momentarily suspended when she discovers an embroidered panel, sewn shortly after the battle of Kosovo by Euphemia, the widow of a Serb prince who had been killed by the Turks. And this text appears to her as a manifesto of nationalist revival. With her embroidery needles, Euphemia had written an outcry for liberation, a prayer for religious and political freedom, and an exhortation to resistance. I quote a short passage from West's English translation of this embroidered poem:

> Many troubles and sufferings have fallen on [Prince Lazar's]
> beloved children, and their lives are passed in sorrow, for the
> sons of Ismail rule over them, and we sorely need your help. . . .
> So bow your knee before the Heavenly King who bestowed on you
> the martyr's crown; beg Him that your beloved children may live
> long and be happy and do His will; beg Him that the Orthodox
> Church may stand firm in the land of our father; beg Him, who is
> the Conqueror of All, that He give your beloved sons, Prince Ste-
> phen and Prince Vuk, the victory over all their enemies, seen and
> unseen. If the Lord gives us His help, we shall give you praise and
> thanks for it. (518)

Pleading for Serbia's return to sovereignty, Euphemia asks for secular as well as religious victory over Serbia's oppressors.

Although Euphemia's poem is a written text, it has been integrated into the heroic lore surrounding the battle of Kosovo, and this requiem, beautifully embroidered on rich crimson velvet, becomes for West the very model and inspiration for her own aestheticized view on national liberation. In her explicit comment on Serbia's balladry, she forges a connection between this people's poetic and political impulses:

> These poems are not quite so artless as they seem. They were composed by the Serbs, more or less collectively, quite a century after the battle of Kosovo, on the model of the "chanson de geste." . . . Thereafter the full force of the artistic genius of the nation, denied all other outlet, poured into this medium; and the late eighteenth century, which marked the decline of folk-song in the West, here brought it new strength, for the nationalist and liberal ideas popularized by the French Revolution found their perfect expression ready-made in the laments of this enslaved people. (519)

Based on these observations, West begins to develop an extended analogy between Serbia's nationalist liberation and its poetic genius. In fact, she frequently substitutes the word *poem* for the term *Serb self rule.*

The "poem" she invokes when discussing Serbia's history is both a metonymy for Serbia's nationalist revival and for the heroic song cycles that treat of Prince Lazar's defeat in the battle of Kosovo: "The Serbians, to live in modern Serbia, must realize the poem that was written in the monasteries of the Frushka Gora, that was embodied in the dark body of the Tsar Lazar. They had not to choose whether they would make a day-dream into fact: they were under the necessity of choosing between life with that day-dream and death without it" (576).

Up to this point, West links Euphemia's prayer and other heroic songs with resistance and national resurrection rather than with defeatism. In this she is in complete agreement with the many Serbian historians who draw the exact same inference from the traditional poetry of old Serbia. I quote from the online version of *Kosovo* (1992), a collection of historical essays written by Serb nationalists:

> The bard, the storyteller, and, eventually, the traditionalist historian depicted the Battle of Kosovo as the catastrophic turning point in the life of Serbia; it marked the end of an independent, united Serbia and the beginning of 500 years of oppressive Otto-

man rule. The legend of the battle became the core of what we
may call the Kosovo ethic, and the poetry that developed around
the defeat contained themes that were to sustain the Serbian
people during the long centuries of foreign rule.[11]

The nationalist spirit voiced here by Thomas Emmert in the 1990s
squares with West's linking of bardic poetry with actual history some
sixty years earlier.

But West goes perhaps even further than most Serb propagandists
by foregrounding the poetic quality of Serbia's nationalistic dreams.
When Serbia was again threatened with war, during the Balkan wars of
1912, West states: "The Serbians, knifed in the back, continued within
their dream, to achieve their poem. The powerful magic of that dream,
that incantatory poem, blunted the knife. They beat back the Bulgarians" (578). But the onset of World War I brought Serbia once again to
its knees. In October 1915, "the Serbian Army, which now numbered
a quarter of a million men, was faced with three hundred thousand
Austro-German troops . . . and as many Bulgarians. It was now necessary for the country to die" (584). At this point, West inserts a celebration of the heroic withdrawal of the Serbian forces before an enemy that greatly outnumbered them, as Kosovo once again fulfilled its
function as Serbia's nemesis: "The retreating army made its last stand
on the field of Kosovo, where a short time before, in a different dream
of the Creator [i.e. in 1912], it had known victory: where Tsar Lazar had
proved that defeat can last five hundred years" (585). West follows this
with a highly aestheticized description of the retreat, which climaxes
in the pathos of resurrection: "On Corfu the Serbian Army fell down
and slept. Some never awoke. . . . A year after they had been driven
out of Serbia they were back on Serbian soil, fighting the Bulgarians"
(586–87). After a victorious campaign, the Serbs announced "that the
Austro-Hungarian Empire was destroyed and that out of its ruins they
were making a kingdom of the South Slavs, such as had inherited the
glory of Byzantium eight hundred years before. The poem was now
written. . . . The more poetic nation was in Belgrade thirteen days before the Armistice" (587).

Recent developments on the Balkans have shown that the poetry of
nationalism is a double-edged sword that can be used for the purpose
of defense as well as aggression. Indeed, Serb propaganda during the
1990s frequently invoked Tsar Lazar and the poem of the grey falcon.[12]

It is surprising that West did not sense the danger lurking at the core
of such aestheticizations of war.

• • •

But West was not content to celebrate the triumphalist effects of
Serbia's national resurrection and leave it at that. In a later section of
the book she claims that the Serbian song of Prince Lazar and the grey
falcon (i.e., the very core of the so-called Kosovo ethic) is actually
based on an ideology of defeatism. As soon as West arrived on the actual Battlefield of the Blackbirds, where the struggle between the Serbian and the Turkish armies was carried out in 1389, she became convinced that the song was about defeat and self-sacrifice rather than
resistance. In fact, she connected the symbol of the grey falcon with
the Augustinian principle of atonement, which had not only corrupted
the leaders of Old Serbia but also affected contemporary politicians (in
the 1930s).

The particular song from which West derived her political symbolism, "The Fall of the Serbian Empire," retells the myth of Prince Lazar's defeat on the plain of Kosovo. In this ballad, Prince Lazar is visited by the prophet Elijah in the form of a falcon. The poem begins:

> From that high town, holy Jerusalem,
> there comes flying a gray bird, a falcon,
> and in its beak a small bird, a swallow.
> Yet this gray bird is not just a falcon;
> it is our saint, the holy Saint Elijah.
> And the swallow is not just a swallow,
> but a message from the Holy Virgin.
> The falcon flies to Kosovo's flat field.

In the verses that follow, the holy messenger presents Prince Lazar
with a choice:

> Which of the two kingdoms will you embrace?
> Would you rather choose a heavenly kingdom,
> or have instead an earthly kingdom here?

Tsar Lazar, after pondering the options, decides in favor of the heavenly kingdom. In accordance with divine orders, he builds a church in
Kosovo and gives a mass for his armies (an instance of temporal tele-
scoping allowable in oral poetry) before leading them into battle.

If, here and now, you choose the earthly kingdom,
. . . .
Then their army, all the Turks, shall perish.
But if, instead, you choose the heavenly kingdom,
. . . .
Then every man, all soldiers will perish,
and you, their prince, will perish with your host.
. . . .
No sooner have the orders been given
than the Turks come and assault Kosovo.
. . . .
Prince Lazar, then, bids his great host go forth.
The Serbian host is numerous and mighty,
some seventy and seven thousand men,
and they scatter the Turks at Kosovo.
. . . .
Prince Lazar, then, would overwhelm the Turks,
But may God's curse be on Vuk Brankovic!
for he betrays his prince and his wife's father,
and Lazar's host is overwhelmed by the Turks.
Now Lazar falls, the Serbian Prince Lazar,
and with him falls the whole of his brave host,
his seventy and seven thousand men.
All this was done with grace and honor there,
before the eyes of God the Lord Almighty.

                    (trans. Holton and Bormanshinov, 95–98)

After listening to Constantine's recital of this poem, West "realized
fully why this poem had stirred [her]" (912). Hence, the poem's significance for West rests on its ultimately dystopian rather than utopian
implications. Although, in an earlier passage, West had associated Lazar with the utopian qualities of "honour and freedom and harmony"
(912), she now feels compelled to abandon her belief in Lazar's goodness. Instead, the impulse to be gentle and honorable is seen as merely
a disguise for the morbid desire to be obliterated. West exclaims that
pacifists and appeasers alike "want to receive the Eucharist, be beaten
by the Turks, and then go to Heaven. . . . I began to weep, for the left-
wing people among whom I had lived all my life had in their attitude
to foreign politics achieved such a betrayal" (913). The betrayal, one

may add, is of the life force, of freedom, and, ultimately, of the socio-political utopia.

In the epilogue of *Black Lamb and Grey Falcon*, where West returns one more time to the poem of Tsar Lazar, she insists on the connection between the battle of Kosovo and her contemporary historical moment. She says in the epilogue that "quite without irony it could be said that in Mr. Neville Chamberlain's Cabinet and in Whitehall all was holy and honourable. . . . Again the grey falcon had flown from Jerusalem, and it was to be with the English as it was with the Christian Slavs; the nation was to have its throat cut as if it were a black lamb in the arms of a pagan priest. . . . We, like the Slavs of Kossovo, had come to a stage when that fantasy becomes a compulsion to suicide" (1121).

In this context, the connection between defeatism and dystopia is brought home with full force: "As I looked round on this desolate historical landscape, which was desert beyond my gloomiest anticipation of where my ill fortune might bring me, it was not unfamiliar. 'I have been here before,' I said; and that was true, for I had stood on the plain of Kossovo" (1118–19). The analogy developed in this passage is clearly not only between England and Kosovo and between Turkish rule and Nazi oppression, but also between defeatism and dystopia.

• • •

Before discussing West's presentation of Serb history, it is necessary to point out the questionable historical premises of her argument. First of all, she accepts the conventional view that after the Turkish victory on the Field of the Blackbirds, "there followed five hundred years when no man on these plains, nor anywhere else in Europe for hundreds of miles in any direction, was allowed to keep his soul" (911). This is an often repeated theme in her book: "The Turks ruined the Balkans, with a ruin so great that it has not yet been repaired and may prove irreparable" (1066). Historians have challenged both premises; that is to say, the centrality of the Kosovo myth in Serbian history as well as the wholesale condemnation of Turkish rule. Noel Malcolm, for one, states that "in most Balkan countries, the popular view of Ottoman rule is almost entirely negative. The Ottomans are depicted as Asiatic barbarians who destroyed, in each of their possessions, a flourishing national culture. . . . All these claims are at best misleading and at worst completely false" (93). Malcolm also argues that "it was nineteenth-century Serbian ideology that created a cult of the medieval battle of Kosovo as some sort of nationally-defining historical and spiritual event" (xxx).

But even on its own terms, West's argument about the defeatist meaning of the Kosovo ethic is flawed. The Serbs themselves are far from considering the moral and political implications of their oral poetry as being in the least bit defeatist. Indeed, Serbian commentators such as Dimitrije Bogdanovic claim that Prince Lazar made a heroic choice, preferring martyrdom over enslavement: "The Serbian people's spiritual choice of Heaven over earth was manifested most fully and evidently in the fateful oral choice made in the historic battle of 1389, at which the Serbs faced the Turks on the Field of Kosovo. . . . The Serbs did not surrender to the Turks in 1389, nor did they accept the status of vassals. They instead chose to fight." [13]

Concerning the choice as such, it belongs to the realm of legend rather than history. To Noel Malcolm, the antithesis between a heavenly and an earthly kingdom is a rhetorical commonplace that could have been "drawn from any one of a wide range of classical and Christian sources. . . . There is simply no evidence to suggest that any Serb ever drew the idea of a special 'Kosovo covenant' out of these common rhetorical figures before the nineteenth century. Even then, the application of this 'heavenly kingdom' concept must have been somewhat problematical, given that the national ideology to which it was harnessed was concerned very much with the territorial extension of an earthly kingdom" (80).

Thus, when West states "I do not believe in the thesis of the poem. I do not believe that any man can procure his own salvation by refusing to save millions of people from miserable slavery" (911), her argument moves on the plane of legend, not of chronicled history, and it moreover contradicts the Serbs' own interpretation of the same legend. Also, by considering the poem of the grey falcon first as part of a liberationist tradition and then as a sign of defeatism, West strains the logical coherence of the whole book. And she could not have chosen a people less suited to illustrate her point about the Christian desire for self-sacrifice and defeat. West's aberrations in this regard were dictated to a large degree by her deductive political thesis, which she aimed to prove on the Balkans, and by the historical developments of her time, which instilled into her a distinctly dystopian outlook.

But her view of Serbian self-sacrifice did not sit easily with her during the first years of World War II. Even as she was writing about Yugoslavia's collective death wish, events proved her to be wrong:

Yet in this hour the Yugoslavs often repeated the poem of the Tsar Lazar and the grey falcon, which above all other works of art celebrated this appetite for sacrificial self-immolation. 'All was holy, all was honourable'. . . . It was factually inappropriate. In the Yugoslavia of 1941 there was no one who would have bought his personal salvation by consenting to the subjugation of his people, and no one who would not have preferred to be victorious over the Nazis if that had been possible. It was their resistance, not their defeat, which appeared to them as the sacred element in their ordeal. . . . Therefore [the Yugoslavs] chose that Yugoslavia should be destroyed rather than submit to Germany and be secure, and made that choice for love of life, and not love of death. (1145–46)

This shows that West eventually reverted to her earlier interpretation of Serb martyrdom as a form of resistance rather than defeat. Accordingly, her regard for Yugoslavia's resistance causes her to embrace a more hopeful outlook: "The news that Hitler had been defied by Yugoslavia travelled like sunshine over the countries which he had devoured and humiliated, promising spring" (1149).

From our contemporary perspective, having grown accustomed to reports of ethnic cleansing by Serbian forces in Bosnia and Kosovo during the 1990s, the real issue seems not whether the Kosovo songs have a liberationist or a defeatist implication. The real issue is whether these songs can inflame violent nationalism to the degree of murderous warfare. Indeed, while these poems served to motivate Serbian resistance against successive invaders, in the hands of a skilled propagandist such as Slobodan Milosevic the very same songs can be used to legitimize any nationalist action, including genocidal campaigns.

• • •

West's wavering attitude between the two mutually exclusive interpretations of Serbia's balladry is further evidence for the difficulty of maintaining any kind of stable political dichotomy at the end of the 1930s. Liberation and oppression, resistance and defeatism, utopia and dystopia, left and right—such categorical oppositions tended to contaminate each other as the world slid toward a historical disaster of such unprecedented proportions as to defy binary oppositions altogether. And West is emblematic for her invocation of dualistic distinctions and her simultaneous subversion of them. Even while she works out one dualistic contrast after another, West is ultimately fascinated by the fusion of opposites and the ability to overcome antitheses.

This desire for merging actually underpins West's idealization of Byzantine culture. She claims that this culture has managed to dispense with exclusive dualisms in favor of fusion: "The Tiger, blood on its claws, crossed itself; the golden beast became a golden youth; church and state, love and violence, life and death, were to be fused again as in Byzantium" (579). Accordingly, her landscape descriptions are not only informed by dualistic perceptions but occasionally also by a strong impulse to integrate opposites into a harmonious whole: "Here nature was at its most unnatural. . . . It was as if one learned that nightmares might fill not only a troubled hour after midnight but the whole of the night and the day, that a historical epoch might hold horror and nothing else. Yet it was beautiful, so beautiful that the appalled sight could not have enough of it" (1032). This merging, in the above description, of terror and admiration, of the sublime and the beautiful, demonstrates that West was not an inveterate dualist. One could even venture to say that her book strives to foster an ambivalent moral outlook that accommodates simultaneously a tragic and a comic view of human life.

For West, the most powerful agent in fusing the tragic and comic scripts of history into an organic whole was art. In fact, the aesthetic impulse has a medicinal quality for her: "But there is hope that man may change, for two factors work on him that might disinfect him. One is art" (1126). And she goes on to say that in listening to Mozart all our human capacities become involved in the process of experience: " 'Yes,' we say in our beings, heart and mind and muscles fused in listening, 'this is what matters' " (1127). Similarly, West emphasizes in her final reference to the poem of the grey falcon that the artist is distinguished from the common man, the politician, and the capitalist insofar as "his work . . . is often a palimpsest on which are superimposed several incompatible views about his subject. . . . The poem of the Tsar Lazar and the grey falcon tells a story which celebrates the death-wish; but its hidden meaning pulses with life" (1145). This reads actually like a self-absolving statement, applying to West's own art rather better than to the (unspecified) creator of the Serbian ballad. Indeed, *Black Lamb and Grey Falcon* is just such a palimpsest as she describes here, even more so than the poem of the grey falcon, which is a fairly straightforward glorification of a nation's last stand.

In Yugoslavia, then, West found herself in a similar quandary to Graham Greene in Liberia. Both writers were caught in a situation where they appealed to antagonistic principles to deal with their impressions and formulate their political programs, while both recognized that binary political principles were inadequate to deal with the raw data of personal experience. Greene was torn between socialism and capitalism, just as West was torn between liberationism and defeatism. Both writers' opinions sway from one pole to the other, unable to support a coherent political program that would respond to the dictates of experience as well as to the necessities of political ideology.

In the case of *Black Lamb and Grey Falcon,* West's conflicted response to Serbia's balladry was based on two distinct epistemological principles that had become entangled with one another in her thinking: the liberationist thesis derived from an empiricist approach, while the defeatist thesis derived from a deductive principle (i.e., the need to prove her "thesis" that Christian civilization was corrupted by the death wish). The sustained belief in the 1930s that travel was a means for acquiring direct political experience favored the liberationist interpretation, while the penchant of the decade for abstract systems of thought and deductive ideological principles fostered the second stance. Since West's discourse appeals to both epistemological principles at once, the argumentative coherence of her book suffers. It is in this sense that *Black Lamb and Grey Falcon* is at the same time a celebration of dualistic thinking and its ultimate subversion.

Russell Jacoby suggests that the disappearance of political radicalism at the end the twentieth century, together with the death of universal ideals, leads to the *The End of Utopia* (1999). This is actually an apt diagnosis for what also happened at the end of the 1930s, when political radicalism was confounded by historical events and when the rise of totalitarianism threatened any clear distinction between political ideologies. But Jacoby would be well advised also to include in his theory of utopian decline the concept of dystopia, which is crucial to any assessment of utopian beliefs. Not only is one man's utopia another man's dystopia, but all attempts at conjuring up utopian conditions in the "real" world by means of radical politics seem to be destined to turn into a nightmare. In fact, the study of 1930s travel writing would be certain to put a damper on Jacoby's trust in the social merit of utopian pursuits. After all, what is the point of having utopian plans if they cannot be subjected to some form of validation by practical implementation?

As this chapter has shown, the search for utopia in the 1930s turned regularly into a discovery of dystopia. One reason for this was, of course, the worldwide economic depression, which made it almost impossible to find anywhere a sustainable spatial equivalent for the concepts of prosperity and hope. Moreover, as shown above, the rise of totalitarianism proved detrimental to the concept of political dualism, which, as Jacoby has shown, is indispensable for the conception of utopia.[14] Slavoj Žižek has come to the same conclusion, though from a different vantage point, arguing that the psychocultural foundations of totalitarianism are precisely predicated upon the negation of antagonisms.[15] Similarly, Pierre Bourdieu finds it impossible to pair totalitarianism with a dualistic partner.[16] This knowledge was intuited by English intellectuals at the end of the 1930s, and their travel writing bears witness to an experiential kind of deconstruction vis-à-vis oppositional concepts.

Pierre Bourdieu has recently reminded us of the "curse of these ... apparently scientific antinomies rooted in social antagonism" (181) that must be overcome in favor of a recognition of relations.[17] I venture to say that the historical context experienced by 1930s travelers imposed just such an abandonment of dualistic sociopolitical conceptions in favor of relational perspectives on the period's travel writers. Circumstances forced them to acknowledge similarities and *relations* between home and abroad rather than radical differences. Waugh's comparative move at the end of *Remote People*, where London is judged by standards of African hospitality, or West's insistent comparisons between events in the Balkans and events in England, or Greene's lament that Britain's political climate had become a simulacrum of Mexico, constitute gestures toward a relational politics. Although taking sides constituted a strong imperative in the 1930s, the exclusionary emphasis of the dualistic temperament gradually made room for the recognition that self and other, here and there, left and right were actually constituting one another. In terms of traveling, this meant that ethnocentric approaches to foreign societies had to be revised, because it became increasingly apparent that home and abroad were not hierarchically divided but dialectically linked with one another.

6 THE GEOGRAPHY OF FEAR

"Strange Effects of Space"

IN THE 1930s, as we have just seen, travelers returning from their journeys were often haunted by the impression that home looked deceptively like abroad. To Sara Suleri, all narratives of anxiety in the colonial context derive precisely from the "productive disordering of binary dichotomies" (4) such as self and other, home and abroad. Similarly, the travel literature of English intellectuals of the 1930s both registers and produces such a disordering of binaries, and as a result engenders powerful manifestations of anxiety. Concrete historical factors only strengthened these writers' sense of apprehension. Valentine Cunningham, although allowing for a limited amount of fun and games, emphasizes that "early in any approach to the period must come an awareness of the multiplied fears and forebodings and the widespread sadness that make a constant background and foreground" (36). Indeed, the literature of the period reflects, modifies, and sometimes exacerbates apprehensions about contemporary social, economic, and political ills. Entering the fictional lives of Gordon Comstock *(Keep the Aspidistra Flying),* Bernard Marx *(Brave New World),* Tony Last *(A Handful of Dust),* or Conrad Drover *(It's a Battlefield)* (to name only a few of the many available examples) means engaging with a wide range of anxieties. With the notable exception of George Orwell, the novelists who invented these neurotic, haunted, exhausted, and imprisoned characters were not personally suffering from any serious deprivations as a consequence of the Great Depression; but they shared with all social classes a sense of permanent crisis.

Of course, anxiety has many faces, and the expression thereof in travel literature varies from case to case. In his *Haunted Journeys* (1991), Dennis Porter studies the transgressive nature of desires projected onto physical space in texts from the eighteenth century to the present. In *Belated Journeys* (1994), Ali Behdad examines the late-nineteenth-century traveler's anxiety of belatedness—that is, an often-frustrated quest for unmediated experience and first-ness. The feeling of belatedness, in turn, provokes a profound "anxiety of influence," since almost every territory has been worked over, literally and discursively, by previous travelers. Paul Fussell, finally, has elaborated on a properly sociocultural kind of anxiety; namely, the disturbing feeling that "real travel" (whatever that may mean) is being rapidly forced out of existence by postmodernity and its corollary, space/time compression (David Harvey). Then there are the concrete, physical dangers such as falling rocks, snowstorms, and hostile natives, and all these add their share to the anxiety of travel. These are quasi-generic anxieties haunting twentieth-century travelers irrespective of place and time. In contradistinction, what I am interested in here are the specific historical and social conditions that led to the formation of certain ideological and political anxieties that have not yet been sufficiently studied. Such anxieties, I argue, are rife in 1930s travel writing.

English travelers of the 1930s made perhaps the keenest diagnoses of a global political meltdown that resulted from the clash of two ideological paradigms with universal pretensions—socialism and fascism—and from the most serious economic crisis the world had ever experienced. They had a first whiff of the problems facing the traveler in an age of global political, intellectual, and economic developments. At no other time in history had trade, production, and exchange the world over been so thoroughly affected by a single, shared economic dynamic. And as the reverberations of deflation spread throughout the world, so did left-wing radicalism and fascism.

Britain itself formed a microcosm of this global drama as Oswald Mosley's blackshirts skirmished with antifascist opponents. Travel in those days may have suggested the possibility of an escape from the cramped and tense conditions at home, but for the traveler it was conducive to a sense of déjà-vu: the uncanny feeling that one was returning to familiar social and political conditions, but displaced, in a foreign land. This was an almost inevitable by-product of politically conscious traveling in the 1930s.

There were also other, even more ideologically determined factors causing many 1930s travelers to feel anxious while traveling. Indeed, the anxieties registered in their books often arose out of a recognition that their political beliefs were completely incompatible with the foreign social and political context or, more troubling yet, that they were actually engaging in acts of bad faith. The need to assert specific kinds of political views in a culturally estranged environment caused a painful strain to activists intending to bring the benefits of an English liberal mentality to what Greene had termed the "Lawless Roads."

In yet a different sense, the concept of anxiety has acquired importance in recent studies of colonial encounters. Ranajit Guha, for example, argues that the "register of anxiety" evidenced in George Orwell's antiimperial story "Shooting an Elephant" originates in "an indefinite and pervasive anxiety about being lost in empire" (484). Similarly, Sara Suleri shows in *The Rhetoric of English India* that the need to interact with cultural others always presents the danger (or opportunity) of crossing over and of self-abandonment, something the colonizer both fears and desires.[1] In a sense, then, cultural anxiety, imperial anxiety, and ideological anxiety are all related to one another, and it is precisely this compound of anxiety-producing elements that marks the 1930s and its popular literary genre, the travel book.

Among these manifestations of anxiety in 1930s travel writing, some are more openly uncanny, or more obviously driven by psychological dynamics, while others are more specifically political in nature. Both kinds of anxieties, however, can be studied from the perspective of Sigmund Freud's work on the uncanny and on the discontents produced by political and civilizational phenomena. The concept of the uncanny in particular offers a surprisingly adequate means of analysis, with regard to both the link between repetition and anxiety and the cultural context of decadence, which is closely linked to notions of cultural anxiety.

For all four travel writers discussed in this study, the experience of anxiety had a destabilizing effect on their ideological discourses. Graham Greene's loss of ideological "orientation" in the Liberian hinterland triggered a discursive oscillation between proimperial and antiimperial arguments; Evelyn Waugh found that the home/abroad dichotomy he wanted to impose on Africa was subverted by a counter-discourse of universal cultural decadence; George Orwell strove for a social and political realism yet could not help imaginatively "exploiting" his experience of lowlife; and Rebecca West voiced her liberationist support for Yugoslav nationalism amid assertions about the defeatist turn of the Serbian mind. These contradictions are exacerbated in the same degree that feelings of anxiety take hold of these writers' imaginative and discursive means: the more anxious they are, the more their discourse of travel begins to fold into ambivalence, and the more its constitutive logical and ideological frameworks begins to sag.

Haunted by Ideology: Journey without Maps

The haunting quality of repressed ideological potentialities is a muted subtext in *Journey without Maps*. Indeed, Greene's attempt to detract from the political significance of his trip through Liberia is a constant symptom of this ideological anxiety. Although *Journey without Maps* has distinct political overtones, Greene strives to keep these aspects under cover (see chapter 3). The result is a book that downplays political issues, masquerading instead as a psychological regression: "The method of psychoanalysis is to bring the patient back to the idea which he is repressing: a long journey backwards without maps" (96–97); "here one was finding associations with a personal and a racial childhood" (93). This approach promises to yield a coherent enough framework for Greene's journey. Indeed, he concludes that the journey helped him to get in "touch with the true primitive source" (244). In keeping with that attitude, Greene suggests that the center of West Africa (the interior) represents a form of human authenticity that the margin (the coast and, by implication, the imperial metropolis) has lost through corrupt and repressive civilizational mechanisms.

With this attitude, Greene ranks among those who, according to Freud, "have come to take up [a] strange attitude of hostility to civilization" (*Civilization and Its Discontents,* 87). Certainly, Greene makes perfectly clear where England figured on his psychologized map of the world. His trip to Africa was to find out "to what peril of extinction centuries of cerebration have brought us" in an attempt "to discover if one can from what we have come, to recall at which point we went astray" (21). The echoes to Freud's *Civilization and Its Discontents,* an essay that emphasizes the repressive and neurosis-producing demands that civilization makes upon human beings, are unmistakable.

Although Greene differs from other primitivist writers about Africa (including Rider Haggard, Joseph Conrad, and André Gide) in the degree of explicitness with which he bares the psychological device of his approach, he is perpetuating a conventional pattern that equates the journey into Africa with a psychological descent, and both with a cultural regression. Most postcolonial readings of *Journey without Maps* emphasize the conventionality of Greene's approach.[2] But what such critical studies have hitherto failed to register are the deep currents of doubt, mistrust, and anxiety that undermine the supposed arrogance of Greene's primitivist discourse. Indeed, the reality of West Africa remains intractable to this idealizing psychological approach, and Greene eventually had to own up to his political role as a radical intellectual faced with social injustice and oppression.

Instead of enjoying the liberating implications of his encounter with "bareness, simplicity, instinctive friendliness, feeling rather than thought" (192), Greene soon realized that the interior of West Africa offered quite familiar—indeed, all too familiar—patterns of economic exploitation and political corruption: "Civilization here remained exploitation" (61). Even worse, "[the natives] were left alone to their devils and secret societies and private terrors, to the paternal oppression of their chiefs" (107). At this point, it seems that the coast/interior dichotomy has played itself out. All the more surprising, therefore, that Greene falls back on this model again and again. However, the price for his unwillingness to abandon this spatialized system of evolutionary psychology is precisely a return of repressed ideological potentials. This development can be traced in Greene's gradual conversion from antiimperialist skeptic, at the beginning of the narrative, to, in the book's central sections, representative of pure capitalism and racial superiority.

One of the most telling incidents that registers this conversion is the strike scene in the middle of the narrative. I commented on this incident in chapter 3, and I return to it because it has crucial implications for the development of Greene's ideological anxiety. As will be remembered, Greene's carriers were dissatisfied with their low salaries and tough working conditions: "I was no longer a patriarch among my retainers; I was the unjust employer" (147), says Greene. The confrontation is keen, but the resolution quick and drastic. Greene, who admits that he "was exploiting them like all their other masters" (148–49), threatens to fire all his carriers at once. But this incident marks the return of a repressed experience and the onset of political guilt. Indeed, Greene had taken an active part in opposing Britain's general strike in 1926. The sudden recurrence of the strike scenario within the African jungle must have appeared to Greene as an uncanny visitation of political patterns he believed to have overcome. Although he considered himself a leftist liberal, he admitted after a confrontation with a local village chief, "I was very Imperialist" (188). Hence, the deeper that Greene penetrated into the realm of the "primitive," the more he reverted to a political ethos that marked the return of an earlier "system of belief" accompanied by a strong sense of hauntedness.

This connection between the return of a repressed ideological belief and the feeling of anxiety confirms a special aspect of Freud's explanations about the origins of uncanny sensations. Freud, in his essay "The Uncanny" (1919),[3] included among the kinds of repressed psychic contents that can return to haunt us whole "belief systems," or ideologies. I quote a passage from Freud's essay: "Nowadays we no longer believe in it [the animistic omnipotence of thoughts], we have *surmounted* these modes of thought; but we do not feel quite sure of our new beliefs, and the old ones still exist within us ready to seize upon any confirmation. As soon as something *actually happens* in our lives which seems to confirm the old, discarded beliefs we get a feeling of the uncanny" (247–48). If we substitute *ideology* for *modes of thought* and *middle-class ethos* for *animistic belief system*, we can directly apply Freud's analysis of anxiety to Greene's troubled experience in Liberia. Indeed, Greene was haunted by the return of an older political attitude during the African strike.

Evidence for an uncanny mode of perception follows directly in the wake of that scene. Greene continues his narrative by saying, "The next day wasn't so good" (150). Surrounded by natives whose stares "worked a little on the nerves" (154), Greene begins to develop near-hallucinatory visions of a topsy-turvy world: "This was one of the revelations of Africa, the deadness of what we think of as alive, the deadness of nature, the trees and scrubs and flowers, the vitality of what we think of as dead, the cold lunar craters" (154). Haunted by this contradiction, Greene continues, in a section entitled "The Dead Forest," to wonder "if [this forest] had ever been alive" (158), complaining about the "quality of deadness" (157) that pervades everything, a quality he associates with the uncanny feelings associated with uninhabited houses: "No one had ever transferred to *this* forest any human emotion at all. Like the shell of a house on a bankrupt estate it had never been lived in" (157).

In an act of transference, then, Greene projects upon the African scene the uncanniness that the return of his bourgeois, capitalist, and authoritarian social practice had generated in himself. A Freudian reading of Greene's response to the surfacing of his own repressed ideology is particularly appropriate in this context, since Greene himself refers to psychoanalysis in the very passage that includes the lament on the deadness of Africa's nature. Even while he transfers the uncanniness originating from the return of his repressed conservatism onto the surroundings, he speculates whether "if one stayed longer . . . [in] this Liberian forest . . . one might have relearned the way to live without transference, with a lost objectivity" (158).

Greene knows what he is doing, but only up to a point. His uncanny impressions bespeak an unacknowledged guilt about the abandonment of his socialist principles in the jungle of West Africa. Indeed, he felt "crazy to be here in the middle of Liberia when every thing I knew intimately was European. It was like a bad dream" (208). This "bad dream," resulting ostensibly from the traveler's physical inadequacy to his foreign surroundings, also suggests an ideological misfit. *Journey without Maps* is a travel book whose author belies his progressive commitment when dealing with natives and in doing so manifests the guilty consciousness of bad faith.

But try as he may, Greene cannot escape the conundrum of ideological self-betrayal as he metamorphoses from a progressive to a conservative traveler. The very title of the book, *Journey without Maps,* is a declaration that Greene was traveling, both literally and ideologically, in an uncharted and unpredictable territory.[4] The ideological anxiety stemming from the return to previously rejected ideological "premises" surfaces most gloomily in the grim assessment of his journey by reference to T. S. Eliot's *The Waste Land* ("I was fishing in the dull canal") at the end of the narrative, and in an allusion to Sir Walter Raleigh's *Discoverie of Guiana* ("the graves not opened yet for gold, the mine not broken with sledges"). These references make clear that Greene was haunted simultaneously by the cultural legacies of a conservative pessimist, Eliot, and of a frustrated empire builder, Raleigh. Simon Gikandi comments that "[Greene's] return to England is not prompted by any renewed desire for the culture of Englishness but is propelled, as we have already seen, by melancholy and cultural angst" (193).

The notion of travel as self-therapy had badly backfired on Greene, both in a psychological and a political sense. But significantly, Greene did not give up on this economy of desire. His Mexican journey was motivated by a renewal of essentially the same motives.

Uncanny Encounters: The Lawless Roads

What haunts Greene's *The Lawless Roads* is not so much the trauma of ideological anxiety as the awareness of collapsed cultural boundaries and the feeling of religious alienation. Underlying Greene's cultural anxiety is a profound disenchantment with Mexico and its people. Greene hardly stops complaining during the entire book. Already in San Louis Potosí, at an early stage of the journey, Greene recorded "the day I began to hate the Mexicans" (48). In Mexico City, he is wearied by "this boyishness, this immaturity" he observes among "grown men [who] cannot meet in the street without sparring like schoolboys" (69). The ruins of Teotihuacan inspire little more satisfaction (Greene compares the sculptures of the plumed serpent with "gas masks" and "Lewis guns or flame-throwers" [82]), and the allegorical murals of Rivera and Orozco are loathsome to him. The screw of disenchantment receives one more turn when Greene enters the "beautiful city" of Villahermosa in the state of Tabasco. Here he finds conditions of depravity that make him feel as though he "was drawing near to the centre of something—if it was only of darkness and abandonment" (114).

Paradoxically, however, in this anarchic place where "the police are the lowest of the population" (114), Greene is suddenly haunted by the feeling of familiarity. He receives a first shock when the local chief of police declares roundly, "You've come home. Why, everybody in Villahermosa is called Greene—or Graham" (115). But the namesakes are all Mexicans, Mestizoes or distant relatives of English immigrants, a circumstance that strikes Greene as a strange perversion of his sense of cultural and personal belonging. What is even more alarming is that having passed one day in the stifling atmosphere of Villahermosa, Greene suddenly notices that "it is curious how the most dismal place after twenty-four hours begins to seem like home" (118). Greene develops this notion further by musing how Dr. Fitzpatrick, an immigrant Scotsman in Villahermosa, "had been absorbed nearly as completely as the Greenes and Grahams," and he concludes gloomily that "there was something rather horrible and foreboding in this—for an unabsorbed Greene" (118). While Villahermosa's police chief parades the town's population of Greenes and Grahams before him, Greene suddenly finds himself "haunted by fancies, as if fate intended to take in its octopus coils yet another Greene" (119).

This connection between anxiety and the collapse of boundaries believed to be fixed confirms once again Freud's explanations of the origin and the nature of the uncanny. In his essay "The Uncanny," Freud points out that the German equivalent of the word *uncanny—unheimlich—*contains the negation of a spatial concept; namely, the *heim,* or home. Freud explains that "we can understand why linguistic usage has extended 'das Heimliche' into its opposite, 'das Unheimliche;' for this uncanny is in reality nothing new or alien, but something which is familiar and old-established in the mind and which has become alienated from it only through the process of repression" (241). Therefore, each time we undergo an experience of uncanniness, what actually happens is that an aspect of the repressed that was not conscious before asserts itself as part of our conscious psychic life. This process is also at work when we meet a doppelgänger or experience déjà vu. Both phenomena are uncanny because something that seems strange turns out to be no less than familiar.

That which is canny, or *heimlich,* could now be seen as an extension of one's cultural and social home, whereas the strange and "other" comes to signify abroad, or any space that is ethnically or racially different from one's own background. This is a somewhat more general application of Freud's uncanny to the experience of travel compared with the gendered reading some critics have given to the traveler's anxiety. Paul Zweig, for instance, has suggested that the reason men become adventurers lies in their need to escape the (feminized) home in order to fulfill their true masculinity. Yet the minute they are totally cut off from home, they begin to romanticize the foreign territory as feminine, replete with mysterious caves, breast-shaped hills, and forested crevices (as in Rider Haggard's *King Solomon's Mines* and Joseph Conrad's *Lord Jim*), thereby indicating an uncanny return to the (biological) place of origin.[5] This reading, though perfectly coherent in itself, is not capable of accounting for female travelers' anxieties. Moreover, many manifestations of the traveler's uncanny simply cannot be explained by recourse to this sexual model. Quite frequently, it seems, uncanny sensations abroad arise from a sudden awareness that the cultural (rather than sexual) "other" is hauntingly familiar or, conversely, that the home is culturally stranger than the foreign realm.

Freud himself established such a cultural dimension in his essay. In order to elucidate the uncanny effect of repetition, for instance, he referred to his experience of being lost "in a provincial town in Italy" (237) and returning again and again to the same disreputable neighborhood; also, he refers to an uncanny "encounter" with his own mirror image, an event that happened significantly during a train ride.

Greene's cultural anxiety in Mexico was caused partly by the doppelgänger-effect of meeting his strange namesakes and partly by the feeling of being at home in the most depraved of contexts. Even more troubling to him was the realization that he could not understand the religious spirit of the country. The very nature of Mexican Catholicism struck Greene as anomalous and outlandish. Especially in the southern provinces, where the native population had turned "his" religion into a hybrid of animism and Catholicism, Greene finds himself in strange territory precisely where he had most hoped to meet familiarity. In Las Casas, where the Easter proceedings feature a ritual killing of Judas and his "jolly brother," Greene despairs: "Nothing meant anything anymore; it was just sentiment . . . the Host wasn't there" (173). This feeling of alienation within Catholicism leads inevitably to moments of stark anxiety. At times, Greene is "overcome by an immense unreality: I couldn't even recognize my own legs in riding-boots" (132).

Confronted with anxiety and alienation, Greene strives to alleviate his uneasiness by externalizing its source—that is, by aligning the moral and social conditions of Villahermosa with the general state of the human condition. Now Mexico takes on the characteristics of an eschatological symbol, signifying the fall from grace and the ultimate cultural collapse. The "meaning" of this symbol is relatively vague, but some of its implications are based on Greene's impressions of "idolatry and oppression, starvation and casual violence" (184) among Mexicans.

But the more Greene insists on Mexico's symbolical significance, the more he voids this sign of any specific meaning. The notion of Mexico as a symbol for a global sociopolitical and spiritual malaise becomes quite meaningless once the boundaries between what is contaminated by that condition and what contrasts with it are muddled. In other words, the symbol becomes the thing itself, as the boundary between signifier and signified, 'vehicle' and 'tenor,' is blurred. Interestingly, this very phenomenon is identified by Freud as a frequent cause of uncanny sensations: "An uncanny effect is often and easily produced when the distinction between imagination and reality is effaced, as when something that we have hitherto regarded as imaginary appears before us in reality, or when a symbol takes over the full functions of the thing it symbolizes, and so on" (244). A discursive symptom for the semantic breakdown between the symbol and what it stands for is Greene's undifferentiated use of certain qualifiers toward the end of his narrative. Indeed, words such as *hideous* (which appears eleven times), *odious, ugly,* and *dreadful* are almost hysterically splashed on the last pages of the book. Rather surprisingly, however, these qualifiers are not only reserved for "this country which I hated" (195) but strongly color Greene's impressions on returning home: "One was jolted through the hideous iron tunnel at Vauxhall Bridge" (223) and: "One sat in the hideous little convent gymnasium ... and a man explained how our children were to be evacuated" (224).

The realization that Mexico was the world and the world Mexico must have come to Greene on the return trip to England. First, the ship that carried him back to England was full of enthusiastic volunteers going to join Franco's forces in the Spanish civil war. Second, upon arriving in London he was greeted by ARP (air raid precaution) posters, and he felt repelled by "the grit of the London afternoon, among the trams, in the long waste of the Clapham Road" (223). After seeing newspaper posters proclaiming "a crime of violence" (233), Greene asks rhetorically, "How could a world like this end in anything but war? I wondered why I had disliked Mexico so much: *this* was home" (233).

The collapse of Greene's symbolical operations is completed with his gloomy meditation that "perhaps we are in need of violence. Violence came nearer—Mexico was a state of mind" (224). The impression of the inseparability between home and abroad undermines the rhetorical function that Mexico had to play for long stretches in the book. As the whole globe becomes engulfed in the same destructive development, any "part" of the world, even England itself, could serve as a figure of the condition that Greene strives to represent. In a sense, then, the symbol has fallen back on the head of its inventor, and the quintessential figure of alterity (Mexico) turns into nothing less than a facet of the self. It is this recognition that casts such a long and deep shadow over the end of *The Lawless Roads.*

Cultural Decadence: Remote People

Why is it that so many 1930s travelers systematically selected as their destinations the poorest, most crime-ridden, most underdeveloped, and unhealthiest places they could think of? It was not just pure masochism that drove them there. Indeed, all the travelers to wretched places mingled their expressions of anxiety with gloomy cultural forebodings. This fascination with decline and anarchy has something in common with the cultural condition of decadence, an attitude that is shot through with a mixture of catastrophism and a concomitant enjoyment of degradation.

Waugh's *Remote People* presents the reader with the two antithetical, yet related, facets of the decadent mood. First, we are introduced to the playfully ludicrous and cheerfully debunking attitudes that characterize the lighter side of decadence. In the sections touched by this spirit, Waugh tries to stay aloof from his own experiences, although one senses occasionally a more serious concern with the alleged incompetence and banality of Ethiopia's cultural manifestations. Generally, however, a rather charming sense of "crazy enchantment" (20) is the traveler's dominant mood: "It is to *Alice in Wonderland* that my thoughts recur in seeking some historical parallel for life in Addis Ababa" (20). Indeed, Waugh develops scenes worthy of Lewis Carol: "At every corner were half-finished buildings. . . . A foreman circulated among [the laborers], carrying a long cane. When he was engaged elsewhere the work stopped altogether. The men did not sit down, chat, or relax in any way, they simply stood stock-still where they were, motionless as cows in a field, sometimes arrested with one small stone in their hands" (25). And a bit further on: "Attempts are even made, with canes and vigorous exchanges of abuse, to regulate the foot-traffic, a fad which proves wholly unintelligible to the inhabitants. The usual way for an Abyssinian gentleman to travel is straight down the middle of the road on mule-back with ten or twenty armed retainers trotting all round him" (26).

Waugh complements these amusing vignettes (which are contradicted by other testimonies) [6] with a farcical episode recording his visit to the remote Abyssinian monastery of Debra Lenos. Strangely, however, after all the fun, the reader is confronted with the darker side of decadence, because the next section of the book is entitled "First

Nightmare." This indicates that not all was well and that Waugh's jocular discourse merely concealed a higher level of anxiety than could be mitigated by satire.

Waugh's invocations of anxiety within a context of cultural decadence have implications that resonate, once again, with Freud's thoughts on anxiety, in particular with the cultural context from which they sprang. Although the essay on "The Uncanny" is dated 1919, Freud was deeply rooted in the decadent tradition of fin-de-siècle Viennese culture, and this element can be traced throughout his work. Indeed, cultural anxiety was widespread during the last decades of the nineteenth century and the first decade of the twentieth. Vienna in particular eclipsed London, Paris, and Prague toward the end of the nineteenth century in the depth of the despair felt by its intelligentsia. This was partly due to the pervasive sense of political and imperial decline then haunting the Habsburg monarchy. Carl Schorske has linked the feelings of decline with the precarious situation of the Austrian middle classes at the turn of the century: "The Christian Social demagogues began a decade of rule in Vienna which combined all that was anathema to classical liberalism: Anti-Semitism, clericalism, and municipal Socialism. On the national level as well, the liberals were broken as a parliamentary political power by 1900, never to revive. They had been crushed by modern mass movements, Christian, Anti-Semitic, socialist, and nationalist" (6). While the aristocratic class had been chastened by the scientific rationality of bourgeois liberalism, the political power of the middle classes was itself being undermined by various populist and special interest groups.

Hand in hand with the decline of Austria's liberal tradition went the disintegration of the Austrian Empire. By the turn of the century, Austria-Hungary had lost several decisive battles on its territory: "The imperial glamour of Vienna appeared to be diminished after the 'Ausgleich' and . . . [the city] had suffered greatly in prestige as a result of the Austro-Prussian War. . . . The urban intelligentsias of Austria-Habsburg considered the Monarchy to be in a state of chaos and decadence" (Pynsent, 118). Indeed, by about 1900, Vienna's ruling social, political, and cultural classes were in the throes of a powerful anxiety caused by the uncertainties of a decaying empire whose political structures were petrified, whose administration had become a byword for *Schlamperei* (carelessness), and whose racial and social tensions were eating away at the fabric of the state.

But the phenomenon has many facets. As an artistic movement, decadence had its roots in Paris, with Baudelaire, Rimbaud, and Verlaine as its most famous exponents. Other artistic movements of the late nineteenth century are often associated with decadence, in particular British aestheticism (Oscar Wilde), naturalism (Emile Zola, Joris-Karl Huysmans), and Austrian fin-de-siècle realism (Arthur Schnitzler, Hugo Hofmannsthal, and, later, Robert Musil). The sensibility that these artists shared was a feeling Alfred de Musset had already identified in the 1830s when he coined the term *maladie du siècle*. This maladie was an ambivalent mixture of pessimism derived from a feeling of cultural and political decline and a simultaneous emphasis on playful and hedonistic exuberance. But decadence has never sparked protest or political rebellion; indeed, "the Decadent was horrified at the impending doom of European civilisation, and luxuriated in that horror" (Pynsent, 112). "Stylish" language and Dandyism were the outward forms of this sensibility (Pynsent, 112), and its inward manifestation was a brooding, uncanny mood such as that evidenced in Kafka's stories.

Social historians of this period agree that "anxiety, impotence, a heightened awareness of the brutality of social existence" (Schorske, 6) were dominant elements of turn-of-the-century Viennese society. During this time, Freud emerged as the moral consciousness of a narcissistic, decadent, sex-obsessed society: "[Freud] offered a cure for fin-de-siècle anxiety, and that was to release one's repressed childhood anxiety or trauma and thus, usually, one's repressed libido" (Schorske, 157). This "cure," it must be noted, was rooted in the sociopolitical conditions of Freud's time. However, Freud's ahistorical approach to anxiety reflects his withdrawal from the political scene due to his complete frustration with fin-de-siècle politics in Vienna.

Now, it can be argued that the 1930s bore distinctive similarities to the cultural scenario of the fin-de-siècle. Indeed, Pynsent called the 1930s the "only real revival [of Decadence]" (225). This can be verified in the discourse of Londoners such as Waugh and Greene who rehearsed a cultural script that had been current in Vienna some thirty to forty years earlier. Their cultural pessimism derived partly from the contemporary crisis in politics and economy and partly from the aftermath of World War I, seen by many as the collapse of liberal humanism. The Roaring Twenties had revived hopes in the possibility of sociopolitical and economic renewal in Europe. But everything that had

appeared promising during the 1920s was thrown into a state of chaos
during the 1930s: Britain's Labour Party suddenly courted the Conservatives, atheists became Catholics, members of the bourgeois intelligentsia adopted a socialist rhetoric, aristocrats turned fascists. At
no other time in recent memory had the British experienced such a
mounting sense of crisis and disorientation.

Pynsent's definition of "The Decadent" fits Waugh nearly perfectly:
"Decadents protest and reject, but they do not rebel. . . . The Decadents protested against the contemporary decay of civilization, but
they also enjoyed protesting and thus enjoyed decay or the exploitation of decay. They were also pessimists. . . . The Decadents created
their 'paradis artificiels'" (147). Indeed, Waugh's travel writing is permeated by rejection. In his first travel book, *Labels,* he lampooned the
entire Arabic world of art, denouncing it as infantile and tedious. And
in *Waugh in Abyssinia,* he declared roundly that Addis Ababa was "pre-
ternaturally forbidding" (231). As far as his enjoyment of protest goes,
nothing could be more to the point. Waugh is at his comical best when
he describes his own awkwardness abroad or the embarrassment of
others. The coronation of Ethiopia's Haile Selassie was a welcome
occasion for situation comedy. But while Waugh indulged his farcical
vein by reference to Addis Ababa's public life, he was ultimately repelled by the "barbarism" that he saw as the defining characteristic of
Ethiopian society. Indeed, Waugh's cultural decadence, which implies
an almost sadistic enjoyment of cultural decline, was weakened as the
war approached. His explorations of social anarchy, as in *Decline and
Fall* and *Vile Bodies,* gradually made room for more sober assessments
of the human condition. In his last 1930s travel book, *Robbery under
Law,* Waugh invoked the image of the Waste Land as an analogy for
Mexico's political anarchy, and he wonders, "Is civilization, like a leper,
rotting from its extremities?" (3).

As David Lodge has pointed out, the very title of Waugh's first
novel, *Decline and Fall,* could be applied to almost any of Waugh's novels: "The myth of decline provided Evelyn Waugh with a sliding scale
of value on which almost everything is found in some way defec-
tive. . . . There *is,* in fact, behind Waugh's fictional world, a consistent
point of view—that of a dogmatic Christian anti-humanism" (11–12).
As mentioned in chapter 2, the decadent aspect of Waugh's antihumanism was checked by his conversion to Roman Catholicism, which lent
a more serious moral perspective to his 1930s writings. But Waugh's

travel writing is more complex than his fiction in this respect, since his gleeful pessimism about the "barbarity" of foreign nations is occasionally counterbalanced by a streak of sincere political idealism, something that is missing in his novels.

Another aspect of Waugh's travel writing that aligns him with the practice of cultural decadence is his occasional celebration of a pastoral enclave within a world rank with barbarity and corruption. Hence the *paradis artificiel* has its definitive place in Waugh's life, not only in the form of his carefully tended garden at Piers Court (the country house he received as a wedding present in 1937), but also in celebrations of utopian sociopolitical conditions in his travel writing. One of the most memorable celebrations of this sort of paradise is Waugh's description of the colony of Kenya: "I found myself falling in love with Kenya" (156), he exclaims in *Remote People,* and elaborates: "It was lovely at Naivasha; the grass ran down from the house to the water, where there was a bathing-place with a little jetty to take one clear of the rushes. We used to swim in the morning, eat huge luncheons and sleep in the afternoon" (169). According to Pynsent, the decadents' need to create an artificial paradise was an expression of the desire to escape both the ugliness of industrial society and the horrors of quotidian boredom (147). In *Remote People* the implications are very similar. Waugh's "Happy Valley" (156) of Kenya is "constructed" as a bastion against boredom and against the decline of the aristocratic order of society, in England as well as in Arabia. Against these odds, Kenya offered an anodyne for the decadent nostalgic longing to return to "the traditional life of the English squirearchy" (160).

The picture of decadence in *Remote People* is rounded off by the "Third Nightmare," discussed in the context of Waugh's cultural politics of place in chapter 5. Here I would like to stress the uncanny dimension attached to what is after all a fairly "common" London pub: "It was underground. We stepped down into the blare of noise as into a hot swimming-pool, and immersed ourselves; the atmosphere caught our breath like the emanation in a brewery over the tanks where fermentation begins" (211). Something was truly brewing in the center of "civilization," and despite his travels Waugh's homecoming was not a welcoming or joyful experience. Having lost his faith in the achievements of the old generation of political and economic leaders, having been too young to become a war hero, and having experienced the collapse of the global capitalist economy, Waugh could not help being haunted by impressions of decline wherever he went. After the first enchantment of travel had vanished in Addis Ababa, Waugh found himself looking into a bottomless pit of sloth, incompetence, and cultural banality—aspects that he associated with the encroachment of "barbarism" from the cultural margins to the center of civilization.

• • •

In *Remote People,* Waugh's condescending discourse of cultural and racial superiority is undercut by that book's discourse of anxiety. First there is a sense of general cultural decline ("what a mess we have made of civilization in Europe" [180]), causing Waugh to despair of the West's cultural legitimacy and, indeed, of its ability to stem the flood of barbarism. Waugh's anxiety also has a psychocultural foundation. The feeling of ennui that had already haunted Baudelaire and was to beset Musil's decadent "man without qualities" caught up with Waugh in a remote town in Ethiopia. While stranded in the nondescript railway town of Dirre Dowa for two days, Waugh complains that "never in Europe have I been so desperately and degradingly bored as I was during the next four days; they were as black and timeless as Damnation" (100). Such feelings of boredom go far beyond regular symptoms of understimulation. Their power is so compelling as to control all aspects of Waugh's life, rather like a waking dream or a nightmare. In keeping with Freud's realization that the uncanny arises from compulsive repetition, Waugh associates the feeling of stark boredom with the meaningless rituals and social habits of life at home: " 'Never again,' I say on the steps of the house, 'never again,' I say in the railway carriage, 'will I go and stay with those people.' And yet a week or two later the next invitation finds me eagerly accepting" (100). Waugh recognizes that boredom has become a culturally ingrained form of self-denial that not even travel could banish.

But Waugh's anxiety has yet another root; namely, anticolonial national resistance movements. Waugh aptly notes a "slight infection of persecution mania about all political thought in the colonies" (*Remote People,* 163), a feeling he might share to a greater degree than he admits. Indeed, he says elegiacally that "it is uncertain whether the kind of life which the Kenya settlers are attempting to re-establish is capable of survival; whether there may not be in the next twenty-five years a general Withdrawal of the Legions to defend Western civilization at its sources" (168).

That this apocalyptic vision is engendered in a British colony is relevant. It is Waugh's imperial anxiety properly speaking (i.e., the feeling that the Western hold on Africa is slipping) that infects even his customarily sure-footed, domineering discourse. Indeed, *Remote People* contains perhaps more passages of cultural and epistemological uncertainty than the rest of Waugh's travel writing taken together. He often breaks into admissions of his own incompetence as a describer of the foreign culture: "No catalogue of events can convey any real idea of these astounding days" (51); "I will not attempt any description of the ritual; the liturgy was quite unintelligible to me" (73); or "How wrong I was, as things turned out, in all my preconceived notions about this journey" (109). From this basis of insecurity and imperial anxiety, it is only befitting that the book should end on such a downbeat note. Like boredom, travel is no cure for the malaise of anxiety: on the contrary, Waugh found that it could only exacerbate it.

Social and Imperial Guilt: The Road to Wigan Pier

The signs of anxiety that punctuate George Orwell's travel writings derive from a guilt complex acquired during his service as an imperial officer in Burma and from a fundamental uneasiness about his middle-class upbringing. Orwell's book of social exploration, *The Road to Wigan Pier,* is therefore a testimony of ideological atonement—a process that is explicitly figured in terms of a journey, both literal and figurative. But it is also a journey of deracination that produces the exile's "anxiety of arrival." Up to his Spanish expedition, Orwell remained indeed an outsider to the social class whose membership he so strongly coveted. The result is, not surprisingly, a sense of anxiety, generated by the simultaneous desire for and repulsion from the object of his (political) desire.

As mentioned in chapter 1, the opening section of *Wigan Pier* is dominated by Orwell's inventory of the unsavory conditions that he encountered in the Brookers' boardinghouse. Quite tellingly, however, such details are accompanied by images of a haunted nature: "The place was beginning to depress me. It was not only the dirt, the smells and the vile food, but the feeling of stagnant meaningless decay, of having got down into some sub-terranean place where people go creeping round and round, just like blackbeetles, in an endless muddle of slovened jobs and mean grievances" (19). This almost Kafkaesque rendering of a working-class home is followed directly by references to repetition and boredom that echo Waugh's concerns with social routine in *Remote People:* "The most dreadful thing about people like the Brookers is the way they say the same things over and over again. It gives you the feeling that they are not real people at all, but a kind of ghost forever rehearsing the same futile rigmarole" (19). The images are telling: working-class people pictured as inhabiting a subterranean place, behaving like beetles, or, alternatively, as automaton-like creatures. Such representations manifest a high level of uneasiness, if not of outright anxiety, that Orwell himself experienced while dwelling among members of the working class.

Thus, in *Wigan Pier,* anxiety operates within a field of tensions that is generated by the disjunction between Orwell's intellectual desire for ideological assimilation and his inability to completely transcend his own class-consciousness.[7] Indeed, Orwell admits in *Wigan Pier* that there is an inseparable gap between him and the lower classes: "All my notions—notions of good and evil, of pleasant and unpleasant, of funny and serious, of ugly and beautiful—are essentially *middle-class* notions; my taste in books and food and clothes, my sense of honour, my table manners . . . are the products of a special kind of upbringing and a special niche about half-way up the social hierarchy" (162). The whole question of social justice, egalitarianism, and solidarity is bound up with the psychosocial construction of our very identity. And Orwell visibly recoils from the consequences of his own program: "For to get outside the class-racket I have got to suppress not merely my private snobbishness, but most of my other tastes and prejudices as well. I have got to alter myself so completely that at the end I should hardly be recognizable as the same person" (162).

Although Orwell desired an ideological transformation for himself, he presented this prospect ultimately in terms of self-alienation bordering on schizophrenia. Orwell even invokes the archetypal anxiety motif of darkness when referring to the removal of class distinctions. He calls "this class-breaking" a "wild ride into the darkness, and it may be that at the end of it the smile will be on the face of the tiger" (169), thereby linking "class-breaking" to being swallowed up and incorporated into the "other."

Orwell's reflections on social mobility and ideological transformation appear to be a rational, detached assessment of his own ambivalent feelings. But his analysis may become potentially harmful when one ponders the ultimate consequences it has for the lower classes.

For it means in effect that hermetic class barriers are erected around the lower and the middle and higher classes, making it virtually impossible for members of the proletariat to escape the confines of their social class. And if that is so, then the whole argument of social mobility, improving one's lot, gaining acceptance, and homogenizing society is defeated from the outset. Thus, although Orwell's honesty protects his social consciousness from the charge of hypocrisy, it also leads him into an ideological impasse in which ideas of rigid class structures assert themselves as the dominant factors of social life.

But the rift between Orwell's expressed sympathy for the working classes and his sense of ingrained class status goes deeper yet. Whenever he deals with "competitors" in this cause, especially other bourgeois socialists, he has only contempt for them. The famous diatribe against the "cranks" in the socialist movement (i.e., the "fruit-juice drinker, nudist, sandal-wearer, sex-maniac, Quaker, 'Nature Cure' quack, pacifist and feminist in England" [173–74]) reveals once again a high level of anxious demarcation of his own embattled ideological position and a defensive resentment against various marginal groups or social "others." Both his emphasis on the self-alienating results of social equality and his heated polemic against the supposed insincerity of organized socialism make it clear that Orwell felt threatened by the existence of "otherness," be it only the otherness of political schisms and subcategories within the leftist spectrum.

•   •   •

The relationship between guilt and anxiety has been spelled out in *Civilization and Its Discontents,* where Freud argues that "the sense of guilt is at bottom nothing else but a topographical variety of anxiety" (135). For Orwell, the process of ideological confession in *Wigan Pier* is a way of coming to terms with the anxiety that his guilty involvement with imperialism had entailed. And not surprisingly, recollections of guilt are frequently associated with feelings of hauntedness: "Innumerable remembered faces—faces of prisoners in the docks, of men waiting in the condemned cells, of subordinates I had bullied and aged peasants I had snubbed, of servants and coolies I had hit with my fist in moments of rage . . . haunted me intolerably" (149). For Orwell, serving in the British Empire was not so much an empowering as a haunting task. Indeed, his feelings of anxiety are intensified by the insistent repetition with which guilt-producing incidents follow one another. The need to enforce oppressive authority on a daily basis makes for a powerful sense of guilt, which the political system of imperialism strives to neutralize by appeal to justifications such as the "civilizing mission." But in the case of Orwell, the repression of his guilt was never successful, since his confrontations with local people reminded him constantly of the injustice he helped to perpetuate. Accordingly, by sympathizing with the oppressed and downtrodden, Orwell strives both to "expatiate . . . an immense weight of guilt" (149) and to combat his sense of anxiety.

The question of cultural, rather than class, boundaries becomes crucial in the context of Orwell's imperial experience. During his service in Burma, Orwell claims, he was ideologically paralyzed by the contradiction between his racially conditioned role as a master and his innate antipathy toward all forms of domination. The resulting crisis of identity is particularly evident in Orwell's famous essay "Shooting an Elephant." Due to his position of colonial overlord, Orwell complains, he had to perform the act of killing an elephant on the loose, although he was convinced that that action was quite pointless:

> They did not like me, but with the magical rifle in my hands I was momentarily worth watching. And suddenly I realised that I should have to shoot the elephant after all. The people expected it of me and I had got to do it. . . . And it was at this moment, as I stood there with the rifle in my hands, that I first grasped the hollowness, the futility of the white man's dominion in the East. Here was I, the white man with his gun, standing in front of the unarmed native crowd—seemingly the leading actor of the piece; but in reality I was only an absurd puppet pushed to and fro by the will of those yellow faces behind. ("Shooting an Elephant," 2231)

The contradiction between empowerment and disempowerment shows to what degree the colonial officer has himself been enslaved by the ideology he has come to represent. Ranajit Guha claims that at this very moment of indecision, pondering the task of shooting the elephant against his own will, Orwell is "seized by anxiety" (492) because he could have opted out of the colonial system at this point by throwing down the rifle. But, in Guha's view, only a high degree of complicity with the colonial system would produce such a conflict to begin with:

"Orwell's observations are simply the record of a common, if grum-
bling, compliance of the worker ant which carries the grain and the
honey of empire industriously, incessantly, and ever so obediently to
its queen" (490).

I agree with Guha that Orwell was to some degree posturing as an
antiimperial in "Shooting an Elephant." The roughly ten-year gap between the incident described in the essay and the writing of the story
throws a fictional coloring over the whole episode, thereby possibly
dramatizing a moral dilemma that was not perceived as such at the
time of the incident. One may wonder, for instance, if there were really
as many as "two thousand" bystanders crowding in on Orwell? Or is
his inadequate education really to blame for his complicity with imperialism as he suggests (after all, he graduated from Eton, one of England's top schools)? Was he really such an incompetent rifleman (the
protagonist of *Burmese Days,* closely modeled on Orwell, is an excellent shot)? Such matters of dramatization actually tend to distract
from the strange mix of antiimperialism and racism that pervades this
story. Chinua Achebe has famously attacked the implied racism of Joseph Conrad's supposedly antiimperial novella *Heart of Darkness,* and
one could mount similar arguments with regard to Orwell's tale, which
is replete with images like "sneering yellow faces" (2228). Moreover,
his novel *Burmese Days* capitalizes on the stereotypical image of the
despotic oriental ruler (represented by U Po Kyin)—elements that are
charged with what Guha calls "racial loathing" (489).

Undeniably, however, Orwell's use of these racially charged figures
is more self-conscious than Conrad's racially degrading imagery. By
openly admitting to his racist impulses, Orwell strives to control and
defuse "the intolerable sense of guilt" ("Shooting an Elephant," 2228)
that his dealings with the subjects of imperialism had caused. But as
in his relationship to the lower classes, his relationship to oppressed
races was not free of complications. In a strange passage in *Wigan Pier,*
Orwell compares the bodily features of Europeans like him with the
appearance of native Burmans:

> The white man has lank ugly hair growing down his legs and the
> backs of his arms and in an ugly patch on his chest. The Burman
> has only a tuft or two of stiff black hair at the appropriate places;
> for the rest he is quite hairless and is usually beardless as well.

The white man almost always goes bald, the Burman seldom or
never. The Burman's teeth are perfect, though generally discol-
oured by betel juice, the white man's teeth invariably decay. The
white man is generally ill-shaped, and when he grows fat he
bulges in improbable places; the Mongol has beautiful bones and
in old age he is almost as shapely as in young. Admittedly the
white races throw up a few individuals who for a few years are supremely beautiful; but on the whole, say what you will, they are
far less comely than orientals. (144)

This is an interesting variation on the theme of colonial desire. Although Orwell seems at first sight to produce a counterdiscourse that
exalts the "other" at the expense of the "self," the discursive parameters of a dominant stance assert themselves with a vengeance. For one
thing, Orwell displays an amazing confidence in lumping together "the
Burman" with "the Mongol" and, finally, "orientals," just as he essen-
tializes his own racial background ("white man," "white races"). Moreover, Orwell furnishes here an example of the fact that the colonizer "is
eclipsed by his fixation on and fetishization of the Other: the self becomes a prisoner of the projected image" (JanMohamed, 20).

   In other words, Orwell's idealization of the Burman body can be
read as an expression of colonial desire (and anxiety) that reduces the
"other" to a physical object and then provides it with desirable attributes that the self ostensibly lacks. In this manner, the "other" (of
whom Orwell says in another passage, "I felt towards a Burman almost
as I felt towards a woman" [*Wigan Pier,* 144]) turns out to be simultaneously the object of desire and a cause for self-loathing. Orwell's
supposed admiration of the Burman physique is further undercut if
we consider Orwell's attitude to the "yellow faces" he so intensely resented in "Shooting an Elephant."

   Thus, Orwell deals with racial difference in a manner similar to that
in which he deals with social difference—namely, by oscillating between deprecation and idealization. It seems that the ambivalence of
desire and guilt fosters a response to social or racial difference that
follows a predetermined path. It is a path that disregards relative difference, overlapping modes of identification, and subtle assessments
of dissimilarity. Even if we are to read the above passage as a reversal
of the colonial's stance of absolute superiority, it is impossible not to

consider the corollary of anxiety that attends this reversal. Indeed, Orwell's exultation of "the Burman" has a touch about it of envy, not to
say self-hatred, that betrays a deep sense of anxiety about the possibility of being eclipsed by members of another race.

Thanatos Looms: Black Lamb and Grey Falcon

Anxiety is almost too mild a term to designate Rebecca West's anguished confrontation with the historical record of violence, oppression, and betrayal in the Balkans. Even her outstanding rhetorical abilities failed her sometimes in dealing with the historical burden that
haunted this region. Occasionally *Black Lamb and Grey Falcon* contains scarcely articulate exclamations such as "Murder. Murder. Murder. Murder" (152) when the emotion overwhelms her, or convoluted
syntactical structures when the facts seem to contradict the principles
of logic.

These are exceptions, however: West's prose is generally lucid and
controlled, if not unpolemic. For instance, she calmly reports that her
host in Skopje "came back and sat by the lamp, his head on his hand,
and spoke of Mussolini in the West and Hitler in the North. It was clear
that he knew that perhaps no other pictures would hang on these
walls, that these pictures in front of us might some day be brought to
the ground with the slash of a bayonet and die under the hot tide of
their own glass when the smoke rose from the burning walls" (819).
But the real anguish lurking behind such controlled diction can be felt
on almost every page of the book. And it may be this constant tension
between West's sense of acute danger and the dictates of her refined
prose style that caused her to say that "this has seemed to me at times
an unendurably horrible book to have to write" (1126). On almost every page, *Black Lamb and Grey Falcon* registers the apprehensions that
had accumulated throughout the 1930s as a result of political and social tensions in Europe. Moreover, to write the narrative of Balkan history (a history she compared "with the smell of skunk" [127]), was a
hard, anxiety-ridden task.

The very proliferation of historical narratives in *Black Lamb and
Grey Falcon* bears witness to West's overwhelming sense of historical
anxiety, as she tries to make sense of the most horrible scenarios in the
history of Europe, including the prospect of another world war. Her
deliberate plunging into the sordidness of history parallels to some

degree the tendency of other 1930s travelers such as Greene or Orwell, who traveled to witness the worst social and political conditions they could think of. Of course, West's Fabian heritage caused her to look for traces of a meliorative historical narrative; but her experience as a woman and as a traveler on the Balkans made her realize that the destructive element was very deep, indeed, and that suffering and injustice held the upper hand in the history of mankind.

As a manifesto of liberation politics, *Black Lamb and Grey Falcon* propagates visions of national liberation and female emancipation; but as an account of history, the book offers a bleak perspective of the potential success of any liberationist project. It appears that all the evidence of her historical investigations pointed in the direction of a complete triumph of man's innate brutality, a fact that produces not only frustration in the present but also fear for the future. Accordingly, the epigraph of *Black Lamb and Grey Falcon* is deliberately phrased as an elegy: "To my friends in Yugoslavia, who are now all dead or enslaved."

All her fears, both historical and moral, past and contemporary, come to a head in the two sections of the book containing the key to the title's symbolism. In Macedonia she witnessed the ritual slaughter of lambs and cocks by Christian and Muslim supplicants, an incident that provided her with the emblem for her philosophical and religious thesis. Indeed, the sacrifice appears to her the very antithesis to the pursuits of beauty, compassion, and peace. Her loathing of this ritual is so strong as to cause an anguished response that borders on hysteria. West and her husband were invited by a Macedonian couple to witness the annual rite at the "Sheep's Field," where numerous animals are killed at Saint George's Eve to procure for childless women and unprosperous peasants the boon of fertility. But were it not for the fact that "the place had enormous authority" (823), West would have turned and fled the scene right after her arrival, so repulsive was the prospect: "The grass we walked on from the car was trodden and muddied and littered with paper, and as we came nearer the rock we had to pick our way among a number of bleeding cocks' heads. . . . It was the body of our death, it was the seed of the sin that is in us, it was the forge where the sword was wrought that shall slay us" (823). The controlled biblical diction of these sentences, fraught with references to the book of Matthew,[8] soon gives way to a flood of invective whose register and rhythm betray an immense force of apprehension and anxiety:

> The rite of the Sheep's Field was purely shameful. It was a huge
> and dirty lie. . . . Women do not get children by adding to the
> normal act of copulation the slaughter of a lamb, the breaking
> of a jar, the decapitation of a cock, the stretching of wool through
> blood and grease. . . . Those who have invented it and maintained
> it through the ages were actuated by a beastly retrogression, they
> wanted again to enjoy the dawn of nastiness as it had first broken
> over their infant minds. They wanted to put their hands on some-
> thing weaker than themselves and prod its mechanism to funny
> tricks by the use of pain, to smash what was whole, to puddle in
> the warm stickiness of their own secretions. (826)

It is in such instances of verbal "violence" that West's language departs from the discourse of metaphysics, aesthetics, and history to de-
scend to the regions of pure viscerality.

Her attack on the sordidness of the Sheep's Field ritual is studded
with nouns denoting concrete physical details: "act of copulation,"
"blood and grease," "stale and stinking blood," "the warm stickiness
of their own secretions." Here as elsewhere, West's feelings of anxiety
are channeled through the body. This is commensurate with her overall approach to Yugoslavia, which is indeed physical and personal in
spite of the often detached-seeming stylistic veneer of its discursive
rendering. Her first stay in that country (in 1936) had made her literally
sick, and it took her weeks to recover from the rigors of the trip. In a
certain sense, then, West's own body stands in for the country of Yugoslavia. Indeed, she personally felt the trauma of its impending vio-
lation by fascist aggressors, just as she identified herself with the black
lamb expiring on the sacrificial stone: "I knew this rock well. I had lived
under the shadow of it all my life" (827).

Clearly, for West the public domain of history resonates deeply in
the private echo chamber of her own life, causing what Montefiore defined as the "deliberate intertwining of individual and collective memory" (186) in *Black Lamb and Grey Falcon*. The mixing of public and
private spheres is carried over into a mixing of physical and spiritual
dimensions, as West often deploys a deftly physical, bodily rhetoric in
passages that deal with the moral and spiritual implications of sacri-

fice, death wish, and political resistance. After all, her attack against sacrifice and bloodshed in the service of goodness is not so much directed against the people who perform the ritual as it is against a particular form of spiritual corruption that constitutes the precondition for their behavior. West attacks a spiritual principle that pervades "all our Western thought"—that is, "the repulsive pretence that pain is the proper price for any good thing" (827). In engaging the body to discuss a moral and spiritual condition, West shows that, at the end of the 1930s, anxiety was not only socially pervasive but that it was felt beneath the skin, causing more than just ideological quandaries or political apprehensions.

In passages such as the above, where West drops her usual guard and abandons stylistic decorum, anxiety stares us in the face unmediated. It is an anxiety that often marks the return of a repressed, shadowy awareness about one's own social and moral position. Sometimes, West implicates herself in processes that she holds responsible for perpetuating the power of the death wish: "Then I cried out, for I had forgotten the black lamb, and it had stretched out its neck and laid its cold twitching muzzle against my bare forearm. All the men laughed at me. . . . I returned their laughter, but I was frightened. I did not trust anybody in this group, least of all myself, to cast off this infatuation with sacrifice which had caused Kossovo, which, if it were not checked, would abort all human increase" (917). As much as the current political threats, especially the rise of fascism and the specter of war, frightened her, the ultimate anxiety came from within. It is West's fear of giving in to the death wish herself, a fear that implies the return of a repressed desire, that constitutes the biggest anxiety felt throughout the book.

Even the great emperor of Old Serbia, Stephen Dushan, she says, "died in his prime as many die, because he wished for death; because this image of bloody sacrifice which obsesses us all had made him see shame in the triumph which seemed his destiny" (916). In a related section, West brings home the same point by associating English appeasement policy with "a compulsion to suicide" (1121). These words clearly indicate Freud's influence, especially his work in *Civilization and Its Discontents,* on the death wish and the struggle between Eros and Thanatos. But in contradistinction to Freud, who stressed the transhistorical, universal elements of psychic life, West emphasizes the contingency of emotional and historical orders of experience. For her, the death wish and the pacifist movement derive from specifically Christian, Augustinian doctrines, and thus from historical causes, and not from an innate, unchangeable destiny.

• • •

The personal perspective of West's approach to history also determines her presentation of Gerda, whom she constructs as an allegory for Germany's fascist regime. Gerda is the German wife of Constantine, West's Serbian guide (who in fact was the poet Stanislav Vinaver). Gerda delights in degrading the very virtues that West finds so attractive in the Slavic peoples. Whereas West says approvingly that "the Slav, who seems wholly a man of action, is aware of the interior life, of the springs of action, as only the intellectuals of other races are" (916), Gerda has only scorn for them: " 'It is stupid to be like that,' she said, 'you cannot like people who are stupid' " (464). In due course, the phrase "Gerda's Empire" (805) comes to stand metonymically for the treachery and destructiveness of empires everywhere. Thus, West uses Gerda as a personification for the arrogance of imperial domination, casting herself, by implication, in the shape of a liberal antagonist of Gerda's absolutist pretensions.[9] Accordingly, one of the climactic passages in the book is orchestrated as a personal confrontation between England's liberal ethos and Germany's totalitarian politics.

Gerda's praise of a war memorial at Bitolj, which reminded the local population of their own defeat at the hands of German invaders, causes West to fume with rage. But for once she leaves it to her husband, Henry Andrews, to put matters straight. In an angry speech, he upbraids Gerda on the memorial's bad taste, a reproach that triggers a chauvinist answer: " 'Now he has insulted my people! . . . It ought to be published in the newspapers that English people say such things. . . . But we Germans don't do such things, because we are too kind, and we want to be friends with England. But think of it, here I am, far from my home, and he insults my blood, the German blood!' " (763). Thinking back to this experience, West muses that " 'Gerda's empire cannot last long. But while it lasts it will be terrible' " (805), an apt prediction of coming events. In West's description, then, Gerda does not stand for female concerns and experiences, but rather represents all that is reprehensible in patriarchal, authoritarian power structures. This is to show that the destructiveness of the masculine ethos is not restricted to the male sex, but rather that it constitutes a spiritual and political force that also appeals to women.

In her attention to and simultaneous abhorrence of power politics, West's narrative fuses two separate strands that dominated England's discourse of history toward the end of the 1930s. From 1936 to 1938— that is for the duration of the Spanish civil war—politics could still be seen as a means of positive resistance and of possible renewal. However, a sense of resignation and even, at times, of nihilism began to spread after Franco's victory in the spring of 1938, a feeling intensified by Stalin's purges between 1936 and 1938. Then followed the "days of shame and bewilderment that followed Munich" (1118) in the fall of 1938, when Chamberlain made large concessions to Hitler. West toured Yugoslavia precisely during those years of gradual disillusionment with politics. But the writing of the book (certainly part of it) was contemporaneous with the London Blitz and the Battle of Britain.

Black Lamb and Grey Falcon, therefore, presents the reader with a complex mixture of activism and pessimism. It is neither a wholly resigned book, such as Graham Greene and Evelyn Waugh produced, with their invocations of universalized violence and historical "Waste Lands," nor is it a revolutionary book of unmitigated hopes and utopian aspirations. *Black Lamb and Grey Falcon* straddles the margins of both hope and despair, just as it invokes life and death as the defining characteristics of Yugoslavia's mystery.

• • •

In the foregoing discussions, I have outlined the particular dynamics of anxiety that were sparked by the historical and ideological tensions of the 1930s. Bad faith produced an intense feeling of ideological anxiety for Graham Greene during his trip in Africa; in Mexico, it was the feeling of collapsed cultural and racial boundaries that put the stamp of a haunted experience on his traveling. In both cases, anxiety signaled an elision of a difference, both ideologically (he fell back on middle-class values) and racially (he saw himself reflected in the Mexican condition). For Evelyn Waugh, feelings of anxiety resulted from a decadent cultural perspective that caused him to mock the very precepts of civilization that he implicitly relied on to rationalize his own sense of racial and cultural superiority abroad. His discourse of mastery is destabilized by the cultural anxiety breeding at the back of his mind, an anxiety that is duly acknowledged in the nightmarish quality of his journey and the realization that home and abroad are only mirror images of one another. In the travel writing of George Orwell, guilt is the sign of an incomplete social transformation (the ideology lagging behind the belief, as it were). In facing the poor and the colonized, Orwell is constantly torn between his liberationist, egalitarian ideals and his bourgeois background. And each time the repressed middle-class consciousness rears its head, the result is an uncanny impression. Rebecca West, finally, feels anxious because she recognizes the formidable power that the subconscious death wish holds over the human mind—a wish that colors both Christian and patriarchal belief systems, but also lodges in her own psyche. In all cases, however, it is the experience of spatial displacement that allows the repressed to surface and thereby causes the eruption of anxieties. In this sense, then, foreign surroundings had a catalytic effect on all four authors: they contributed to the destabilization of what had seemed settled and helped bring about important realizations as a result of these feelings of anxiety.

CONCLUSION

ALTHOUGH BRITISH travelers of the 1930s were os-
tensibly interested in political issues abroad, their observations and
judgments were deeply anchored in the historical imperatives and
dominant ideologies of their own society. For instance, the disjunction between Britain's rightists and leftists during the 1930s is clearly
reflected in Waugh's and Orwell's respective travel books. Evelyn
Waugh's travel writing spoke to the heart of those who yearned for authoritarian solutions to the specter of revolution, both at home and
abroad. He shrewdly used his authority as a traveler to further conservative, imperialist, and racist arguments. By comparison, George
Orwell's travel books were conceived as instruments of social change,
reassuring those who saw in the economic slump an indication that
social changes were impending. Using travel as a form of social exploration, Orwell tried to promote an ideological reorientation among
the members of the British middle classes, although this project was
hampered by the tenacity of his own bourgeois mentalities. Graham
Greene's progress from a search for innocence in Africa to the recognition of sin and fallenness in Mexico mirrors the transition of the
1930s from revolutionary hopefulness at the beginning to pessimistic
resignation at the end of the decade. Rebecca West, in turn, used her
travels to mount an attack against defeatist policies and to outline an
emancipatory program based on core British liberal values.

The destinations chosen by these travelers are indicative of their
homegrown ideologies as well, rather than reflecting a disinterested

approach to foreign politics. Leftists tended to go to places that were embroiled in class struggles or engaged in antifascist resistance. It was the London tramp circuit, the Chinese city under Japanese fire, the Spanish trench, or the war-ravaged Balkans that attracted politically engaged leftists such as Orwell, West, Auden, Isherwood, Spender, and others. Conservative travelers, on the other hand, tended to visit faraway places (mostly British colonies) that still exercised an exotic appeal (Waugh went to Africa and Latin America, Peter Fleming to Brazil and Central Asia).

This ideological affinity (or incompatibility) of certain locations with certain political convictions alone disqualifies any assumption about travel itself being inherently progressive or conservative. Although the experience of displacement and local conflict invariably impacted on the ideological beliefs of political travelers in the 1930s, there is no rule of thumb as to how it influenced them. Surely, going abroad did not make a leftist out of a conservative person, nor did it always contribute to a strengthening, in leftists, of reactionary social and cultural potentials. What it did, however, was to bring to the fore the travelers' most deeply felt, though not always openly admitted, ideological positions. In a sense, then, going abroad was the test that revealed the traveler's true political mettle. What Eric Leed said about the mind of the traveler in general is also applicable to the political identity of those who venture abroad. "In the difficult and dangerous journey, the self of the traveler is impoverished and reduced to its essentials, allowing one to see what those essentials are" (8).

• • •

One issue remains to be broached, however, and that is the question of whether the books treated in this study had any measurable political effects. This is not such an arcane line of inquiry as it might at first appear. In her book *Questions of Travel* (1996), Caren Kaplan maintains that "any effort to link world and text must begin by deconstructing the opposition between politics and aesthetics" (9).

I have been attempting throughout to deconstruct the perceived opposition between the aesthetic order of literature and the tangible dimension of historical reality. Surely, the texts covered in this study were precisely trying to breach the gap between the textual and the worldly realms. For instance, *The Road to Wigan Pier,* distributed to the members of the Left Book Club, was written and published with the

intent of furthering social change in Britain. Several other 1930s travelers also believed that their journeys would affect the paradigms of a
given political situation by tipping the balance of power in one direction rather than another. Their erstwhile enthusiasm faded, however,
as the desired results failed to materialize and the decade began to
slither toward its cataclysmic end. Hence, Waugh's *Robbery under Law,*
one of the decade's last travel books, displays little confidence in the
integrity and usefulness of its own political purpose: "Politics, everywhere destructive, have here dried up the place, frozen it, cracked it,
and powdered it to dust. . . . Today we are plague-stricken by politics.
This is a political book" (3). The frustration underlying Waugh's simultaneous invocation and denunciation of politics is based on the realization that despite dozens of politically motivated travel books, the
course of history was not affected by the busy traveling and writing of
a whole generation of authors.

   In fact, it was precisely the conservative travel books that were the
most spectacular failures in producing any tangible sociopolitical results. Evelyn Waugh's profascist rhapsodies were, many contemporaries felt, in addition to being rather embarrassing, mere effusions of a
conservative mind that would not prolong the lifespan of Italy's fascist
rule anywhere by so much as a single day. Indeed, Waugh's diligent
attacks on Ethiopian culture and its political figurehead Emperor Haile
Selassie proved to be ironically futile: Haile Selassie's term as emperor
even outlasted Waugh's own lifespan. Finally, the effect of Waugh's
Robbery under Law on the course of Mexico's oil expropriation was virtually nil, partly because the outbreak of World War II shortly after its
publication posed much more urgent threats than the economic fate
of the Cowdray petroleum estate. Even Greene's African travelogue
contributed little to the debate over slavery in Liberia and did not bring
an end to the country's repressive minority politics.[1] Greene's Mexican travelogue, finally, had no impact whatsoever on the fate of Mexico's Catholics, nor did it do much to raise anti-Cárdenas sentiments
in England.

   What about leftist travel books? By the criteria of Pierre Bourdieu's
model of cultural production, left-wing art should be eminently capable of producing measurable results: "The fact remains that the cultural producers are able to use the power conferred on them, especially in periods of crisis, by their capacity to put forward a critical

definition of the social world, to mobilize the potential strength of the dominated classes and subvert the order prevailing in the field of power" (*The Field of Cultural Production*, 44). But in a political reckoning of 1930s travel writing, progressive travel books do not fare much better than their conservative counterparts.

The impressive statistical evidence of *The Road to Wigan Pier*, combined with its descriptive vivacity, may have raised middle-class awareness about the calamitous social and economic conditions in England's primary industries, but it almost certainly did not influence people at the political command posts. Sir William Beveridge, the founder of Britain's collective social-security scheme, does not pay any tribute to *The Road to Wigan Pier* in his speeches and publications. The famous Beveridge Report, which was to become the blueprint for Britain's welfare state, instead relied on government-sponsored "social surveys" as the basis for his plan, not on publications such as Orwell's.[2] Eventually, Orwell's political testimony about the crisis in Catalonia did indeed contribute to discredit Stalinism in the West; and his "politics of truth," as Lionel Trilling termed it in 1952, even inspired anti-communist rhetoric in McCarthy's America. But the book had no effect on the political fate of the left-wing faction in the Spanish civil war, and its usefulness for the House Un-American Activities Committee (HUAC) cannot have been more than remote.

Of all the 1930s travel books treated in this study, only *Black Lamb and Grey Falcon* produced lasting effects. As a recent spate of books and reports on Bosnia, Serbia, and Kosovo has proven, no writer about the region can ignore the political and historical arguments set forth in *Black Lamb and Grey Falcon*. Not all references to the book are congratulatory, though. Those interested in practical political solutions denounce what they consider West's underlying ideology of tribalism. Richard Holbrooke, President Clinton's special envoy to the region in the 1990s, complained that "West's openly pro-Serb attitudes and her view that the Muslims were racially inferior had influenced two generations of readers and policy makers" (*To End a War*, 22). Similarly, Branimir Anzulovic states that "*Black Lamb and Grey Falcon* was inspired by hatred" (*Heavenly Serbia*, 171) and that the book, together with others, contributed to "the propagation of Serbian myths by hosts of Western writers, scholars, reporters, analysts, and politicians, result[ing] in monumental ignorance, which contributed to the outbreak of the war and did enormous harm to Serbia, among others" (171).

Naturally, Serbs themselves feel differently about this matter. Predrag Simic, for one, takes a highly complementary stance toward Rebecca West's Yugoslav book, arguing that

> the US had a positive opinion about the Serbs for decades. This was due to the wonderful book *Black Lamb and Grey Falcon* by Rebecca West, who was a friend of H. G. Wells and Stanislav Vinaver, and who described Yugoslavia and Serbian people in an almost epic way. Practically, the content of that book was the basis for American relations toward Yugoslavia; it had more influence than politics. Every American ambassador in Belgrade had that book—the possession of it was a sign of how serious one looked upon the mission of an ambassador in Serbia.[3]

Simic's comment highlights two crucial matters; namely, first, that *Black Lamb and Grey Falcon* is above all else a great work of literature, and second, that its effects are even more pervasive than politics. Surely, these two aspects are inherently related to one another, since the sustained popularity of the book was based primarily on its high literary merit rather than on its value as a factual guide to Balkan history—a function that could be fulfilled by any number of other publications. In a manner of speaking, the political influence of *Black Lamb and Grey Falcon* rode into posterity on the wings of its own epic aspiration.

But the political trajectory of *Black Lamb and Grey Falcon* is a complicated tangle of effects and side-effects. As indicated in chapter 4, it inspired the very man who turned out to be one of Serbia's most notorious nationalist politicians—Nikola Koljevic.[4] But it was through the mediation of another traveler that *Black Lamb and Grey Falcon* became once again enmeshed in the political process. Indeed, Robert D. Kaplan acknowledges *Black Lamb and Grey Falcon* explicitly in his influential book *Balkan Ghosts* (1993): "So [West] came to Yugoslavia to investigate the nature of the looming cataclysm, just as I came to investigate the nature of another looming cataclysm" (8). But while Kaplan's emphasis on the supposed immutability of old hatreds in the Balkans resembles West's take on the matter, *Balkan Ghosts* actually deviates in an important respect from *Black Lamb and Grey Falcon*.

Instead of being pro-Serb, as West's book certainly is, Kaplan's study takes a different approach. In the eyes of Predrag Simic,

> *Balkan Ghosts* . . . was just the opposite of Rebecca West's book. Kaplan hypothesizes that the Balkans generate hatred and that even Hitler learned to hate through the influence of Balkan, Slovenian, and particularly, Serbian people. With that he wanted to say that Serbs are no longer a freedom-loving, honorable, small nation striving to achieve the same ideals as America. On the contrary, he describes Serbia as an evil, genetically deformed nation. Among other influences, this book was the reason that the American public so easily accepted [NATO's] bombardment of Belgrade, Kragujevac, Cacak, etc. At the end of all this, it was concluded that the Serbian nation is the source of all problems and evil.[5]

Based on Simic's evaluation, *Black Lamb and Grey Falcon* had two entirely contradictory effects: first it fostered pro-Serb attitudes in the United States, and then, in the same country, through the mediation of Robert Kaplan, a strong anti-Serb bias. To add an additional layer of complexity: President Clinton is said to have read *Balkan Ghosts* while deliberating in 1993 whether or not to use force in Bosnia.[6] Ironically, though, Clinton derived the impression that the age-old tribal hatreds in the Balkans rendered any foreign intervention futile, an opinion that flatly contradicted Kaplan's own position on the matter.[7]

It all goes to show that political travel writing works in mysterious ways and that the authors of such books do not have a great deal of control over the eventual effect of their works in the public sphere. Compared with the discursive instability and the overall complexity of literary travel books, such as those analyzed in this study, the more straightforward rhetoric of investigative journalism allows less room for interpretive maneuvers. Moreover, the contents of news reporting can more easily be disseminated by a host of mass media with far greater range and visibility. Hence, the often spectacular results of news coverage, which manages to topple political figureheads (e.g., Watergate), bring whole industries to their knees (European boycotts of the fur trade), or launch global political protests (e.g., news of the Tiananmen massacre). The travel book, on the other hand, is primarily a work of art, whose mixture of empirical and symbolical discourses based on both objective and ultrasubjective insights ultimately defies the utilitarian purpose to which political travel writers themselves may want to put the genre. Moreover, by the time a travel book sees the light of publication, the political turmoils it reports on may either have subsided or mutated into new shapes, adding a further element of temporal distancing to this notoriously belated genre.

• • •

The faith of 1930s travel writers in the political utility of their books was a relatively short-lived phenomenon, too. Instead of offering straightforward political analyses and confident policy recommendations (as Kaplan does), the discourse of 1930s travelers was amalgamated by psychosocial anxieties, self-deconstructing dualisms, and political propaganda. As shown in chapters 5 and 6, any purposive political rhetoric in these travel books was systematically undercut by the destabilizing effects of psychological processes and by the epistemological disruptions caused by unstable binaries. At the end of the 1930s, travel writing as a form of political rhetoric had run its course, and World War II fostered the cynical opinion that politics was ultimately a game of power played by a few political figureheads—namely, Stalin, Hitler, Mussolini, Churchill, and Roosevelt.

After the war, political art and political traveling was little appreciated and perhaps even deemed an anachronism. It was a setback from which most 1930s travel writers did not recover: George Orwell lost interest in travel writing altogether; Rebecca West left her only other attempt at travel writing, a book about Mexico, unfinished; and Evelyn Waugh's only travel book written after the 1930s is of inferior quality. Indeed, *A Tourist in Africa* (1960) lacks the zest, originality, and interest of his 1930s travel writing. There remains Graham Greene, whose attempts at travel writing after the war also failed quite markedly. *In Search of a Character* (1961) and *Getting to Know the General* (1984) lack the compelling quality of his two 1930s travel books. Both works are primarily accounts of Greene's struggles with his imaginative resources. The bulk of *In Search of a Character* is dedicated to Greene's research among Congo's leper colonies as he was preparing to write *A Burnt Out Case* (1961). And *Getting to Know the General* chronicles Greene's friendship with the idiosyncratic dictator of Panama, General Omar Torrijos. Especially the rather tedious *Getting to Know the General* is little more than a substitute for a novel about Panama that

Greene never managed to write. Clearly, then, these authors' impetus
to write travel books had been spent almost completely once the 1930s
were over.

During the 1950s, books that tried to combine travel and politics
were not in demand, as travelers no longer fancied risking their necks
over political issues. Although the 1960s saw an outpouring of partisan
journalism about Cuba and China (see *Political Pilgrims*), it took the
civil wars in Central America during the 1980s to revive the tradition of
political travel writing, properly speaking. Both Joan Didion (*Salvador*
[1983]) and Salman Rushdie (*The Jaguar Smile* [1987]) produced fine
travel books about the region that were once again politically engaged
in a way that 1930s travel books were. Then followed the Balkan crisis
of the 1990s, which triggered an even larger number of politically motivated accounts of travel. Thus Carol Traynor Williams's observation
that in the 1990s "politics is more than ever the content of travel
books" (*Travel Culture,* xv) holds true. But there is a noteworthy absence of British writers among contemporary political travelers. It appears, indeed, that the tradition of political travel writing has passed
from British to American and postcolonial travel writers, and that the
shift has entailed a noteworthy and salutary renewal of this kind of
travel book.

For instance, the recent writings of V. S. Naipaul manifest an impulse to reorient the travel writer's perspective on foreign societies.
Naipaul investigates the closely knit interstices between the cultural
and the political spheres, and in doing so adopts a new tone—that is,
a blend of various discourses, specifically travel writing, investigative
journalism, biography, history, and anthropology. His excellent *India:
A Million Mutinies Now* (1990) and a clutch of articles for the *New
Yorker* dispense with the claptrap of adventure and the self-inflation
that have customarily been the stock-in-trade of conventional travel
writers. Instead, Naipaul cuts right to the chase of the political reality
in India or Iran, something he achieves by supplying his own perceptions with patient and inquisitive interviews among local people. By
shifting from the role of dominant commentator to a more humble
position of inquiry and observation, the situation of a given country is
allowed to come alive instead of being caricatured through overbear-
ing cultural biases.[8]

At a time when information about anything is all-pervasive and instantly accessible on the worldwide web, contemporary travel writers

have to give their subjects a new spin, either by piercing to levels of information that have not been previously mined or by judging, synthesizing, and questioning available data in unconventional ways. Several contemporary travel writers have risen to the challenge and produced remarkable travel books that embrace a more sophisticated cultural politics than the older examples of the genre. The best among them shed light on the subtle interrelations between people's personal lives and their political and economic contexts (V. S. Naipaul), they explore the local in its interconnection with transnational cultural and political processes (Pico Iyer), or they deconstruct media presentations of political hot spots such as El Salvador (Joan Didion) or Ethiopia (Robert Kaplan).

While all of these travel writers are politically engaged, only Robert Kaplan seems to be willing to cross the threshold from investigating and reporting to explicitly calling for political interventions to resolve conflicts abroad. This procedure is fraught with its own ideological problems, not to speak of the practical complications surrounding actual interventionist politics. In fact, it would be easy to denounce Kaplan's interventionism as a piece of neocolonial thinking that uses humanitarian motives as a smoke screen. Consider, for instance, the following statement in *Surrender or Starve* (1988): "Despite what African rulers say, the lack of an imperial tradition in the United States has hindered, rather than helped, its ability to be a force for positive change in Africa" (130–31). This comes dangerously close to vindicating American imperial ventures. But although Kaplan's call for military intervention in Africa recalls similar statements by Waugh, his ethical stance differs appreciably from that of his 1930s predecessor. While Waugh's attitude to Ethiopia was fueled by generalizing racist sentiments and a corrosive antihumanism, Kaplan's interventionism is based on a fundamentally humanistic, liberal impulse. Where Waugh denigrated both the Ethiopian government and its population, Kaplan targets the reprehensible politics of the country's leadership. Kaplan's dystopian account of Ethiopia ("Ethiopia is a *thugocracy:* thugs rule it" [*Surrender or Starve,* 9]) is not meant to discredit Ethiopia's cultural legacy, nor to ridicule the human dignity of its inhabitants. Instead it simply repudiates the conventional wisdom that a people gets the kind of government it deserves, because reckless warlords and cleptocratic rulers in postcolonial Africa just do not have the legitimacy of democratically elected governments elsewhere in the world.

Despite Kaplan's obvious efforts to be a fair, culturally sensitive, and self-critical observer of foreign societies, his work remains controversial. Richard Holbrooke sharply criticized the fact that "*Balkan Ghosts: A Journey through History* . . . left most of its readers with the sense that nothing could be done by outsiders in a region so steeped in ancient hatreds" (*To End a War*, 22). And the authors of a recent study on contemporary travel writing, Patrick Holland and Graham Huggan, attack Kaplan on account of his determinism ("Even climate and geography point to violence and atrophy" [*Tourists with Typewriters*, 211]) and because he is a cultural pessimist ("The travel account swerves into disaster journalism" [211]). Holland and Huggan also reject Kaplan's emblematic method—because "the constant deployment of vivid metaphor, in which such natural phenomena as seeds, eruptions, and conflagrations produce cultural effects, occludes both historical terms and the consideration of economics and politics" (211–12).

I am more willing than those two critics to commend Kaplan on his political and economic analyses. It is to his credit, for instance, that he does not usually proceed deductively in his explanations (as most 1930s travelers did). For instance, while Graham Greene tried to fit his impressions of West Africa onto a simple psychodynamic, spatial model, Kaplan's impressions in West Africa lead to the realization that "traveling . . . inevitably complicated my paradigm" (9). In fact, Kaplan's attempt to form a coherent theory about West Africa always entails a conceptual "mop-up operation" (9), as the model fails to explain the reality satisfactorily. Instead of imposing a predigested explanatory scheme upon any particular area of the globe, Kaplan vows to investigate how "culture, politics, geography, history, and economics were inextricable. Rather than a grand theory, the best I could now hope for was a better appreciation of these interrelations" (9). Moreover, in a critically productive move, Kaplan starts *The Ends of the Earth* (1996) by questioning the cultural authority and ideological hegemony inherent in cartographic projections: "Maps, so seemingly objective, are actually propaganda. They represent the lowest common denominator of the conventional wisdom. But what if the conventional wisdom is wrong? What if the Mediterranean basin is no longer the center of civilization?" (5) Such questions are indicative of a certain humility in the traveler, a stance that is rarely evidenced in the more cocksure travel accounts of the 1930s. Arguably, Kaplan's travel writing can be seen as harboring the seed for a new kind of cross-cultural rhetoric, one that is rooted in a self-reflexive kind of inquiry that constantly questions the premises of its own ideological and epistemological apparatus.

Moreover, even such "shortcomings" as Kaplan's determinism, pessimism, and his use of figurative language, hardly compromise the humanitarian aspect of his writings; nor do they diminish the artistic merit of his work. In fact, the very same "shortcomings" could be traced easily in what Peter Wolfe has called "the masterpiece of travel literature in our century" (*Rebecca West,* 26); namely, *Black Lamb and Grey Falcon.* West's book, too, has a strong pessimistic undercurrent, it is chock-full with figurative language, and the author's explanatory method frequently swerves toward determinism.[9] Also, the number of contradictions in West's "self-correcting masterpiece" (209), as Carl Rollyson termed *Black Lamb and Grey Falcon,* would equal or even exceed the number of inconsistencies that Holland and Huggan have spotted in Kaplan's *The Ends of the Earth* (*Tourists with Typewriters,* 212). Given these parallels, it is no surprise that Kaplan has found inspiration in Rebecca West's travel writing. In fact, he inherited West's basic method as well as her own self-image of the travel writer as a visionary cultural hero.

In a sense, then, the circle has been closed. Like many 1930s travelers, Kaplan feels that a global crisis is brewing, although the malaise he chronicles does not have the clear-cut political implications that attended the worsening international climate at the end of the 1930s. Nevertheless, Kaplan is convinced that a subtle sickness is spreading throughout parts of the world—a sickness that could end up undermining the very core of civic society if it is not recognized and opposed. In his diatribes against the politics of hunger, organized crime, and warlordism, Kaplan remains faithful to his American, liberal ideas of freedom, accountablity, compassion, and civil rights. But while he offers scathing opinions, he is no demagogue. Rather, he sees his role as that of a prophet warning those who stay moored in their private security "that we inhabit one increasingly small and crowded earth" (*The Ends of the Earth,* 9), and that it is better to register the warning signs before it is too late.[10]

Right now, it looks as though the gap between the industrialized societies and the underdeveloped nations is growing apace, with the digital divide acting as a powerful catalyzer for further divisions. It may not be a bad idea at such a time to pay attention to political travelers who, like Kaplan, traverse areas of conflict with the intention of recognizing a pattern and distilling a Zeitgeist from their observations in different places and among plural societies. As with 1930s travel books, the question to be asked should perhaps not so much be "What has been gained by political travel writing?" but rather, "What would have been lost without it?"

Contemporary political travelers such as Kaplan, Naipaul, Didion, and Rushdie provide a welcome corrective to the self-congratulatory, unpolitical journey narratives that are pouring onto the market. As James Clifford has put it, "there is no politically innocent methodology for intercultural interpretation" (19), and everybody who departs from the world's most industrialized nations to report on conditions in the less stable and less prosperous places of the world faces a host of ideological challenges. Moreover, due to the economic power wielded by such travelers, they also make de facto social and economic interventions. Now, if one's impressions abroad are dominated by injustice, maladministration, sickness, hunger, poverty, and war, then it is surely commendable to explore the roots and causes of such conditions — without, however, indulging superficial racist or ethnocentric views. Only an approach that is well-informed, discriminating, and politically sensitive can foster a perspective on foreign places that goes beyond selfish, unreflected appeals to exoticism, adventure, and simple sentiment.

NOTES

PREFACE

1. As Laurie McMillin observes, "from James Hilton's *Lost Horizon* to Peter Matthiessen's *The Snow Leopard,* something significant was supposed to happen to Western travellers in Tibetan lands" (49).
2. For a detailed account of these events and their political aftermath, see Ronald D. Schwartz's essay "The Anti-Splittist Campaign and Tibetan political Consciousness" (1994).

INTRODUCTION

1. Referring to the Victorian age, Andrea Lewis insists that "travel discourse during this time helped to accomplish and maintain Britain's empire because it gave voice to the actual geographical movement of British citizens through colonized territory" (47).
2. *Fellow traveler* is a translation of Trotsky's Russian term *popútchik.* A popútchik was someone who supported the general aims of the communists without specifically endorsing all of their policies. In his book *Fellow Travellers of the Right: British Enthusiasts for Nazi Germany, 1933–39,* Richard Griffiths applies *fellow traveler* to fascist sympathizers.
3. See Mark Cocker's account of the intelligence work performed by Eric Bailey.
4. From the comprehensive bibliography of travel books compiled by Michael Kowalewski, one can derive the following distribution of English travel books published per decade: 1900–1909: 23 titles; 1910–19: 29 titles; 1920–29: 52 titles; 1930–39: 72 titles; 1940–49: 22 titles.
5. Among the ten authors Fussell discusses in depth, only D. H. Lawrence and Norman Douglas wrote travel books before the 1930s.

6. This very ambivalence is the subject of Auden's poem "A Voyage" (1938), where the search for a "Good Place" is no sooner invoked than it is branded as an "illness," a "fever":

> Alone with his heart at last, does the fortunate traveller find
> In the vague touch of a breeze, the fickle flash of a wave,
> Proofs that somewhere exists, really, the Good Place,
> Convincing as those that children find in the stones and holes?

> No, he discovers nothing: he does not want to arrive.
> The journey is false, his unreal excitement really an illness
> On a false island where the heart cannot act and will not suffer
> He condones his fever; he is weaker than he thought; his weakness is
> real.

7. Richard Johnstone comments that "Communism and Catholicism were increasingly singled out in the thirties as the alternative cures for the sickness of a generation" (3).

1 GEORGE ORWELL

1. Paul Fussell points out that "etymologically a traveler is one who suffers 'travail,' a word deriving in its turn from Latin 'tripalium,' a torture instrument consisting of three stakes designed to rack the body" (39).
2. According to David Harvey, the geography of capitalism is "strongly differentiated. 'Difference' and 'otherness' is *produced* in space through the simple logic of uneven capital investment and a proliferating geographical division of labour" (6).
3. The Means Test allowed every household a fixed total income. Everything—savings, relatives' incomes, casual earnings—was counted toward the total sum allowed to each household, a sum that was barely above starvation level.

2 EVELYN WAUGH

1. "The world outside the Roman Empire was, in the eyes of the Imperial citizen, a sort of waste. It was not thickly populated, it had no appreciable arts or sciences, it was *barbarous*" (Belloc, 23).
2. Although Marxist critics such as Terry Eagleton (e.g., in *Literary Theory: An Introduction*) have consistently attacked the ideology of liberal humanism, they have not recognized that its opposite (i.e., antihumanism) may foster even more noxious social attitudes.
3. Samuel Johnson's first book, *A Voyage to Abyssinia,* is a translation from the French of Jerónimo Lobo's travel narrative. Lobo, a Portuguese Jesuit, entered Ethiopia in 1625 and stayed there, on and off, until the expulsion of the Jesuits.
4. The Ethiopian section of *Remote People* is clearly the central and most coherently developed part of the book, although *Remote People* is not only about Ethiopia. Waugh also visited Aden, which at that time was a British

protectorate, the colonies of Kenya, Uganda, and Tanganyika, and the Congo.

5. Waugh did not relish the pun on *War in Abyssinia*. The title was chosen by his editors at Longmans.
6. Waugh wrote to his literary agent that "a very rich chap wants me to write a book about Mexico. I gather he is willing to subsidize it. I am seeing him on Wednesday and will turn him onto you for thumb-screwing" (Sykes, 182).
7. The Sinarquists, a quasi-fascist movement formed in 1938, were never in a position to seize power in Mexico.

3 GRAHAM GREENE

1. Greene's anticommunism comes out clearly in his lampooning of the party functionary in *It's a Battlefield*.
2. Instrumental in this claim was Kathleen Simon's *Slavery* (London: Hodder & Stoughton, 1929), based on her and her husband's private investigations in Liberia.
3. "At gun point, Lieutenant Stockton attempted to convince 'King Peter' and other minor Bassa and Dei chieftains that the settlers came as benefactors, not enemies. . . . Hostility intensified as the settlers later pressed tribal residents into service as field hands and household domestics and imposed American forms of speech, justice, and commerce in the area under their control" (Liebenow, 16).
4. Barbara Greene explained that "it all happened after a wedding. 'Why don't you come to Liberia with me?' I was asked by my cousin, Graham, and, having just had a glass or two of champagne, it seemed a remarkably easy thing to do. I agreed at once" (1).
5. The following are examples of close correspondences between Barbara's and Graham's travel books:

G.G.: Here the women wore little silver arrows in their hair and twisted silver bracelets, beaten by the blacksmith out of old Napoleon coins. . . . The weavers were busy, and every piece of craftmanship we saw was light and unselfconscious. (133)
B.G.: The village blacksmith made rings and bracelets out of old Napoleon coins. . . . The women also wore beautiful little ornaments in their fuzzy black hair. There were men busy weaving cloth on their primitive looms. The patterns were simple, effective, and unselfconscious. (57)

G.G.: The great swallow-tail butterflies . . . rose in clouds round our waists at the stream sides. (157)
B.G.: Little streams we had to cross were covered with butterflies of every shade, that rose in a cloud and fluttered round us as we passed. (36)

G.G.: There was no view, no change of scene, nothing to distract our eyes, and even if there had been, we couldn't have enjoyed the sight, for the eyes had to be kept on the ground all the way, to avoid the roots and boulders. (156)

B.G.: There was nothing more to see. Never a view, never a change. Most of the time it was necessary to keep one's eyes fixed on the path in front, for it was always rough. (86)

6. From *Too Late to Turn Back:* "But they were child-like creatures, easily amused, living in the moment" (32); "Like children they came to us, pointing out their hurts with the utmost confidence that we could make them well again" (71); "This time he reappeared with an old school copy-book, on the outside of which was written in a child's laboured hand-writing, WRITING AND GOGRAPHY. VICTOR PROSSER, LAWFUL PROPERTY. 'I expect,' he said, in his serious, childish way, 'that you would like to read this during tea'" (141).

7. Karen Lawrence pointed out that "the plot of the male journey depends on keeping woman in her place. Not only is her place at home, but she in effect is home itself, for the female body is traditionally associated with earth, shelter, enclosure" (1).

8. Barbara Greene said about her cousin that "his brain frightened me. It was sharp and clear and cruel. I admired him for being unsentimental, but 'always remember to rely on yourself,' I noted. 'If you are in a sticky place he will be so interested in noting your reactions that he will probably forget to rescue you'" (6).

9. Mary Suzanne Schriber comments that nineteenth-century women travelers "marshal[ed] the discourse of colonialism . . . [and] 'produced' in their texts the European, African, and Middle Eastern, among 'Other' natives, particularly the native Woman, and then reveled in the privileges and superiority of American womanhood" (xxii).

10. However, this does not preclude the existence of psychological differences between male and female travel writing. Marianna Torgovnick has argued convincingly that women travelers can more easily convince themselves to "cast off . . . models of selfhood that were completely normative back home," while male travelers regularly "backed away from the oceanic, perceiving it as a danger to what Jung called 'the mature European self'" (*Primitive Passions*, 16).

11. Jean A. Meyer stresses the mutual basis of these *arreglos:* "the State acknowledged the impossibility of extirpating the Church and religion, and the Church legitimised the state and lent it its authority to domesticate the subject people" (211).

4 REBECCA WEST

1. Many of these articles are collected in *The Young Rebecca: Writings of Rebecca West, 1911–17*, edited by Jane Marcus.

2. In *Twilight in Italy*, D. H. Lawrence mentions his companion, Frieda, only in passing. Graham Greene, in *Journey without Maps*, virtually writes his cousin Barbara Greene out of existence, and Evelyn Waugh, in *Labels*, flatly denies the existence of his former wife as fellow traveler.

3. West insists that "there is not the smallest reason for confounding nationalism, which is the desire of a people to be itself, with imperialism, which is the desire of a people to prevent other peoples from being themselves" (*Black Lamb and Grey Falcon*, 843).
4. West emphasizes that churches built in the Serbo-Byzantine fashion "crouch low in the earth . . . housing something that should not be where people live, something that needs to be kept in the dark. . . . But shadow is also a sensible prescription for good magic, and Christianity as a religion of darkness has its advantages over our Western conception of Christianity as a religion of light" (*Black Lamb and Grey Falcon*, 710).
5. "Nineteenth-century writers of literary epic in the Balkans were asserting a nationalism in their writing that lauded the liberation and removal of foreign oppression. These ideals were equated almost exclusively with male identity" (Beissinger, 81).
6. Richard Tillinghast suspects "that Rebecca West, in rejecting suffering and sacrifice as a redemptive part of life, was kicking against the misery of her own early years, including the endless difficulties presented by her unhappy love affair with H. G. Wells" (21).
7. <http://www.srpska-mreza.com/mlad/>
8. The Serb translation of *Black Lamb and Grey Falcon* is only 420 pages long. The translator explains that those parts that constitute the common historical and cultural knowledge of Yugoslavs have been omitted. Koljevic also omitted many of the long digressions dealing with the history of Austria-Hungary.

5   THE TROUBLE WITH DUALISM

1. At the time of Victorian travelers such as Trollope, Froude, and Burton, the dualism between self and other was firmly modeled upon ethnocentric distinctions that were dictated by the imperial mindset and its distinctions between the metropolitan center and the savage periphery of empire. Such distinctions could not be maintained easily at a time of mounting unrest in the colonies, increased social tension at home, and adverse economic and political developments all around the world.
2. Anthony Trollope found in Jamaica the "one true and actual Utopia of the Caribbean Seas—the Transatlantic Eden" (128).
3. In an essay entitled "Marrakech," George Orwell wrote that "all people who work with their hands are partly invisible. . . . [And] where the human beings have brown skins their poverty is simply not noticed. . . . For several weeks, always at about the same time of day, the file of old women had hobbled past the house with their firewood, and though they had registered themselves on my eyeballs I cannot truly say that I had seen them" (27–29).
4. "In a world of diaspora, transnational culture flows, and mass movements of populations, old-fashioned attempts to map the globe as a set of culture

regions or homelands are bewildered by a dazzling array of postcolonial simulacra. . . . In this culture-play of diaspora, familiar lines between 'here' and 'there,' center and periphery, colony and metropole become blurred" (Gupta and Ferguson, 38).

5. This expression is dated slang based on the proverb "one can't change the spots on a leopard." Waugh uses this expression to indicate that London even outdoes Africa in terms of savagery.

6. "If things can really happen in Utopia, if real disorder, change, transgression, novelty, in brief if history is possible at all, then we begin to doubt whether it can really be a Utopia after all, and its institutions—from a promise of the fulfillment of collective living—slowly begin to turn around into their opposite, a more properly dystopian repression of the unique existential experience of individual lives" (Jameson, 95).

7. Richard Johnstone observes that "for Waugh, the individual's attempt to discover some temporal justification of his own significance is as illusory as Tony's search for the city. No justification exists. The final destination of the search is absurdity" (91).

8. Eschatology concerns "the teaching of the last things, such as the resurection of the dead, the Last Judgment, the end of this world and the creation of a new one." (Metzger and Coogan, 192).

9. Despairing comments about the fate of humanity are sprinkled throughout the book: "It's typical of Mexico, of the whole human race perhaps—violence in favor or an ideal and then the ideal lost and the violence just going on" (47); "caution returned—the expecting the worst of human nature as well as of snakes, the dreary hopeless failure of love" (143–44); "the blind eyes of the Spanish volunteers [to the civil war] were now beginning to open, like those of new-born children opening on the lunar landscape of the human struggle. . . . How could a world like this end in anything but war" (223).

10. For more background information on the figure of the whisky priest, see Sherry, *The Life of Graham Greene*, 1: 712.

11. <http://www.srpska-mreza.com/bookstore/kosovo/kosovo11.htm>.

12. For an example of this, visit the internet site Kosovo Heritage: <http://www.srpska-mreza.com/mlad/index.htm>.

13. <http://www.srpska-mreza.com/bookstore/kosovo/kosovo12.htm>.

14. "The cliché that left and right converge seems accurate. All parties share an aversion to utopian thought and universal concepts, although each is driven by a different logic" (Jacoby, 116).

15. Slavoj Žižek maintains that "the aspiration to abolish [radical antagonisms] is precisely the source of totalitarian temptation: the greatest mass murders and holocausts have always been perpetrated in the name of man as harmonious being, of a New Man without antagonistic tension" (5).

16. "Take for instance, the opposition between the individual and society, or

between individualism and holism, or totalitarianism: I really don't know what to put at the other pole" (Bourdieu, 179).

17. Loïc Wacquant explains that "Bourdieu affirms the *primacy of relations*. In his view such dualistic alternatives reflect a commonsensical perception of social reality of which sociology must rid itself" (15).

6 THE GEOGRAPHY OF FEAR

1. Sara Suleri insists that "the story of colonial encounter is in itself a radically decentering narrative that is impelled to realign with violence any static binarism between colonizer and colonized. . . . The necessary intimacies that obtain between ruler and ruled create a counter-culture not always explicable in terms of an allegory of otherness" (2–3).

2. "For all his eagerness to confront the primitive on its own terms, for all his professed contempt for England's contemporary civilization, Greene cannot break loose from his cultural world. He constantly uses familiar terms of reference to describe the strange land. A striking feature of the narrative is the succession of similes comparing Africa to England" (Monnier, 66). Referring to African books by Greene, Gide, and Waugh, Thomas Knipp argues that "imaginative Westerners imposed on Africa a collection of values and characteristics dredged up from their own subconscious by their own psychological needs. Africa was a state of mind" (3).

3. "The Uncanny" was published in 1919, but Freud explained in a letter that he had found the draft of this essay among old papers in a drawer. His reference to *Totem and Taboo* in the essay would situate its genesis at a time before 1913.

4. On this point I am at variance with Simon Gikandi, who concludes that Greene's "'journey without maps' has been pre-mapped all along" (189). Although Gikandi recognizes the "failure of [Greene's] own project" (188), especially his inability to validate the "primitive source" he had come to find, Gikandi does not register the confusion and contradiction at the heart of Greene's cultural and ideological undertaking.

5. For a full treatment of this anxiety motif, see *The Adventurer* (1974), by Paul Zweig.

6. According to historian Harold Marcus, "miracles were everywhere: triumphal arches rose on the main thoroughfares, electric lines suddenly appeared, telephones were installed in strategic locations, streets were graded and paved overnight, and, in some cases, sidewalks were laid down. The preparations were completed in the nick of time [for Haile Selassie's coronation], and many remarked about the capital's relative newness" (132).

7. Richard Hoggart states that Orwell "was reacting intensely against his social and educational background [and] was much of the time trying to cast off his class. But he always respected certain characteristic virtues of his

class, such as fairmindedness and responsibility. . . . In some deep-seated ways Orwell was himself characteristic of his class" (vii).

8. Janet Montefiore offers an in-depth discussion of the religious implications of this (and related) passages in *Men and Women Writers of the 1930s*, 197–99.

9. In her close comparison between West's travel diary of 1937 and *Black Lamb and Grey Falcon,* Janet Montefiore has disclosed the extensive amount of fictionalization that went into the making of "Gerda:" See *Men and Women Writers of the 1930s*, 209–15.

CONCLUSION

1. By comparison, André Gide's *Voyage au Congo* (1927) led to a parliamentary inquiry into the business practices of the French Compagnie Forestière and, eventually, to the revocation of their trading license for the Congo. If nothing else, this suggests that French intellectuals had a greater purchase on their country's political elite than their peers had in England. One is reminded of the great stir caused by Satre, de Beauvoir, et al. when they opposed France's war in Algeria.

2. In all the literature that I surveyed, the development of Britain's social-security system in the early 1940s is nowhere linked explicitly to Orwell's writings. Even a study whose title could be taken to allude to *The Road to Wigan Pier*—Karl de Schweinitz's *England's Road to Social Security* (1943)—does not contain a reference to Orwell.

3. <http://news.suc.org/interviews/Simic/index.html>, translated from Serbo-Croatian by Sandra Orsulic.

4. Nikola Koljevic was for a while the right-hand man of Radovan Karadzic, an indited war criminal. After losing his influence with the Bosnian-Serb leadership, in 1997 Koljevic committed suicide.

5. <http://news.suc.org/interviews/Simic/index.html>, Orsulic trans.

6. "In 1993, just as President Clinton was contemplating forceful action to halt the war in Bosnia, he and Mrs. Clinton are said to have read *Balkan Ghosts.* The history of ethnic rivalry I detailed reportedly encouraged the President's pessimism about the region, and—it is said—was a factor in his decision not to launch an overt military response in support of the Bosnian Moslems" (Kaplan, x).

7. Kaplan protests that "since the first half of 1993, I have publicly advocated military action in support of the Bosnian Moslems, even raising the possibility of U.S. ground troops" (*Balkan Ghosts*, xi).

8. Naipaul's recent travel writings contrast sharply with the travel books he wrote at an earlier stage of his career: *An Area of Darkness* (1964) and *The Middle Passage* (1962), especially, display a disturbing amount of opinionated comment in the imperial manner. Beginning with *India: A Million Mutinies Now* (1990), Naipaul reinvented his approach to travel writing, taking a more flexible, inquisitive, and fair-minded approach to foreign societies.

9. In *St. Augustine,* written shortly before her trips to Yugoslavia, West states that "we exercise what looks like a free faculty of choice, but the way we exercise that faculty depends on our innate qualities and our environment, and these always bind us in some way or another to the neuroses which compel us to choose death rather than life" (215).

10. Robert Kaplan warns that "if the past is any guide, in too many places there will be a time lag between extreme social deterioration and strategies which might have prevented it. The long-range future might be bright, but the next few decades will be tumultous" (*The Ends of the Earth,* 437).

BIBLIOGRAPHY

Achebe, Chinua. "An Image of Africa: Racism in Conrad's *Heart of Darkness.*" In Joseph Conrad, *Heart of Darkness*, ed. R. Kimbrough, pp. 251–62. New York: Norton Critical Edition, 1988.

Anderson, R. Earle. *Liberia, America's African Friend.* Chapel Hill: University of North Carolina Press, 1952.

Anzulovic, Branimir. *Heavenly Serbia: From Myth to Genocide.* New York: New York University Press, 1999.

Auden. W. H. *Collected Poems.* Ed. Edward Mendelson. London: Faber & Faber, 1976.

Authors Take Sides on the Spanish War. London: Left Review, 1937.

Bailey, David. *Viva Christo Rey! The Cristero Rebellion and the Church-State Conflict in Mexico.* Austin: University of Texas Press, 1974.

Beauchamp, Gorman. "Zamiatin's *We.*" In *No Place Else: Explorations in Utopian and Dystopian Fiction*, ed. Eric Rabkin, Martin Greenberg, and Joseph Olander, pp. 56–77. Carbondale: Southern Illinois University Press, 1983.

Behdad, Ali. *Belated Travelers: Orientalism in the Age of Colonial Dissolution.* Durham: Duke University Press, 1994.

Beissinger, Margaret. "Epic, Gender, and Nationalism: The Development of Nineteenth-Century Balkan Literature." In *Epic Traditions in the Contemporary World: The Poetics of Community*, ed. Margaret Beissinger, Jane Tylus, and Susanne Wofford. Berkeley: University of California Press, 1999.

Belloc, Hilaire. *Europe and the Faith.* London: Burns & Oates, 1920.

Bergonzi, Bernard. "*Nineteen Eighty-Four* and the Literary Imagination." In *Between Dream and Nature: Essays on Utopia and Dystopia*, ed., Dominic Baker-Smith and C. C. Barfoot, pp. 211–28. Amsterdam: Rodophi, 1987.

Bhabha, Homi. *The Location of Culture.* London: Routledge, 1994.

Blunt, Alison. *Travel, Gender, and Imperialism: Mary Kingsley and West Africa.* New York: Guilford Press, 1994.

Bogdanovic, Dimitrije. <http://www.srpska-mreza.com / bookstore / kosovo / kosovo12.htm>. Accessed Oct. 15, 2000.

Bourdieu, Pierre, and Wacquant Loïc. *An Invitation to Refexive Sociology*. Chicago: University of Chicago Press, 1992.

Bourdieu, Pierre. *The Field of Cultural Production: Essays on Art and Literature*. New York: Columbia University Press, 1993.

Brandenburg, Frank. *The Making of Modern Mexico*. Englewood Cliffs: Prentice-Hall, 1964.

Branson, Noreen, and Margot Heinemann. *Britain in the Nineteen Thirties*. London: Weidenfeld & Nicolson, 1971.

Camin, Hector Aguilar. *In the Shadow of the Mexican Revolution: Contemporary Mexican History, 1910–1989*. Austin: University of Texas Press, 1993.

Carens, James F. *The Satiric Art of Evelyn Waugh*. Seattle: University of Washington Press, 1966.

Chamberlain, Lesley. "Rebecca West in Yugoslavia." *Contemporary Review* 248, no. 1444 (1986): 262–66.

Clifford, James. *Routes: Travel and Translation in the Late Twentieth Century*. Cambridge: Harvard University Press, 1997.

Cocker, Mark. *Loneliness and Time: The Story of British Travel Writing*. New York: Pantheon Books, 1992.

Conrad, Joseph. *Heart of Darkness*. London: Penguin, 1995.

Crick, Bernard. *George Orwell: A Life*. Boston: Little, Brown, 1980.

Cunningham, Valentine. *British Writers of the Thirties*. Oxford: Oxford University Press, 1988.

Didion, Joan. *Salvador*. New York: Simon & Schuster, 1983.

Dodd, Philip. "The Views of Travelers: Travel Writing in the '30s." *Prose Studies* 5, no. 1 (1982): 127–38.

Dorich, William. <http://www.srpska-mreza.com/bookstore/kosovo/kosovo.htm>. Accessed Oct. 15, 2000.

Emmert, Thomas. <http://www.srpska-mreza.com/bookstore/kosovo/kosovo11.htm>. Accessed Oct. 15, 2000.

Fleming, Peter. "The Man from Rangoon." In *Views from Abroad: The Spectator Book of Travel Writing*, ed. Philip Marsden-Smedley and Jeffrey Klinke, pp. 6–9. London: Grafton Books, 1988.

Freud, Sigmund. *The Standard Edition of the Complete Psychological Works of Sigmund Freud*. Trans. James Strachey. London: Hogarth Press, 1953.

Fussell, Paul. *Abroad: British Literary Traveling between the Wars*. Oxford: Oxford University Press, 1980.

Gardner, Averil. *George Orwell*. Boston: Twayne, 1987.

Geertz, Clifford. *The Interpretation of Cultures: Selected Essays*. New York: Basic Books, 1973.

Gide, André. *Travels in the Congo*. Trans. Dorothy Bussy. New York: Modern Age Books, 1937.

Gikandi, Simon. *Maps of Englishness: Writing Identity in the Culture of Colonialism*. New York: Columbia University Press, 1996.

Gingras, George. "Travel." In *Dictionary of Literary Themes and Motifs*. New York: Greenwood Press, 1988.

Gladt, Karl. *Kaisertraum und Königskrone: Aufstieg und Untergang einer serbischen Dynastie*. Graz: Verlag Styria, 1972.

Glendinning, Victoria. *Rebecca West: A Life*. London: Weidenfeld & Nicolson, 1987.

Gloversmith, Frank. "Changing Things: Orwell and Auden." In *Class, Culture, and Social Change: A New View of the '30s*, ed. Frank Gloversmith. Sussex: Harvester Press, 1980.

Goodwin, Barbara, and Keith Taylor. *The Politics of Utopia: A Study in Theory and Practice*. London: Hutchinson, 1982.

Graves, Robert, and Alan Hodge. *The Long Week End: A Social History of Great Britain, 1918–1939*. New York: Macmillan, 1941.

Greene, Barbara. *Too Late to Turn Back*. London: Settle Bendall, 1981.

Greene, Graham. *Collected Essays*. New York: Viking Press, 1951.

———. *England Made Me*. Heinemann/Bodley Head, 1935.

———. *In Search of a Character: Two African Journals*. London: Bodley Head, 1961.

———. *It's a Battlefield*. London: Heinemann/Bodley Head, 1934.

———. *Journey without Maps*. London: Penguin, 1971.

———. *The Lawless Roads*. London: Penguin, 1982.

———. *The Other Man: Conversations with Graham Greene*, ed. Marie-Françoise Allain. Trans. from the French by Guido Waldman. London: Bodley Head, 1983.

———. *The Power and the Glory*. New York: Penguin, 1940.

———. *Ways of Escape*. New York: Simon & Schuster, 1980.

Griffiths, Richard. *Fellow Travellers of the Right: British Enthusiasts for Nazi Germany, 1933–9*. London: Constable, 1980.

Guha, Ranajit. "Not at Home in Empire." *Critical Inquiry* 23, no. 3 (1997): 482–93.

Gupta, A., and J. Ferguson. *Culture, Power, Place: Explorations in Critical Anthropology*. Durham: Duke University Press, 1997.

Harvey, David. "From Space to Place and Back Again: Reflections on the Condition of Postmodernity." In *Mapping the Futures: Local Cultures, Global Change*, pp. 3–29. London: Routledge, 1993.

Hobsbawn, Eric. *The Age of Extremes: The Short Twentieth Century, 1914–1991*. London: Abacus, 1994.

Hoggart, Richard. Introduction to *The Road to Wigan Pier*, by George Orwell. London: Heinemann, 1965.

Holbrooke, Richard. *To End a War*. New York: Modern Library, 1998.

Holland, Patrick, and Graham Huggan. *Tourists with Typewriters: Critical Reflections on Contemporary Travel Writing*. Ann Arbor: University of Michigan Press, 1998.

Hollander, Paul. *Political Pilgrims: Travels of Western Intellectuals to the Soviet Union, China, and Cuba, 1928–1978*. Oxford: Oxford University Press, 1981.

Holton, Milne, and Vasa Mihailovich. *Serbian Poetry from the Beginnings to the Present.* New Haven: Yale Center for International and Area Studies, 1988.

Huxley, Aldous. *Beyond the Mexique Bay.* London: Chatto & Windus, 1974.

Hynes, Samuel. *The Auden Generation: Literature and Politics in England in the '30s.* London: Bodley Head, 1976.

Isherwood, Christopher, and W. H. Auden. *Journey to a War.* London: Faber & Faber, 1939.

Iyer, Pico. *Video Night in Kathmandu and Other Reports from the Not-So-Far-East.* New York: Alfred Knopf, 1988.

Jacoby, Russell. *The End of Utopia: Politics and Culture in an Age of Apathy.* New York: Basic Books, 1999.

James, JoAnn, and William J. Cloonan, eds. *Apocalyptic Visions Past and Present.* Tallahassee: Florida State University Press, 1988.

Jameson, Fredric. *The Ideologies of Theory: Essays, 1971–1986,* vol. 2: *The Syntax of History.* Minneapolis: University of Minnesota Press, 1988.

JanMohamed, Abdul. *Manichean Aesthetics: The Politics of Literature in Colonial Africa.* Amherst: University of Massachusetts Press, 1983.

Johnson, Samuel. *A Voyage to Abyssinia.* Trans. Joel J. Gold. New Haven: Yale University Press, 1985.

Johnstone, Richard. "Travelling in the Thirties." *London Magazine* 20, nos. 5 and 6 (1980): 90–96.

———. *The Will to Believe: Novelists of the Nineteen-thirties.* Oxford: Oxford University Press, 1982.

Kaplan, Caren. *Questions of Travel: Postmodern Discourses of Displacement.* Durham: Duke University Press, 1996.

Kaplan, Robert D. *Balkan Ghosts: A Journey through History.* New York: Vintage Books, 1993.

———. *The Ends of the Earth: A Journey to the Frontiers of Anarchy.* New York: Vintage Books, 1996.

———. *Surrender or Starve: The Wars behind the Famine.* Boulder: Westview Press, 1988.

———. "What Makes History." *Atlantic Monthly* 285, no. 3 (2000): 18–20.

Knipp, Thomas. "Gide and Greene: Africa and the Literary Imagination." *Serif* 6, no. 2 (1969): 3–14.

Koljevic, Nikola. Foreword to *Crno Jagnje i Sivi Soko,* by Rebeke Vest. Trans. Nikola Koljevic. 4th ed. Belgrade: BIGZ, 2000.

Kosovo Heritage 1. <http://www.srpska-mreza.com/mlad/index.htm>. Accessed Oct. 15, 2000.

Kowalewski, Michael, ed. *Temperamental Journeys: Essays on the Modern Literature of Travel.* Athens: University of Georgia Press, 1992.

Lawrence, Karen. *Penelope Voyages: Women and Travel in the British Literary Tradition.* Ithaca: Cornell University Press, 1994.

Leed, Eric J. *The Mind of the Traveler: From Gilgamesh to Global Tourism.* New York: Basic Books, 1991.

Lewis, Andrea. "A 'Nasrani' Woman Goes Native: Englishness in Rosita Forbes's *The Secret of the Sahara Kufaru.*" *Ariel* 27, no. 4 (1996): 47–67.

Liebenow, Gus J. *Liberia: The Quest for Democracy.* Indianapolis: Indiana University Press, 1987.

Lodge, David. *Evelyn Waugh.* New York: Columbia University Press, 1971.

London, Jack. *The People of the Abyss.* Ed. I. O. Evans. New York: Archer House, 1963.

Malcolm, Noel. *Kosovo: A Short History.* New York: New York University Press, 1998.

Marcus, Harold. *A History of Ethiopia.* Berkeley: University of California Press, 1994.

Marcus, Jane. *The Young Rebecca: Writings of Rebecca West, 1911–17.* New York: Viking Press/Virago, 1982.

Mayhew, Henry. *The Morning Chronicle Survey of Labour and the Poor: The Metropolitan Districts,* vol. 1. Sussex: Caliban Books, 1980.

McMillin, Laurie H. "Enlightenment Travels: The Making of Epiphany in Tibet." In *Writes of Passage: Reading Travel Writing,* pp. 49–69. New York: Routledge, 1999.

Mercer, Wendy. "Gender and Genre in Nineteenth-century Travel Writing: Leonie d'Aunet and Xavier Marmier." In *Travel Writing and Empire: Postcolonial Theory in Transit,* ed. Steve Clark, pp. 147–63. London: Zed Books, 1999.

Metzger, Bruce M., and Michael D. Coogan. *The Oxford Companion to the Bible.* Oxford: Oxford University Press, 1993.

Meyer, Jean A. *The Cristero Rebellion: The Mexican People between Church and State, 1926–1929.* Trans. Richard Southern. Cambridge: Cambridge University Press, 1976.

Mockler, Anthony. *Graham Greene: Three Lives.* Arbroath: Hunter Mackay, 1994.

Monnier, Jean-Yves. "Myth and Reality: Graham Greene's View of Africa." *Commonwealth* 11, no. 1 (1988): 61–69.

Montefiore, Janet. *Men and Women Writers of the 1930s.* London: Routledge, 1996.

Mowat, Charles Loch. *Britain between the Wars, 1918–1940.* London: Methuen, 1955.

Muggeridge, Malcom. *The Thirties: 1930–1940 in Great Britain.* London: Collins, 1940.

Musgrove, Brian. "Travel and Unsettlement: Freud on Vacation." In *Travel Writing and Empire: Postcolonial Theory in Transit,* ed. Steve Clark, pp. 31–44. London: Zed Books, 1999.

Naipaul, V. S. *An Area of Darkness.* New York: Macmillan, 1964.

———. *India: A Million Mutinies Now.* London: Minerva, 1990.

Ogude, S. W. "In Search of Misery: A Study of Graham Greene's Travels in Africa." *Odu* 11 (January 1975): 45–60.

Oliver, Roland A., and J. D. Fage. *A Short History of Africa.* 5th ed. Harmondsworth: Penguin, 1975.

Orwell, George. *Burmese Days*. London: Victor Gollancz, 1935.

———. *Collected Essays*. London: Secker & Warburg, 1961.

———. *Down and Out in Paris and London*. London: Victor Gollancz, 1933.

———. *Homage to Catalonia*. San Diego: Harcourt Brace Jovanovich, 1952.

———. *Keep the Aspidistra Flying*. London: Victor Gollancz, 1936.

———. *The Road to Wigan Pier*. London: Victor Gollancz, 1937.

———. "Shooting an Elephant." In *Norton Anthology of English Literature*, vol. 2, 6th ed., ed. M. H. Abrams, pp. 2228–33. New York: W. W. Norton, 1993.

Porter, Dennis. *Haunted Journeys, Desire and Transgression in European Travel Writing*. Princeton: Princeton University Press, 1991.

Pratt, Mary Louise. *Imperial Eyes: Travel Writing and Transculturation*. London: Routledge, 1992.

Priestley, J. B. *English Journey*. Chicago: University of Chicago Press, 1934.

Pynsent, Robert B., ed. *Decadence and Innovation: Austro-Hungarian Life and Art at the Turn of the Century*. London: Weidenfeld & Nicolson, 1989.

Rabkin, Eric S. "Atavism and Utopia." In *No Place Else: Explorations in Utopian and Dystopian Fiction*, ed. Rabkin, Greenberg, and Olander, pp. 1–10.

———. "Why Destroy the World?" Introduction to *The End of the World*, ed. Eric S. Rabkin, Martin H. Greenberg, and Joseph D. Olander, pp. vii–xv. Carbondale: Southern Illinois University Press, 1983.

Rancière, Jacques. "Discovering New Worlds: Politics of Travel and Metaphors of Space." In *Travellers' Tales: Narratives of Home and Displacement*, ed. George Robertson, Melinda Mash, Lisa Tickner, Jon Bird, Barry Curtis, and Tim Putnam, pp. 29–37. London: Routledge, 1994.

Rollyson, Carl. *Rebecca West: A Saga of the Century*. London: Hodder & Stoughton, 1995.

Rosslyn, Felicity. "Rebecca West, Gerda, and the Sense of Process." In *Black Lambs and Grey Falcons: Women Travellers in the Balkans*, ed. John B. Allcock and Antonia Young, pp. 102–15. Bradford: Bradford University Press, 1991.

Rushdie, Salman. *The Jaguar Smile: A Nicaraguan Journey*. London: Picador, 1987.

Schorske, Carl E. *Fin-de-Siècle Vienna: Politics and Culture*. New York: Knopf, 1980.

Schriber, Mary Suzanne. *Telling Travels*. Dekalb: Northern Illinois University Press, 1995.

Schwartz, Ronald D. "The Anti-Splittist Campaign and Tibetan Political Consciousness." In *Resistance and Reform in Tibet*, ed. Robert Barnett, pp. 207–37. London: Hurst, 1994.

Shelden, Michael. *Orwell: The Authorized Biography*. New York: Harper Collins, 1991.

Sherry, Norman. *The Life of Graham Greene*. Vols. 1–3. New York: Viking Press, 1989.

Simic, Predrag. <http://news.suc.org/interviews/Simic/index.html>. Accessed Oct. 15, 2000.

Simon, Kathleen. *Slavery*. London: Hodder & Stoughton, 1929.

Skelton, Robin, ed. *Poetry of the Thirties.* Harmondsworth: Penguin, 1964.

Smith, Grahame. *The Achievement of Graham Greene.* Sussex: Harvester Press, 1986.

Spender, Stephen. *The Destructive Element.* London: Jonathan Cape, 1935.

Sperber, Murray A. " 'Marx: G. O.'s Dog': A Study of Politics and Literature in George Orwell's *Homage to Catalonia.*" *Dalhousie Review* 52 (1972): 226–36.

Stannard, Martin. "Debunking the Jungle: The Context of Evelyn Waugh's Travel Books, 1930–39." *Prose Studies* 5, no. 1 (1982): 105–25.

———. *Evelyn Waugh: The Early Years, 1903–1939.* London: J. M. Dent & Sons, 1986.

Stec, Loretta. "Female Sacrifice: Gender and Nostalgic Nationalism in Rebecca West's *Black Lamb and Grey Falcon.* In *Narratives of Nostalgia, Gender, and Nationalism,* ed. Jean Pickering and Suzanne Kehde, pp. 138–58. New York: New York University Press, 1997.

Stevenson, Catherine B. *Victorian Women Travel Writers in Africa.* Boston: Twayne, 1982.

Suleri, Sara. *The Rhetoric of English India.* Chicago: University of Chicago Press, 1992.

Sykes, Christopher. *Evelyn Waugh: A Biography.* London: Collins, 1975.

Symons, Julian. *The Thirties: A Dream Revolved.* Westport Conn.: Greenwood Press, 1960.

Tillinghast, Richard. "The Tragedy of Yugoslavia." *New Criterion* 10, no. 10 (1992): 12–22.

Torgovnick, Marianna. *Primitive Passions.* New York: Alfred Knopf, 1997.

Trilling, Lionel. "George Orwell and the Politics of Truth." In *George Orwell: A Collection of Critical Essays,* ed. Raymond Williams. Englewood Cliffs: Prentice-Hall, 1974.

Trollope, Anthony. *The West Indies and the Spanish Main.* London: Cass, 1968.

Van den Abbeele, Georges. *Travel as Metaphor: From Montaigne to Rousseau.* Minneapolis: University of Minnesota Press, 1992.

Wacquant, Loïc, and Pierre Bourdieu. *An Invitation to Reflexive Sociology.* Chicago: University of Chicago Press, 1992.

Waugh, Evelyn. *Black Mischief.* London: Chapman & Hall, 1932.

———. *Decline and Fall.* Boston: Little, Brown, 1946.

———. *The Diaries of Evelyn Waugh,* ed. Michael Davie. London: Weidenfeld & Nicolson, 1976.

———. *The Essays, Articles, and Reviews of Evelyn Waugh,* ed. Donat Gallagher. London: Methuen, 1983.

———. *A Handful of Dust.* London: Chapman & Hall, 1934.

———. *Labels: A Mediterranean Journey.* London: Duckworth, 1930.

———. *A Little Learning: The First Volume of an Autobiography.* London: Sidgwick & Jackson, 1964.

———. *Ninety-two Days.* London: Methuen, 1991.

———. *Remote People.* London: Methuen, 1991.

———. *Robbery under Law: The Mexican Object Lesson.* London: Chapman & Hall, 1939.

———. *Scoop*. Boston: Little, Brown, 1937.

———. *Tourist in Africa*. London: Chapman & Hall, 1960.

———. *Vile Bodies*. London: Chapman & Hall, 1930.

———. *Waugh in Abyssinia*. London: Longmans, Green, 1936.

———. *When the Going Was Good*. Boston: Little, Brown, 1947.

West, Rebecca. *Black Lamb and Grey Falcon*. New York: Penguin, 1941.

———. *A Celebration: Selected from Her Writings*. London: Macmillan, 1977.

Williams, Carol Traynor. *Travel Culture: Essays on What Makes Us Go*. Westport: Praeger, 1998.

Wolfe, Peter. *Rebecca West: Artist and Thinker*. Carbondale: Southern Illinois University Press, 1971.

Yaeger, Patricia. Introduction to *The Geography of Identity*, ed. Patricia Yaeger. Ann Arbor: University of Michigan Press, 1996.

Žižek, Slavoj. *The Sublime Object of Ideology*. London: Verso, 1989.

Zweig, Paul. *The Adventurer*. New York: Basic Books, 1974.

INDEX